The Best
AMERICAN
ESSAYS®
2023

GUEST EDITORS OF THE BEST AMERICAN ESSAYS

The Best AMERICAN ESSAYS® 2023

Edited and with an Introduction
by Vivian Gornick

Robert Atwan, Series Editor

MARINER BOOKS
New York   Boston

HarperCollins books may be purchased for educational, business, or sales promotional use. For information, please email the Special Markets Department at SPsales@harpercollins.com.

FIRST EDITION

ISSN 0888-3742
ISBN 978-0-06-328884-3

23 24 25 26 27 LBC 5 4 3 2 1

Contents

Foreword

"I enter into discussion and argument with great freedom and ease, inasmuch as opinion finds in me a bad soil to penetrate and take deep root in. No propositions astonish me, no belief offends me, whatever contrast it offers with my own. There is no fancy so frivolous and so extravagant that it does not seem to me quite suitable to the production of the human mind."

—Montaigne, "On the Art of Discussion," 1588

"Argument is to me the air I breathe. Given any proposition, I cannot help believing the other side and defending it."

—Gertrude Stein, as a Radcliffe student in 1895

"Freedom is the freedom to say that two plus two make four. If that is granted, all else follows."

—George Orwell, *Nineteen Eighty-Four*, 1949

"One task of literature is to formulate questions and construct counter-statements to the reigning pieties. And even when art is not oppositional, the arts gravitate toward contrariness. Literature is dialogue; responsiveness."

—Susan Sontag, "Literature Is Freedom," 2003

CENSORSHIP MAY BE as old as literature itself. "You can't say that!" I imagine someone sitting around an evening fire suddenly shouting to the community's favorite storyteller. "If you say that, tomorrow we will return empty from the hunt," exclaims another. And so for the next gathering, the storyteller modifies the tale, omits a few details, changes some words and expressions. His listeners seem happy, his critics appeased.

Yet our ancient storyteller is frustrated. He wants to say what he wants to say. And precisely in the way he wants to say it. But that is now forbidden by the elders: prohibited, verboten, taboo. Then, gradually, he discovers different ways to communicate what he wants, maybe through a parable or analogy, an unusual figure of speech, a subtle circumlocution, an ironic joke—and he smiles to himself knowing his listeners are none the wiser. Most, that is; he also notices that a small part of his clan understands what he's done. They silently "get it" and a bond is now formed between them. These few "insiders" have done what alert audiences would do throughout all succeeding generations. We call it "reading between the lines." What does it mean to "read between the lines"? Essentially, it's to realize that what we are hearing—or reading—is not what it appears to be, that hidden inside what is being said is another message or implication, one the ostensible audience doesn't, or hopefully doesn't, recognize. The exciting tale of how the woolly mammoth was cunningly trapped and killed is really—as some listeners infer—a story about ridding themselves of their vicious leader. As cultures and societies everywhere augmented the scope and range of linguistic skills, the dynamics of expression and suppression became a key feature of human communication. And the history of thought and opinion became inseparable from the history of censorship.

One of the most penetrating essays on "reading between the lines" appeared at a very dangerous moment: November 1941, just weeks before our declarations of war against Japan and Germany. The essay is "Persecution and the Art of Writing" by the classics scholar and political philosopher Leo Strauss, a German Jew who immigrated to the United States in 1937 and became a leading intellectual at the University of Chicago. Like another writer he knew with a shared background, Hannah Arendt, Strauss unfortunately is not as well known to literary students than he should be and, like many complex thinkers, he is largely misinterpreted politically. But it's not his narrower political or broader philosophical views I'm interested in here but his contribution to literary studies.

A "truly independent" thinker, Strauss maintains, who cannot be persuaded to accept orthodox or "government-sponsored views," can, nevertheless, "utter his views in public and remain unharmed, provided he moves with circumspection." Moreover, he "can even utter them in print without incurring any danger, provided he is capable of writing between the lines." This common expression, he reminds us, "is clearly metaphoric." To try to explain what writing between the lines means "in unmetaphoric language," he argues,

> would lead to the discovery of a terra incognita, a field whose very dimensions are as yet unexplored and which offers ample scope for highly intriguing and even important investigations. One may say without fear of being presently convicted of grave exaggeration that almost the only preparatory work to guide the explorer in this field is buried in the writings of the rhetoricians of antiquity.

Strauss's thesis is that sanctioned persecution, whether by state, church, or prominent institutions, inevitably "gives rise to a peculiar technique of writing, and therewith to a peculiar type of literature, in which the truth about all crucial things is presented exclusively between the lines." Although in this seminal essay Strauss neither offers a close analysis of actual surreptitious literary techniques nor provides enough concrete examples to illustrate his point— and much of the time seems to use the term *literature* to cover history, philosophy, and science—the essay nevertheless clearly proposes an absorbing new way of reading creative works. Assuming, as he does, that the suppression of unorthodox opinion has occurred often throughout history, he suggests that we may therefore "wonder whether some of the greatest writers of the past have not adapted their literary technique to the requirements of persecution . . ." To read these works as they were meant to be read requires the development of the appropriate critical tools.

To the best of my knowledge, Leo Strauss's suggestion has never been implemented by any critical school. I don't know of any literary movement that focuses on reading and writing between the lines. (Though Derrida has broached the topic and quite a few contemporary writers and artists implement techniques of erasure and blackout.) Surely no current critical school has produced a Quintilian or Cicero to taxonomize the rhetorical schemes and tropes that would allow those who desire to express unorthodox opinions to ingeniously evade decipherment and persecution. Yet, returning to the "rhetoricians of antiquity" may be a start. A key principle of free expression rests on the supposition that exceptional writers and their intended readers are more attuned to the intricacies of language than the censor. Presumably, one might learn from such a critical method to understand and appreciate the political subtlety of Shakespeare's history plays or perhaps decode the erotic enigmas of Gertrude Stein's *Tender Buttons.*

Today, more than eighty years after Strauss's essay, with public support for freedom of expression in the United States waning (a phenomenon I've covered in previous forewords and one amply documented by various polls and international monitoring organizations[*]), writers may want to learn some of the skills Strauss's essay outlines but doesn't specifically identify. As free expression becomes increasingly deprioritized, how will we—as readers, listeners, and viewers—fully understand what is and what is not being disseminated, especially from authoritarian sources, and how will writers and artists with nonconformist views manage to find ways to express them without being prevented or punished. What works will be the next *Lady Chatterley's Lover, Ulysses, Lolita,* "Howl"? In ten years, or five, what will be prohibited? Will Orwell's anti-totalitarian classic, *Nineteen Eighty-Four*—whose protagonist may be literature's first "stealth editor"—hit too close to home for a widening authoritative state? Will school systems find good reasons to ban *Jonathan Livingston Seagull?* Another day passes and suddenly another "offensive" book is identified for condemnation, removal from publication or circulation, or silently sanitized.

One of the best essays I've encountered on the subject of writing and reading between the lines—and one that offers a practical model of how such analysis could be done—is J. M. Coetzee's brilliant "Zbigniew Herbert and the Figure of the Censor."[†] Coetzee looks at Herbert's poems "less as responses to the Polish censorship" of that specific time, but "as instances of the complex general problem of writing within a regime of censorship." Within such

---

[*]   Salman Rushdie: "We live in a moment, I think, at which freedom of expression, freedom to publish has not in my lifetime been under such threat in the countries of the West," May 2023.

[†]   The essay was originally published in *Salmagundi* in 1990/91 and collected in Coetzee's *Giving Offense: Essays on Censorship* (1996). For anyone interested in censorship and literature this remarkable book is indispensable.

regimes, writing becomes "an act with a different and heightened social meaning, while reading is a more complex, more suspicious, and perhaps more alert activity." The essay is much too subtle and complex for summary here but I recommend it to anyone who wants to understand how to "read" the dynamic interplay between the creative artist and authoritative censor. For Coetzee, as poets intensify the artifice required to evade an ever-escalating censorship, they risk compromising the authenticity that makes language human. Finally, to resist the absolutists, who need to know what a poem "really means" (its "truth" or its "message"), the poet, in order to remain genuinely human, may decide to defy the tyranny of interpretation itself.

Evading censorship may be a less complicated matter, however, in poetry, fiction, and drama, where the author can often disclaim unpopular positions as part of an imaginative framework. Serious poetry from all eras is opaque to most readers and much can be hidden by clouds of obscurity. Novelists and dramatists (and of course screenwriters) can express inconvenient opinions through various personae or unreliable narrators, or through the voices of discredited characters. Disfavored political comment can escape detection also by diverting it into episodes or scenes that seem peripheral to the central action. But, as Vivian Gornick reminds us in her introduction, the essayist can't hide behind an unreliable narrator or insincere persona for "the reader must be convinced that the persona is writing as honestly as possible."

In other words, the essayist would appear to have far fewer opportunities to distract and deceive the censor. And this leaves us with my central question: If we are as a society slouching toward enforced conformity and an unprecedented restriction of free inquiry and public discourse (many former free speech advocates appear to have ditched John Stuart Mill and Walter Lippmann), how will essayists respond? Of course numerous writers—I would guess the majority—will not be concerned about censorship and for many reasons: They have fully assimilated or "internalized" censorial strictures; they are accommodating and perfectly willing to de-amplify or modify content and phrasing simply to be published; they have no threatening, unorthodox views to begin with; they have willingly embraced prevailing opinions to be more readily approved and applauded. Essayists and memoirists surely feel the pressures of self-censorship more than other writers. The instinctive desire to be liked, admired, to be considered virtuous (an impulse perhaps more common today) doesn't always mesh with the goal of complete honesty and candor. Mark Twain expressed this internal conflict well: "I have been dictating this autobiography of mine daily for three months; I have thought of fifteen hundred or two thousand incidents of my life which I am ashamed of but I have not gotten one of them to consent to go on paper yet."

Obviously, the path of least resistance, the well-worn road, is easier than "the one less traveled by." But what of those who can't affirm the established, mainstream opinions, whose thoughts may stray outside of their political packaging, who recoil at self-censoring, who, like Thoreau, hear "a different drummer" and hold or simply entertain positions and ideas that are "unacceptable," "objectionable," "offensive," "inappropriate," "impermissible"—the list can go on and on. To avoid persecution, will they, like Isaac Babel, turn to the "genre of silence"? Or will they take a lesson from Leo Strauss and explore the methodologies of subterfuge? Will they discover ways of expressing "dangerous" ideas in essays that appear innocuous? Or will they employ one of the essayist's most hackneyed tactics, the bold assertion of a safe audacity: that is, expressing the commonly acceptable opinions of your intended audience as though they were truly risky.

It's often forgotten that the word "essay" is also a verb; to essay is to try, to attempt, to venture. It involves, even invites, risk. Essays were not intended to be "safe places." Yet one of the primary aims of today's censorship is safety, whether imposed sincerely to protect or deviously to suppress. Must anything that makes readers feel "unsafe" be censored? "Safety First" may be a commendable slogan for an industrial workplace or a nuclear power plant but it should have no place in the arts. Safe creative writing strikes me as an oxymoron. The title of Harold Lloyd's wonderful comedic film *Safety Last!* may be the more appropriate motto for the arts.

As this will be my final foreword (I've decided to step down after thirty-eight years as the editor of this series), it felt appropriate to consider here my deepest concerns about where the essay is headed as we enter the second quarter of the twenty-first century. The genre, I'm happy to say, is in a much healthier state than when I began work on the first volume, in 1985. That's not to say that this edition contains "better" essays than the first one—it doesn't—but that the genre is no longer dismissed as a form of subliterature as it once was. When I first proposed the idea of an annual series devoted to essays in the early 1980s, editors visibly winced at the word. The very term "essay" seemed so prohibited industry-wide that I began referring to the "E-word." Once the series was finally launched, my central challenge was to persuade readers that the essay was a vital literary genre—that essays were indeed literature—and, perhaps more important, that enough of them were being written to justify an annual collection. At the time these assumptions could not be taken for granted.*

This stubborn resistance to essays surprised me at the time and I covered it often in my earlier forewords. But today, there's no longer any need to whisper the "E-word." The essay is now a fully reputable genre and essayists are no longer what E. B. White called in 1979 "second-class citizens" in the republic of letters. *New York Times* reviews no longer need to be headlined (as one did as late as 1990): "A Book with the Nerve to Use 'Essays' in Its Title." The genre has also reacquired the academic standing it had so strangely lost: not so long ago, critical essays were published only about fiction, poetry, and drama; but now we frequently encounter essays on the essay. I enthusiastically recommend one very impressive contribution to the genre's resurgence: the new *Edinburgh Companion to the Essay*, a comprehensive exploration of the genre from a wide variety of fresh and provocative perspectives.†

So the challenge now no longer involves trying to resuscitate a once vital literary form; it is rather to nurture and cultivate it. One detriment to its growth is surely a restriction of free expression, whether through outright censorship and punishment or through the fear of harsh reprisals for saying the wrong thing or holding the wrong opinion. The aim of censorship is to make its imposition unnecessary; when people are sufficiently intimidated—socially, professionally, economically—they will do their best not to give

---

* Those interested in more of the start-up details can check the account I contributed to *Essay Daily* (December 7, 2015): "The Best American Essays: Some Notes on the Series, Its Background and Origins."

† *The Edinburgh Companion to the Essay*, eds. Mario Aquilina, Bob Cowser, Jr., and Nicole B. Wallack. Edinburgh University Press, 2022.

offense. The censors have then invisibly achieved their goal.* Of course, such fears will immeasurably suppress the creativity of younger, less secure and established writers and artists.

I opened this foreword with pertinent quotations from four of my favorite essayists, four brilliant and courageous ones. I invite you to ponder their thoughts and then ask yourself: How long will their ideals of freedom, skepticism, and open-minded tolerance for opposing views—the essence of essayism—remain sustainable literary values? Or are they already hopelessly obsolete?

My favorite example of the "acknowledgments genre" is a hilarious short story of that name by Paul Theroux that appeared in *The New Yorker* in 1979. I was tempted to imitate it here but I'll censor that impulse and proceed straight on. As I'm covering nearly forty years, this scroll will be more extensive than usual, though not nearly as protracted as today's average film credits.

There would be no *Best American Essays* without its guest editors. So first, I would like to acknowledge all the wonderful writers I've collaborated with over the years. Their names—some of the most prominent in modern literature—are conveniently listed in the front of this book. Together, their introductions comprise an impressive account of the art of the essay from the end of one century through the beginning of another. I expect these introductions—many of them outstanding essays in themselves—will be an invaluable resource for critics and scholars for years to come.

And the series would not exist without the in-house editors who coordinate the many moving parts and sometimes relentless schedule of an annual book. A very grateful thank-you to (in chronological order): Corlies "Cork" Smith, Katrina Kenison, Laurie Parsons, John Herman, Celina Spiegel, Janet Silver, Wendy Holt, Heidi Pitlor, Erin Edmison, Eric Chinski, Deanne Urmy, and, most recent, Nicole Angeloro, who has deftly helped steer each book from start to finish since 2006. It has been a delight to work with all of them as well as a few others—many thanks also to Larry Cooper, Liz Duvall, Mary Dalton-Hoffman, Jessica Vestuto, and Megan Wilson.

---

* See Glenn C. Loury's remarkably prescient paper on "writing between the lines" and the "rules of permissible expression: "Self-Censorship in Public Discourse: A Theory of 'Political Correctness' and Related Phenomena (Rationality and Society, Oct 1994). Of course to critique "political correctness" is itself politically incorrect.

I'm grateful to Gerald McCauley, who patiently pitched the original proposal and has remained my agent since day one.

I can't possibly recall after nearly forty years all those who lent assistance at different times in one way or another—professionally, personally, psychically. But I'll take a stab: Chris Arthur, Donna Ashley, Jin Auh, Karen Babine, Geoffrey Bent, J. Bill Berry, Anne Bernays, Andrew Blauner, Lynn Bloom, Marc Bookman, Kenneth Brief, Peter Brier, Alexander Butrym, Wendy Call, Anthony Cardoza, Alexander Chee, Tracy Chevalier, Charles Christensen, Kelly Coveny, George Dardess, Valerie Duff-Strautmann, Martha Grace Duncan, Hope Edelman, Joseph Epstein, Anne Fadiman, David Fedo, Kyle Giacomozzi, Albert Goldbarth, Mindy Greenstein, Lee Gutkind, Dave Harris, George V. Higgins, Richard Hoffman, Pat Hoy, Allan Hunter, Arthur Johnson, Jane Jubilee, Sandy Kaye, Garret Keizer, Carl Klaus, Mark Kramer, Peter Krass, Mary Laur, David Lazar, David Lehman, E. J. Levy, Mel Livatino, Phillip Lopate, Evan Lushing, Patrick Madden, David Masello, Rebecca McClanahan, Honor Moore, Kyoko Mori, Joyce Carol Oates, Danielle Ofri, Charles O'Neill, Alan Michael Parker, John Reed, Peggy Rosenthal, Rob Stothart, Scott Russell Sanders, Mimi Schwartz, Nancy Sommers, Jill Talbot, Barry Targan, Ellen Thibault, David Ulin, Andrew Unger, William Vesterman, Nicole Walker, Jerald Walker, Nicole B. Wallack, Elissa Weaver, Joel Whitney, Laurance Wieder. And a few sadly missed: Paul Bertram, Brian Doyle, Donald Ellegood, Bruce Forer, James Guetti, John Harrington, Justin Kaplan, David Perler, Richard Poirier, Jon Roberts, Michael Steinberg, Ned Stuckey-French, William Phillips.

One thing I learned as series editor right from the start is that our literary magazines form the foundation of our creative writing. Without the editors of these magazines I'd have no essays to collect each year. So, I'm enormously indebted to the editors (many of whom are also outstanding writers themselves) who keep the essays flowing. There are too many to mention but a special thanks to: Anna Lena Phillips Bell, Susan Bianconi, Sven Birkerts, Sudip Bose, Peg Boyers, Robert Boyers, Deb Chasman, Jill Christman, Laura Cogan, George Core, Lucy Diver, Ellen Duffer, Henry Finder, Hattie Fletcher, Robert Fogarty, John Freeman, David Gessner, Stephanie G'Schwind, David Hamilton, Lauren Hohle, Sacha Idell, Ann Kjellberg, Carolyn Keubler, Mark Krotov,

Wendy Lesser, Joe Mackall, Elizabeth McKenzie, William Meiners, Mary Kenagy Mitchell, Ander Monson, Dinty Moore, Brad Morrow, Askold Melnyczuk, Emily Nemens, Lynne Nugent, Sumanth Prabhaker, Ladette Randolph, Sigrid Rausing, Evelyn Rogers, David Rowell, Sabine Russ, Sy Safransky, Megan Sexton, Andrew Snee, Ronald Spatz, Willard Spiegelman, Kerry Temple, Christina Thompson, Dayna Tortorici, Stephanie Volmer, Robert Wilson, Rachel Wiseman, S. L. Wisenberg, Emily Wojcik, Allison Wright, James Yeh.

I'd especially like to thank someone who has been a longtime supporter of the essay—as a writer, editor, and publisher—and has herself been included in the series, Kim Dana Kupperman. I'm extremely pleased that she will be serving as series editor beginning with the 2024 volume. She will be expanding platforms for the essay and essaying, so keep an eye out for extra features: bestamericanessays.substack.com.

Four friends deserve a special acknowledgment. Peter Lushing has been with me from gate to wire, always ready to lend a hand, help with research, and supply needed magazines. I'm enormously grateful for his friendship and generous assistance. I've been long indebted to another long-time friend, my grad school roommate and my son's godfather—Donald McQuade. The several college writing anthologies we coedited served as the stepping stones to this series. Our conversations and collaborations substantially enriched my understanding of the essay. I can't thank him enough for what amounts to nearly a lifetime of support, guidance, and encouragement. And a special thank you to Matthew Howard and Shelley Salamansky for their years of assistance, support, and innumerable acts of kindness.

Continuing the personal note, I'd like to express my gratitude to Hélène Atwan for all the expert advice and generous support she offered me as a wife and then as a friend. She played a key role in shaping this series from its conception. Our two children, Gregory and Emily, also lent support, as the life of the series—give or take a year or two—has been commensurate with their own lives. Happily, they overcame a childhood of annual spring deadlines and found their own personal space despite rooms continually piled high with magazines.

Finally, it's satisfying that my last edition should be guest edited by a writer I've read and admired for years and whose work served

very early on as an inspiration for many essayists. I read her regularly
in *The Village Voice* as a graduate student and included her now
famous 1969 *Voice* essay "Women's Liberation: The Next Great Moment in History Is Theirs" in the first anthology I ever assembled.*
Her book *The Situation and the Story* has become required reading
for anyone interested in the art of personal narrative. I whole-
heartedly thank Vivian Gornick for this splendid collection, one
that so brilliantly confirms how vibrant and relevant the personal
essay remains in our time.

A final word: Although this is my last foreword, it is not a farewell.
Starting this year, the new series editor, Kim Dana Kupperman,
will be launching an online newsletter where you will find my
contributions among essays about the essay, interviews, reviews,
and more. Please be sure to subscribe—for free—to the *Best
American Essays* newsletter on Substack. Visit bestamericanessays
.substack.com. I'll look forward to seeing you there and continuing
the conversation.

R.A.

*

The Best American Essays features a selection of the year's outstanding essays published in periodical literature. These essays are
works of literary achievement that show an awareness of craft and
forcefulness of thought. Hundreds of essays are gathered annu-
ally from a wide assortment of publications. These essays are then
screened, and approximately one hundred are turned over to a
distinguished guest editor, who may add a few personal discover-
ies and who makes the final selections. The list of notable essays
appearing in the back of the book includes not only essays submitted to the guest editor but also a selection of essays that were not
submitted.

Editors of print journals and magazines are invited to send
subscriptions or tear sheets (with clear citation and contact information) to the following address, to be received no later than
December 31, 2023:

---

* *Popular Writing in America,* edited with Donald McQuade, Oxford University
Press, 1974.

Kim Dana Kupperman, Series Editor
Best American Essays
P.O. Box 569
Hartland, VT 05048

Editors of online journals and magazines are invited to submit up to five nominations per calendar year—by PDF attachment (with clear citation and contact information), no later than December 31, 2023—to: bestamericanessayseditor@gmail.com.

Writers whose work has been included in the series are invited to nominate up to five of their own eligible essays or up to five essays by other writers. These nominations must be submitted as copies or scans from the publication no later than December 31, 2023, by mail or email. We encourage you to check if the publications in which work appears are routinely submitted to the series.

The qualifications for selection are:

• Original publication in nationally distributed print or online American or Canadian periodicals in 2023.
• Publication in English by writers who are American, Canadian, or who have made the United States their home.
• Original publication as a stand-alone essay on a subject of general interest.

Best American Essays will not consider:

• Abridgments and excerpts taken from longer works (and published in periodicals).
• Essays published in book form—such as a contribution to a collection or anthology—but which have never appeared in a periodical.
• Works of specialized scholarship.
• Unpublished work or work appearing in personal online publications such as blogs.
• Submissions that do not include a full citation (name of publication, date, author contact information, etc.).
• More than five submissions from a single author or online publication.
• Submissions that arrive after the December 31 deadline.

Please note:

- All submissions from print magazines must be scanned or copied from the publication (i.e., not in manuscript or printout format).
- Submissions from online magazines should be sent by PDF attachment via email or by mail as a printed tear sheet from the digital source.
- Editors of print journals and periodicals who include the series on their subscription lists need to do nothing further in the way of submissions. Please check that your journal is being sent to the current address. If editors prefer to highlight or nominate certain essays for special attention, they are welcome to do so. If their periodicals also publish original essays in a separate online outlet, they are invited to select and submit no more than five candidates via PDF.
- Unfortunately, we are unable to reply to individual submissions from authors.

Please check for changes to these submission guidelines at best americanseries.com. Scroll down to the Submission Guidelines button.

Introduction

THE READER WHO sits alone with a novel, a poem, or an essay in hand is free to let all her literary prejudices and predilections wander happily where they will. The delightful anarchy of the uncensored, undefended, even eccentric thoughts that spring to mind while she is reading constitute a significant part of the reading experience. "This is wonderful!" she might declare recklessly to herself after ten pages, or "This is going nowhere," or "God preserve us from these sentences!" As there is no opinion to account for, no position to defend, no argument to take on, the declarative mode is hers to make use of without reservation.

But once this same reader opens her mouth about that same novel, poem, or essay to anyone (friend or foe, relative or stranger), she's in for an exchange—"You think this is good? It's trash." "This kept you up all night? It put me to sleep"—that may arouse primitive anxieties not only about one's judgment, but perhaps even some fundamental sense of well-being.

Thus do I, the reader of more than a hundred American essays published last year, put myself at risk by opening my mouth and saying to you, the reader of the current entry of this revered annual collection, "These are the best of the crop," knowing full well that another editor might, with equal justification, have chosen an entirely different set of selections that would have been as satisfying as this one because right now, in America, there is an abundance of superior essay writing being done and the ones I have chosen for *Best American Essays 2023* are simply the ones that gave me great pleasure, or moved me for reasons I can't readily articulate, or were so indisputably well written I had no choice but to include them. What all, however, have in common is the strong, clear sound of a narrating voice that, in and of itself, is the organizing principle behind the essay. That voice—better known as a persona—is the one I here honor.

Every piece of nonfiction (essay, memoir, literary journalism) is characterized by a persona: the narrator one fashions out of one's own ordinary, everyday self to tell the story the writer wants told. For instance, when I myself sat down to write a memoir about me and my mother I knew that of all the many selves I could have used to tell the story I wanted to tell—the me who was a writer or a feminist or a New Yorker—it was me the daughter who was going to tell this story. On another occasion, writing about my relationship to books, it was me the reader who dominated the persona whose presence on the page was, very nearly, the story being told. Through its tone of voice, its angle of vision, the rhythm of its sentences, what it selects to observe and what to ignore, the persona makes itself integral to the subject at hand; becomes, in fact, its instrument of illumination. Whether personal or informal, the essay or memoir is made distinctive through the decisive presence of the persona who lives to tell *this* story and no other.

A great variety of both subject matter and personae is to be found among the essays that make up this volume of *Best American Essays 2023*. Among those classified as informal, there is Phillip Lopate's elegant critique of the New York intellectuals, Laura Kipnis's ironic take on the gender wars, Kathryn Schulz's historically rich tale of the life and death of Bambi, and David Treuer's startling account of an America that could be experienced only by someone growing up the son of a Jewish immigrant father and a Native American mother. Then, among those essays classified as personal, there is Merrill Joan Gerber's remarkable monologue on her marriage of more than half a century, Eric Borsuk's haunting memoir of his teenage prison experience, Angelique Stevens's harrowing account of what it means to be so poor you have to live with rotten teeth half your life, Ciara Alfaro's wondrous meditation on her adolescent discovery that she was a girl not a boy, and Edward Hoagland's edgy report on aging. These are essays that contribute materially to the long and honorable history of the personal essay by way of the value they place on lived experience.

To fashion such a persona out of one's own undisguised self is no easy thing, but it is the most necessary thing, as it both determines and is determined by the subject at hand. Without it there is neither subject nor story. But, in order for the persona of nonfiction writing to be effective it must observe certain rules. First and foremost, it must seem a reliable narrator. In fiction, famously, a narrator may be and often is unreliable; in the memoir or the essay, never. The reader must be persuaded that here, to the best of his or her ability, the narrator is speaking truth. Not that they are necessarily in possession of the truth, only that they are seeking truth. In other words, the reader must be convinced that the persona is writing as honestly as possible; that we can trust it to take us on a journey, make the piece arrive, bring us out into a clearing where the sense of things is larger than it was before.

One of the most affecting of the essays in this collection is Merrill Joan Gerber's "Revelation at the Food Bank," an essay whose speaking voice—that of a woman in her eighties meditating on her lifelong marriage—comes straight at us from the very first sentence: "'Did you ever have sex with another woman?' I asked my husband when he was eighty-five and we had been married for sixty-two years." The reader does not know in what tone of voice this sentence is being spoken, but the sentence is intriguing enough so that one is willing to wait and see to what use it will be put.

Then, in a voice self-consciously patient and struggling to be fair-minded, the narrator unfolds a catalog of large and small complaints about this lifelong connection—Gerber and her husband met when she was sixteen and he eighteen—mixed in with descriptions of the weekly trips she has begun taking to a church-run food bank for the indigent. Gerber knows she doesn't qualify for free food but she can't help herself, she feels *entitled*, and besides, a greeter at the church becomes a friend when she says, "Have a great day, and God bless." Gerber, herself a non-believing Jew, becomes hooked on "God bless." It makes her feel generous. Otherwise, she admits, she's often in a rage at guess who.

One day, after her husband has annoyed her one time too many with a familiar infraction of one of her rules, she finally cries out at him, "I have to know something. I've thought about this from the day I met you. Did you ever have sex with another woman?" He stares at her, clearly thinking she has lost her mind. "Please," he begs, "don't do this to us now, when there is so little time left for us to be happy."

Happy? So little time left for them to be happy?

Gerber's voice throughout her essay is a marvel of strong emotion held in check by a lifetime of virginal restraint. That restraint is integral to the experience being reported. Its power is exceptional. It puts marriage itself in the dock.

And then there is "The Americas They Left Me," David Treuer's startling tale of growing up on a Native American reservation in Minnesota, the son of an Ojibwa mother and a Jewish immigrant father. It is Treuer's gift and achievement to have written us a mother and a father who are supremely themselves and at the same time supremely metaphorical. The father loved this country while the mother could never forgive it. In the goodness of time these positions become symbolically cemented into the character of each parent and, all other things being equal, tear at the son.

Treuer himself identifies as his mother's kind of Native American: "I inherited from her the same distrust, the same belief that it was a matter of time before the country came for me. I did all the 'right' things: I achieved, I barely misbehaved, I earned and kept my hands, metaphorically and literally, where they could be seen. For better or worse," he tells us, he also inherited from this same astonishingly driven mother who became a reservation nurse, lawyer, and judge, "that desperate wanting. Ambition and greed, for her and for me, were the armor that protected us from the spears that would pin us to the ground if they could."

Inevitably, he spent his youth arguing with a father emotionally attached to viewing the United States through rose-colored glasses. One day at lunch the middle-aged David once again demands of the now really aged father, "How can you stand the things this country does . . . How can you live with it . . . You chose this place. You chose this country. So how can you stand the things it does?"

The old man "stopped eating and put down his silverware and spread those great gripping hands of his. 'No one else wanted me,' he said. 'I was hunted down in Austria, barely tolerated in England and Ireland. But America saved my life. It saved my *life*. So it's my job to save it from itself. That's the deal. That's the bargain.'"

These are voices, *real* voices. The book you are holding in your hands is full of them.

VIVIAN GORNICK

CIARA ALFARO

When We Were Boys

FROM *Water~Stone Review*
after Justin Torres

—WE SPENT AFTERNOONS beneath the high golden sun, wiping
its yolk off our summer-burnt backs.

We walked along the wide, lawless Lubbock streets in a pack, heading nowhere, talking everything. We walked and we begged for a
breeze, cursing the sky until we accepted the passing cars' gusty
offerings as prayers answered. We passed Domino's, and Christ the
King, and the skating rink where my parents met as kids, and the
library where Grandma got those slow-talking cassette tapes, and
Church of Christ, and the gleaming lemon-shaped Taco Bueno
sign, where we debated going inside, then decided against it.
We had no money; the oldest amongst us was my eleven-year-old
brother.

We walked until our palms slicked over, my thighs burned in the
middle, and my feet grew itchy inside my pink Converse high-tops.
They were shoes that released a small damp burp with every step I
took. This sound, and its color, drew unwanted attention amongst
the boys; I adjusted my walk, fell to the back of the group, and
focused my gaze in front of me. *Stop sweating*, my head told my
feet. *Stop that right now.*

The backs of the boys were made up of skinny ankles, curved
calves, bony ribs, and probably, eventually, clothes-hanger shoulders. Their sanded jean shorts were loose and sagged; their
baggy T-shirts had been kissed on the front with shiny silver
graffiti symbols that sometimes got them sent home from fifth-
grade homeroom. Their navy and heather Haneses unlayered

themselves, poking out at the butt. All the mothers of the world hated this about the boys.

I loved it. We kept going.

When we were boys, there were four of us.

Mookie spiked his black hair with a plastic comb and clear blue gel. (*Mom* spiked his black hair with a plastic comb and clear blue gel.) He had a polka-dot blood clot birthmark on his spine, the greenest veins I'd ever seen, and hot skin that grew terra-cotta in the summer, khaki in the winter. He was quiet and always leading us somewhere.

Rhino, who was the exact age between me and Mookie, wore puffy skater sneakers that made his feet look like they belonged to a cartoon character. He had a furrowed brow, buzz-cut temples dripping sweat, and a heart bigger than the people in Grandma's soaps. He cried once a day, sometimes before breakfast, and quoted *Dumb and Dumber* all childhood long. This boy was the softest of us.

With the exception of me and his brother, who were also the kind of soft that melts under touch. Matteo was the baby and my best friend. Together, we lay on the carpet beneath Grandma's piano, traced our fingers over cracked-paint canvases in guest-bedroom closets, and played hushed games of house when the older boys grew tired of us. We filled the roles of husband and wife, even when the older boys told us that it was weird, because that was the only way we knew how to play it. Matteo was small, glossy-eyed, soft-palmed, and babyfat-bellied, and had a high-pitched voice that followed me everywhere, all the time: *CC, CC, CC.*

These boys had skin that went from cinnamon to umber between seasons, darker than mine and Mookie's. This both did and did not mean anything to all of us. We knew that Mookie and I were *white Mexican*, and Rhino and Matteo were *Mexican Mexican.* Mostly: our grandma and their papo—the flower shop man—were married, or something like it, and so we all belonged to Grandma and to each other.

These were the first boys I ever learned to love. And, like teeth, like scabs, like flowers, we grew instinctively into this boyhood.

When we were tired, thirsty, and homesick—after we'd worn our route and popped by the droughted green-water lake to poke the sun-dried fish carcasses with sticks—we went home, to Grandma's, where Rhino and Matteo sometimes lived. Inside, we chugged warm, clouded Lipton iced tea. We nudged Grandma, with her smooth skin and round hips pushed up against the counter, asking her *what are you doing, what's that, but why* until she sighed, turned to us, and said, *Why don't y'all go play out back?*

Grandma had a face that time could not catch. Poreless drugstore skin, gorgeous penciled brows, and lashes that never held mascara the way she wanted, but didn't really need to. Her eyes, I'd learn, were my eyes: crinkle-edged and fire brown in the light. Grandma's hair grew and grew, movie star–sized, holding all the family's secret poker chips. These secrets made her curls dance when she walked, bouncing against her shoulders and back up toward the sky. Grandma knew where she was headed next. The world saw her coming—five feet tall and not to be messed with. She cooked with her hands, seasoning her fists. Our whole childhood, she never once sat down to rest. She was a woman you listened to.

And so, we ran out to the back, until the blue-skied stars came out and we were purple-faced, gasping from laughter. When we were here, we were all the boys at once. We were our dads—soldiers, crawling on the floor, throwing sock grenades. We were the Grim Reaper and Ed, Edd, n Eddy, plus one. We were running back into the kitchen, crying for being excluded. We were Grandma's entertainment, all crowded in one stucco-walled room, with her clapping and announcing our names onto the stage: *Now presenting . . , Mookie, Rhino, Matteo, and CC!* We were a mariachi band and a traveling circus and a comedy club and an arm-wrestling arena all at once. We were manly men, made of bones and scars and glory, until Grandma took us down by the knees and tickled us silly.

Or, we were at the big lake far from home, buried in the dusty canyons, watching the water sparkle and the Lubbock rich people ride their boats across the sage shores. The canyon was like an unthawed ice cream scoop removed from the earth. Grandma parked at the top and we all shuffled down. Raucous land: yucca and cholla out to get you. Beer cans tinkered across the dirt, here and everywhere. Inside the gross, gross water, the fish screamed. It was the best we could ask for in a place like ours.

We lived like boys. We climbed into the caves, up and up, back into the darkness, deciphering the graffiti—the boys knew this language—until Grandma called from behind her sunglasses down below, *Everything okay up there?* We squirmed down, our hearts missing her, and held hands with the stickered earth as we scooted. We laid our bellies on the pier and stuck our bare arms in the water, daring a monster to grab us. We were *Ready,* we told the man with whiskers under his bucket hat later, as he knotted pink worms on our hooks. We threw our lines in and waited for a pull; we waited longer, because Grandma had paid for this. It was the kiddy lake, where a reel was guaranteed.

Halfway through the afternoon, I was the last one left. I felt the tug and out of the water came the biggest fish any of us boys had ever seen. It was iridescent silver and so ugly; it was bigger than my face and forearm combined. *CC, oh my god, grab it!* the boys said. *Just grab it!* But it was too ugly and slimy and skittish. I'd never expected *this* to happen. It swung from my pole, threatening everyone in our circumference. I held the pole out even farther; I wanted to throw the whole thing clean into the water, pole and worm and fish and all. It was the captain now.

The boys kicked concrete, pointing at me, howling. Grandma laughed from ten feet's distance. I screamed. I begged the whisker man to get its flopping body away from me. He sighed, made me hold the pole steady and watch. He had severe hands. It was all too close: the paper clip–punctured hole in its tiny fish lips and the fear in its fish eyes. The man threw my fish and its fear right back in for another go.

On the walk home, my heart was waterlogged. I couldn't help but feel I'd witnessed something that the boys and Grandma hadn't. I was sitting inside this, inside those fear-shocked opal eyes, when the boys started crossing a lost piece of plywood. One by one, they held their arms out like butterflies, steadying their balance. *Careful,* Grandma said from up ahead. We hadn't made it far from the water. *We knooow,* we sang back.

Just as it was my turn to step up, to cross the beam last, Matteo stepped too far ahead. We mistimed ourselves, us babies. The beam raised, then came down in place, onto my big toe. Matteo tumbled, I bayed. I fell to the dirt and untied my shoe, peeled off my sock. Like a hookfish through skin, the nail cracked in half and gushed blood. It hurt worse upon sight and burned evil against the air. Grandma sucked her teeth. *What did I say?*

We bowed our heads. The boys picked me up and draped my arms over their shoulders until we made it to the car. They sat me in the center. I didn't realize I'd been crying until it became hard to breathe. The boys curled around me, all three of them holding my hands and forearms. It was an hour-long car ride that'd leave the suede smelling of sour for weeks. When I kept crying, they poked their funny faces at me, telling me, *It's okay, CC, it's okay, it's okay. Did you know that was the biggest fish we've ever seen? That any of us will ever see? That we would've been scared too?* Grandma kept her honey-colored face straight ahead, right on the road, hands choking the wheel, racing to get me to my parents.

At home, the boys kissed my wet cheeks on the porch. Mom drew me a bath. I lay inside, my body a thing full of fear. My foot was pushed up against the wall, out of the water. I was scared of the pain of submersion. When I looked at it there, yellowed nail ripped in half like a canyon, leaking red into the water, throbbing hot, maimed and disgusting, attached to that hairy calf, I thought: Who could possibly want to touch this fish now?

When we were boys—no. When the boys were boys, I had a body too.

The doctor told me I had a body too young for the changes happening to it. What happened to me: I was born a girl but became a bull. I tried to pretend it wasn't happening—a bad habit I'd develop for myself. I'd never seen anyone turn into a bull before. I'd look down at myself every few weeks, in hotel sheets or a best friend's bathroom mirror, and find some new horror: tapeworm-rivers stretched across my muffin-topped hips, flaps of pink and burly hair between my legs, flinty skin of a face that couldn't remember how to stretch, to smile. The bull's belly filled until I couldn't see my feet, and from Grandma's living room, MTV told it: *Yo mama so fat _____! Yo mama so ugly _____!*

And the boys howled. They became wolves. They grew slender and tall and stealthy. They ricocheted down every hall; they got sent to detention; they wanted to be seen and heard and made strong. I traced their shadow yowls with my feet. *Stop that right now,* my head said, when they all sensed me and looked back.

I never knew how to fit inside that body, but baby, I tried. I closed my eyes and laid my neck against the bathtub porcelain; I didn't look at it, the mangled toe. I worried this wouldn't stop happening to me, like Michael in "Thriller." It thrashed inside me at night—fists enclosed around my tendons and bones, shocking muscles, screams pistol-whipping me from my dreams. My body was like a bad summer night—silent, waiting for something to break, to bleed.

Something different was coming for me. The boys couldn't keep me.

In those final days as boys, when it grew dark at Grandma's, dark enough for her to finally shut the garage and close the blinds, she made us quesadillas with sodas on the side. She tickled our backs with her pink-polished fingers. She watched us brush our teeth side by side by side in the foggy bathroom mirror. We all shared a room, us boys. Once there, she kissed our cheeks—all eight of them—and then the cavernous house went quiet.

Once we knew she was asleep, we turned down the TV and flipped on *Nightmare on Elm Street, Friday the 13th,* and *Bride of Chucky.* We debated which monster was the scariest, then made fun of each other's answers. *Chucky isn't scary, CC. That's not the point of him.* The wolves and I never agreed. They said their monsters were scarier than mine; I believed them.

It was around this time that men began jumping Grandma's fence to steal her bamboo. She had a backyard like a small greenhouse— thorny grape vineyards, tangles of green suffocating—held apart from the living room by a sliding pane of glass. At night, the carpet showed its age spots; the two hallways turned frigid; the sixties kitchen exhaled its breath. The neighborhood wasn't like it used to be. She couldn't stay here. We all felt something was about to happen to us. The croak of what the world required from each of us moaned louder, but we couldn't make out what it was saying.

For now, us boys crowded onto the two twin-sized beds the way we'd always done: sweaty and sleepy-eyed. Eventually, the TV turned off and we listened to each other breathe in the dark, protecting one another with our warmth. We believed in the ghost at the end of the hall, watching us. We clawed our covers tighter, kicked each other's calves. We didn't know it, but this is how we built our bravery: by reminding ourselves that we weren't scared alone.

Always, the sun rose. We woke and Grandma let us poke her fresh tortilla dough with our index fingers, then watch it exhale back into place. We sat on the bricked patio, kicking our veiny feet beneath the table, brushing shoulders, waiting for our burritos. My toe was healing. We held on to this. We did everything all again, for as long as we could.

Years later, at the start of middle school, after the boys had truly stopped hanging out with me and Grandma had moved houses, the girls would sometimes slam shut their lockers and turn their heads toward me. They knew something about me. Even though my boyhood had gone stale, the girls could smell it leaking from my skin, the way Grandma's garlic does to Dad.

I bet you've never had anything bad happen to you in your whole sweet life, huh, Ciara? Yas said, two lockers down, her eyes narrowed at me. She was half-and-half like me; our skin had warmed to the color of cumin from the drills we'd been running under the sun. She raised a leg to tie her shoe. *That's why you're always so . . . happy.* The stacks of tiny black hair ties looped around her wrist quaked there.

I'd been in my corner, locker number 3, shimmying out of my shorts. Trying not to cause trouble, I said *ya, I guess so.* Or, I said *no, actually.* It doesn't matter. Her words would become a refrain of my life, taunting me and the smile I'd finally figured out for a long while. But here, we were girls holding secrets, a fish carcass lake between us, both talking about something else.

What I think she meant was that she could sense I'd been loved; that she needed a love like the kind leaking from my skin to believe in. She needed it to be possible for a girl to be loved like a boy.

What she failed to see was that I no longer belonged to the boys and I was not a girl. I was a bloodbath.

Today, the boys ask me when I'm coming home next before I've even left. They tell me, *Be careful up there,* even when they're not sure where I'm moving to next. They linger in Grandma's living room, kitchen, front lawn, and doorway to ask me how I'm doing. We're always catching up, never quite there. We don't talk about where our blood has been, but we know. We can imagine. It's still Grandma's favorite song, listening to us.

Some of the boys have chased the sky down for their lovers. Some of them have babies. All of us have had that waterlogged thing in our chest punctured, hooked, and set back in for another go-around. Sometimes, we remember something great: the sticky of the dollar theater floor, the nectared taste of Grandma's backyard grapes, the way that fish almost took out someone's eye.

I watch their smiles pulse. When we hug, I feel their hearts in their chests: candlelit, graffiti-walled caverns, pumping fresh hot blood that's been places.

It's enough—knowing I'd once belonged there too.

JILLIAN BARNET

Any Kind of Leaving

FROM *New Letters*

KONRAD HARTMAN SLEPT with one eye open. I asked him once why his eye did that. He said one time he was helping Kathleen hang curtains in the front room, and she was up on the ladder with a cigarette in her mouth, like always. In his German accent, as if his thick lips were too relaxed to participate, he explained, "She dropped the hot ash right in my eye. It burnt my eye and now it don't close." Then he smiled like it was nothing. But in the scene my mind created, he hollered, smacked the ladder, and Kathleen teetered in the air.

Konrad often came home late at night and slept most of the morning, but not through breakfast because the trailer was so small—the kitchen table where we ate stood just a couple of feet away from him sleeping there on the sofa. So he'd get up and eat with Kathleen and me, leaning on his meaty forearms, drooping forward over his eggs and bacon as if his back was still sleeping. Then he'd return to sleep on the sofa for the rest of the morning. When I'd come through the door from playing outside, I'd see that eye looking all white like it was dead, or sometimes moving like it was searching for something while he slept. When I was six, it was the creepiest thing I'd ever seen.

I asked Konny, which is what I called him, a lot of questions. I talked to him more than to most other adults on account of the hour-long ride from my house in the city to Kathleen and Konny's trailer in Dennings Orchard Trailer Court. He would come to get me in his big blue Lincoln after his shift managing the pet store. On the drive, we talked about my school, about why bunnies' noses wiggle, and why somebody chose red, yellow, and green for the traffic lights. We talked about everything. He didn't seem to mind my talking, and didn't turn the radio on or say he was too busy, the way other adults did. When Konny stepped on the brake, he always put his arm out to keep me from sliding off the seat.

Kathleen wasn't really Konny's wife. My mother called her his "common-law wife," which I understood to mean they had not stood before a minister or anyone else in charge of such things, but they considered themselves married anyway. Kathleen had probably lived at our house longer than she'd lived in the trailer with Konny. She became my nanny when my baby nurse, Mrs. Tenney, left, around the time I was a year old, and stayed until I turned six. Kathleen made sure I brushed my teeth while I stood on the little stool in the bathroom, put barrettes in my hair, and shined my Mary Jane shoes with Jubilee. She cooked my meals and when she made something special, she let me lick the spoon. At night, Kathleen bathed me, on her knees beside the tub, and blew giant soap bubbles by making an O with her thumb and fingers. When it was time for bedtime stories, she used a magnifying glass because her eyes were so bad that even her Coke-bottle-thick glasses weren't enough. I thought everyone read that way, and when I started to read by myself, I looked for and used her magnifier. Her lap was the only one I can recall sitting on and it felt doughy-soft and smelled like baby powder. Her long gray hair crossed over her head in two plaits and sometimes she let me put the bobby pins in. Kathleen's room was off our upstairs hall and had a twin bed, a tall dresser, and a reading chair, which was all that would fit. But when I was six, my parents moved to a new, more modern house where there wasn't a room for her anymore and she left us to go live with Konny in the trailer.

Just the way Kathleen wasn't really Konny's wife, I wasn't really my parents' daughter. My mother told me the people who had me couldn't keep me. My parents wanted a baby so they asked if they could have me. People seemed to think it was a really good thing, being adopted. They said it made me special, but it didn't feel very special that the people who had me gave me away. I felt bad that I wasn't more appreciative, the way everyone said I should be, but the truth was I didn't much like my family. For one thing, they didn't smell right to me. My mother had a peppery odor that made the back of my throat itch. My parents seemed surprised by me, my blond hair and questions. The very fact of me seemed to startle them, mouths agape and quizzical expressions when I appeared, as if they'd no idea I was still there, or what to do with me now that they knew. Sometimes I pretended that my real parents would come to get me. Sometimes I pretended Kathleen was my mother.

Any kind of leaving feels harder for some adopted children. We already feel like we've been left enough. I don't remember my reaction when Kathleen left us, but I know I hated the new house we moved into. I held it against that house that it didn't have room for her, partly because I had no other explanation for her leaving. I must have made a fuss. All I know is, it ended up that from the time I was six to almost twelve, I spent the better part of every Christmas and Easter vacation and a few weeks each summer with Kathleen and Konny at Dennings Orchard Trailer Court.

Konny was always the one to drive me there, down Lincoln Highway, and then a right turn down a steep U-shaped road to the last trailer on the left—faded blue with little white metal awnings over the windows. In the center of the yard, on a cement pedestal, stood a purple reflective ball, and in the patchy grass around it, blue and green glass nuggets like the kind you see in an aquarium, only each of these was the size of two adult fists. A birdbath and vegetable garden occupied opposite corners, and in winter, a lit-up Santa rocked back and forth, holding his belly as he laughed. A chain-link fence surrounded the yard.

When I got there, Kathleen would come out onto the stoop, gather me and my bag, and help me put everything in order where I could find it in the one bedroom at the back of the trailer. Kathleen and I slept in the queen-size bed there, which gave us just enough room to get out of the bed on one side, turn sideways, and shimmy between the bed and the dresser to get to the bathroom or the kitchen beyond. Kathleen slept on the outside of the bed even though that meant I had to wake her up to go to the bathroom in the middle of the night. She always came with me and stood outside the bathroom door, an accordion pleated plastic divider with a magnetic latch that didn't work. She helped bathe me in that bathroom because, though there was a shower, boxes and tools filled it up. Kathleen heated water on the kitchen stove and brought it in a pot to the bathroom. I stood, shivering, on the toilet lid so that we could both fit, while she bathed me with a washcloth.

Kathleen and Konny's home differed in every possible way from the tidy, spacious one I shared with my parents on a wide, tree-lined boulevard in the city. At home we had no pets, but Konny bred dogs: Tiny, a miniature pinscher, and Cindy, a German shepherd. When they were in heat, Kathleen spread newspapers on all the floors to catch the drops of blood I didn't yet understand. The kitchen had a sheen of yellow-brown grease everywhere, made darker by the nicotine from Kathleen and Konny's cigarettes. Cigarette burns dotted the Formica counter and table where I sat with Kathleen, a cigarette almost always hanging from her lower lip. In the afternoons, we watched Rege Cordic's afternoon movie on the tabletop black-and-white TV in the 7' × 30' trailer hazy with cigarette smoke.

My parents never saw the trailer. They never once saw the kitchen's greased walls and newspaper floor. How they could have let me live in a place they'd never seen, with an unmarried couple, one a man they knew almost nothing about, I have no idea. It pains me now to realize that Kathleen and Konny were paid to watch me and the money must have been important to them. It pains me more to know that my presence created a safety for Kathleen that was even more important.

I heard Konny snap at her morning and evening, call her stupid, slow. I knew she never once left the confines of the chain-link fence, not ever. I knew their eyes rarely met. I felt the danger in that possibility in a nameless place in my belly. I felt it when Konny spit, "Shut up, Kathleen," and I felt it in my own silence.

But Kathleen let me sit on her lap. Konny listened to me when I spoke. Being there was as special as I would ever feel. So I made the bad go away. I saw, and didn't see.

The last time I stayed there, Konny came home after Kathleen and I were in bed. It must have been well past midnight when one of his friends poured him through the door. We heard the dead weight of him hit the floor and his loud, confused rant. Kathleen got up. I followed, peeking out from the bedroom. Kathleen tried to block my view, but I saw her and the friend struggle to get Konny to the sofa. His bloodied face bore little resemblance to the person I knew. His thick arms, unleashed by drink, flailed and punched, taking out everything on the table; a full, heavy glass ashtray flew directly into the TV screen. "Fucking bitch goddamn cunt!" His shouts filled the trailer with a new kind of filth.

The next morning, Konny was supposed to drive me home. Morning became afternoon. His eye that previously wouldn't close swelled to a slit in his scabbed face. His right hand, too, was bandaged and I wondered who or what he'd hit. Now, like Kathleen, I was afraid to meet his eyes. When he finally did drive me home, on the way he kept asking me if the red traffic lights were bigger than the green and yellow ones. I told him yes, because they were, but I felt sick that he was the one asking questions, asking them like he desperately needed the answer.

I don't know whose idea it was that I didn't go back. I never said anything about that night, not even to myself. I simply didn't think about what I'd seen and what I'd already known, on some level, to be an ugliness, a danger. I grew more interested in school activities and friends. But I do remember the phone call from Kathleen nine years later. By then, I was twenty-one, home on a break from college. She simply said, "Please come get me. He's going to kill me."

When I pulled up outside the chain-link fence, Kathleen stood on the stoop in her cotton housecoat and bare feet. A light winter snow was falling. Her shaking hands struggled to unlatch the gate. Konny appeared in the doorway, throwing her shoes out after her. "Take the goddamn bitch," he shouted in my direction. I helped her into the car. She was a smaller, thinner version of herself. The stench of feces coming off her choked me. Her arms were bruised purple.

At home, I made the mistake of not calling the police or social services so they could see the full effect of the abuse Kathleen had suffered. I thought only of making her comfortable. My mother, with whom I still lived, stood with her mouth agape while I stayed in motion. I drew a bath and, just as Kathleen had once done for me, I helped her undress and step over the rim of the tub, then lower herself into the water. The water turned a rusty brown when she hit it. Her hair was so matted washing it was impossible, so she allowed me to cut it there in the tub, then wash it while she sat with her ridged spine curled forward. I kept running new hot water into the tub, partly to keep her warm and partly to change out the filthy water.

Social services eventually did come. They helped place Kathleen in a county-funded senior living facility, but she only lived a few months longer. The doctor called it "failure to thrive." When she died, even though it was illegal, I took the box of her ashes to a remote part of the neighborhood park where she used to take me to play. But when I opened the box, she was not all ash. Chunks of bone fell to the ground, and everything felt like my fault.

Ten years later, I had just gone through a divorce. I was a single mother with three kids and a crummy job selling shoes. I'd given up fighting for decent child support because paying a lawyer was too expensive.

I was coming home from grocery shopping, a steady late October rain falling, soaking the brown paper bags so that they had to be handled from the bottom. Rain slicked the fallen leaves underfoot as I climbed the stairs to the house with my four-year-old son in one arm, a bag in the other, and my six-year-old twin girls circling around me. I could hear the phone ringing from inside the house as I set the bag down to slip the key in the door.

On the phone, a man's voice. "I'm Sergeant Connor from the Westmoreland County police. We're here with the body of Konrad Hartman. You've been named next of kin and we need to know what you'd like us to do with the body."

I'd like to say that what went through my mind at that moment was grief, grief for someone I had known, someone who had been good to me, even if he had not been good to Kathleen. There was some of that, but mostly there was: *Why am I named next of kin? Abuser. Murderer. Some nerve. Why would he think I'd want anything to do with him? Should I even care that he's dead, let alone have to be responsible for his sorry carcass? What DO I want them to do with his body?*

Once I calmed down, I thought about the Konny who had been good to me, who put his arm out when he stepped on the brake, who, not so unlike me, had no other kin to name. I realized I couldn't not give him some sort of funeral. I couldn't afford it, but I figured it would just be me, his ashes, and some prayers. But the thing is, people came. People he worked with at the pet store, people from Dennings Orchard, people he knew from the Shriners, people from I didn't know where.

And every one of them thought I was his daughter, greeted me as his daughter.

I found myself, standing in the funeral home, his urn on the skirted table beside me, playing along with his lie. I didn't really think too hard about it; I didn't have time to. People were coming up to me, reaching for my hand, "You must be Konrad's daughter, Jill. I've heard so much about you. He was so proud of you." My mouth opened to explain, but no explanation came. I must have looked like a fish gulping as I let the story he had created take over. Even posthumously, his lie was so convincing I started wondering what people would think of me for not being closer to "my father" all these years. I even found myself wondering if there was some way Konny could actually be my father, and Kathleen my mother. Of course, they weren't, but it was as if my long-ago fantasy, a fantasy I had never spoken out loud, had osmosed to Konny.

But that wasn't even the strangest part.

A week after Konny's funeral, I was at work, carrying a tower of shoe boxes in both arms, when someone said there was a phone call for me. The man on the phone introduced himself as Konny's lawyer. Then he said, "Are you sitting down?"

"Why? Should I be?"

"Yes, I think you should," he said. I took a seat on the stool behind the front counter. He went on, "Mr. Hartman left you everything. He left you a quarter of a million dollars, his car, and a very valuable coin collection."

I asked the lawyer to repeat himself. And then I asked him again. He said it exactly the same way. Then he told me that Konny had left me the trailer too, but he didn't advise me to see it because "the state of it would be too disturbing." He said he would take care of disposing of it.

It's strange how we remember little details when something life-changing happens. It's as if our brains know to take a snapshot of that moment, because afterward we might need it to remember what life was like before. I remember the fluorescent light, the vague rubbery smell of the carpet padding, the heaviness of my exhausted body on the rough wooden stool. I listened as the lawyer basically told me that Konny died in a hovel, Kathleen lived in that hovel, and somehow because of that my kids would be able to go to college, and I might be able to go to grad school.

None of it made any sense, of course. There was a craziness about it. And what had I done that made him want to leave it to me? I felt a sickening guilt. And a profound relief.

It took months to settle the estate fully. On St. Patrick's Day, the day before what would have been Kathleen's birthday, I arrived at

Konny's lawyer's office. His diminutive secretary stood just four and a half feet tall, a stature that would have garnered stares under normal circumstances, but that day she wore head-to-toe Kelly green for the holiday—dress, stockings, and shoes. The lawyer sent her across the street to the bank to get the coin collection stored in their vault, and when she returned, she stood in his office doorway with a burlap bag full of old coins and a grin. All that was missing was a top hat and a rainbow. I drove away in Konny's car, the bag of coins on the front seat, the check in my pocket.

Back on the day of Konny's funeral, when I'd brought his ashes home, I had planned to leave them in the garage until I could figure out what to do with them, but when I looked around the dingy, cold garage that day, it didn't seem right to leave him there, no matter what he had done. So I brought him inside and put him on a high shelf in the coat closet. After visiting the lawyer, when I drove Konny's car home, I got him out of the coat closet and put him on the front seat of his car, how I remembered us being together, only now I was the one in the driver's seat. We drove around like that for over a year before I finally laid him to rest.

SYLVIE BAUMGARTEL

Fat Man and Little Boy

FROM *Subtropics*

I RECEIVED A pair of earrings as a gift. The person who gave them to me is a friend who works at the Los Alamos National Laboratory. I don't know what she does, except that she has the highest clearance that there is. Her husband doesn't know any more than I do about her work. He doesn't even know where her office is. This is for his own protection. I suspect that her background is in the CIA. I do know that she flies planes and that she speaks German, Russian, Chinese, Arabic, and Hebrew.

The earrings are small silver bombs. One is Fat Man, the other is Little Boy. The atomic bombs dropped on Hiroshima and Nagasaki. They sell the earrings at the gift shop in the Los Alamos History Museum at the Fuller Lodge. The Fuller Lodge was previously the Los Alamos Ranch School, an elite, prestigious boys' school. Gore Vidal is an alumnus, as is J. Robert Oppenheimer. The school was taken over by the US government in 1943 for the scientists working on the Manhattan Project, after Albert Einstein sent a letter to President Roosevelt warning him of the possibility that the Germans could get to nuclear weapons first. The Ranch School was closed, and a group of scientists from around the world moved to the Secret City, known as "the Hill." Nearby land was taken from the Hispanics who had old land grants established by the Crown of Spain, as well as from the Pueblo people, to secure the area.

Oppenheimer and his team successfully made atomic bombs in just two years. One of the reasons they could do this was because of Marie Curie, the early-twentieth-century physicist and chemist. Her discovery of radium and polonium and her work with these elements was essential to the creation and development of atomic weapons. Her work was also enormously helpful for medicine, paving the way for millions and millions of lives to be saved with X-rays and radiation therapy. The remedy is in the poison, the poison in the remedy. I like that a woman's genius birthed such powerful destruction and such powerful healing. Kali is the goddess of creation and of death.

Inside the small Los Alamos History Museum, there is a wedding dress. It is made from parachute nylon. The Manhattan Project physicist Albert Bartlett got the material from an explosives testing site and had the dress made for his wife, Eleanor. There is a penlight, worn in the pocket of one of the bomber pilots on the Nagasaki mission. There is a skin drum that belonged to Richard Feynman. (Back in the day, the scientists would gather after work and play music together.) There are gold teeth caps to protect the physicist Al Graves from his own fillings, which had become radioactive after he was exposed to radiation during an accident that killed the scientist Louis Slotin. There is a photograph of one of the three known spies to have infiltrated the Manhattan Project. They passed the secrets on to the Soviets, which is how they created their own nuclear weapons. The spies were not discovered until after the war.

Looking at these things I feel both curious and uneasy. Looking at the penlight worn by the Nagasaki bomber nauseates me. He lived a long and healthy life after dropping that bomb. My friend who works at the Lab assures me that Fat Man and Little Boy saved far more lives in the long run than they killed. But they killed more than 200,000 people. Those exact lives were not saved; I don't believe in necessary evils. But I also don't know that I am completely against nuclear weapons, as I was when I was a teenager in Santa Fe, protesting the Lab, protesting the Gulf War, seeing things in black and white.

Right outside the Fuller Lodge, there is a twelfth-century Indian pueblo site. There are grids of pale brown volcanic rocks in the grass—the floor plans for the pueblo. The rooms are so small, I don't know how people could really use them. It's amazing to stand inside the ruins of the abandoned city from a thousand years ago, right where Oppenheimer and the other scientists lived and ate and drank and bathed while they built the bombs.

Los Alamos is on a plateau, and there are incredible views of mountains and cliffs in all directions. The air is fresh, the sky bright blue. There are tall pine trees, singing birds.

Not far from the Fuller Lodge is Ashley Pond, full of ducks, geese, carp, and koi. My son and I walk to the nearby Starbucks and get salami, cheese, and hot chocolates, and sit under a huge ponderosa pine tree and look at the pond while we eat. Then we walk around the pond, and my navy-blue sun hat blows off my head and into the water. A man on the other side takes off his shoes and goes into the pond and retrieves my hat for me. Los Alamos is a friendly city. There is very little crime.

Los Alamos feels electric. It's exciting, haunted and ominous. For many years, I never wanted to go anywhere near the place. It feels strange to be here now because it feels good, it feels safe, it's beautiful. It's also fascinating to be in the history and near the secrecy. There's a volcano nearby that erupted one million years ago, spewing debris thousands of miles, all the way to Kansas. There were dinosaurs, including *Tyrannosaurus rex*. Various tribes of Indigenous Americans lived here for thousands of years before the Europeans came. Then it was a deserted mountain with a prestigious boys' school on it and nothing else. Then the site for one of the most significant scientific achievements of all time. Everyone knows about it—everyone knows about the making of the atomic bomb. But that's old history. What are they doing there now? What secrets are they keeping that we will one day learn about, or that perhaps will never be openly revealed? I know there's a lot of space research there. Life on other planets, UFOs.

There have been mysterious sightings of green fireballs over Los Alamos since the 1940s. Scientists and skeptics have verified these sightings, and the fact is that they don't know what they are. The fireballs have been recorded hundreds of times over Los Alamos and also over the Sandia National Laboratories, in Albuquerque, another military lab. In 1951, *Time* magazine published an article called "Green Balls of Fire" about the phenomenon. Recently, there has been more news about the green fireballs, and their unnerving concentration around sensitive military sites. The US government is worried, but not much more is publicly known about exactly *how* worried and what they're doing about it. My friend just smiles when I ask her about it and doesn't say a word.

Los Alamos is a quiet, vibrant, sinister, calm, mysterious, and gorgeous place. There are more millionaires per capita here than anywhere else in the world. Also more PhDs per capita. It's a bit unnerving how good it feels to be here. I really like the feeling—which makes me feel uncomfortable. Really, the essence of the city is death. Los Alamos can't escape the fact that its pretty, rich, safe facade is built on violence and destruction, the annihilation of foreign peoples.

Los Alamos has excellent schools, the best in New Mexico. Nearby Española is incredibly poor, with high crime rates and abysmal schools. The contrast is quite stark. There are tensions between the people in the valley and the people on "the Hill."

There are tensions within Santa Fe, too. Santa Fe hates Los Alamos. Santa Fe is a very liberal city, full of pacifists. It doesn't like that this mecca of weaponry is only thirty minutes away. I grew up hearing that Los Alamos was evil, that the Lab was evil, that Los Alamos was dangerous, contaminated, toxic. A poisonous city. I never wanted to go near it. There is still nuclear waste here, seeping into the land. It will cost billions to clean it up. It's hard to get accurate answers about exactly how much waste there is, how much contamination is in the land and water. Several Indigenous communities have been harmed by the waste, and there is a lot of anger and mistrust about how the cleanup is being handled.

When I was in grade school, I went to Los Alamos with a friend for the day. Her father was a postman there. I felt like I was in danger just being there. Breathing the air. I didn't eat or drink anything.

Where I am living now in Santa Fe, I can see the lights of Los Alamos at night, glowing orange to the northwest. Los Alamos keeps a lot of secrets, and so do I. Maybe this is why I like it. Los Alamos makes powerful, dangerous things. And protective things. Does my government keep me safe? Are we more in danger because of nuclear weapons, or are we safer? Was making them inevitable? This is how humans are, what we do. We discover, we invent, at our own peril. Maybe it is all exactly how it needs to be. Maybe it's all wrong and we must turn things around. But I do like the intensity and power of the Lab. I like that my friend can't tell me what she does. I do not want to know. There's a chance I wouldn't want to be friends with her anymore.

Los Alamos also evokes fear. Fear of cancer, fear of annihilation. Whatever crazy things they're concocting up there, other countries are, too. It's still an arms race. We're a target. If there is a nuclear war, Los Alamos would be a priority target. Sleepy, sweet little Santa Fe is surrounded by powerful, energetic military sites. Part of me likes this, some fighting-a-war part inside me—but it's not good. What if all of that money and all of those geniuses were asked to save our species from the mass extinction we're entering? Or to feed everyone in the world and educate every child? Los Alamos and its neighbors, Pojoaque and Española, are almost feudal. The one percent is getting stronger and richer, and the poor are getting poorer and more plentiful. If intelligence isn't connected to empathy, it's incredibly dangerous.

When I feel that "war part" inside me—it's a fierce part that wants to fight for what is right. Which is against the real mission of LANL. So why do I like it here?

My friend reminds me that if we hadn't dropped the bombs on Japan, there would have been a land war, and she says it would have been far more brutal, and at least a million Japanese people would have died. Not to mention the fact that there has not been a World War III because of the weapons. If that is true, does this justify the existence of the atomic bombs?

Los Alamos is utilitarian. The buildings aren't pretty; they're utilitarian. Los Alamos is rich, but it's not old money. It's new money, money being made right now by doing secret things. Things that might be endangering us, or making us safer. Maybe some of both. Maybe it depends on who you are. The atomic bombs might have kept us and the Soviets safer, but they certainly didn't keep the Japanese safer. The people blown to bits. The people melted, vaporized. The people on the edges of the blast, screaming, poisoned, poised to die slow, painful deaths while remembering the sound and the flash of Fat Man and Little Boy.

I can't imagine ever wearing those silver Fat Man and Little Boy earrings. I can't imagine giving bombs names like that. Fat Man was originally called Mark III. The name "Fat Man" refers to the character played by Sydney Greenstreet in *The Maltese Falcon*. The other bomb, the one dropped on Hiroshima, was first called Thin Man, after the Dashiell Hammett detective novels. But later the name changed to Little Boy. The B-29 bomber named *Enola Gay* carried Little Boy. A Japanese survivor in Hiroshima said he looked up in the sky and saw what looked like a *silver drop*. It was the *Enola Gay*, but he wasn't worried because it was a lone aircraft. Enola Gay was the name of the mother of one of the pilots. I wonder how she felt about her namesake.

I went to school with Oppenheimer's granddaughter, Sarah. She was a few years older than me, so I didn't know her well. I remember that she was kind, and that she had a beautiful and unusual face. She wore her hair in blond dreadlocks. Her last name was an enormous burden for her. Now she has a shaved head and is an accomplished visual artist. She makes large sculptural and architectural pieces, shown in museums and galleries all over the world. It's a brilliant family.

After Fat Man and Little Boy were dropped, J. Robert Oppenheimer opposed any further development of atomic weapons and resigned from the directorship of the Manhattan Project. He didn't agree that it was necessary for the second bomb to be used, he didn't see the purpose; it was gratuitously destructive. He said he had blood on his hands.

"We knew the world would not be the same. A few people laughed, a few people cried, most people were silent. I remembered the line from the Hindu scripture the Bhagavad Gita. Vishnu is trying to persuade the prince that he should do his duty and to impress him takes on his multi-armed form and says, 'Now I am become Death, the destroyer of worlds.' I suppose we all thought that one way or another."

The bombs were an astonishment when they detonated. I watch the film footage taken from the Boeing B-29 Superfortress Bockscar planes. The explosions bloomed upward and out and formed gargantuan blue, luminescent caps. They look like enormous, glowing jellyfish of light.

The dark isn't always bad and light isn't always good.

Oppenheimer was nominated for a Nobel Prize three times but never won. He married Kitty, and had a passionate affair with a young psychiatrist named Jean Tatlock. She was a member of the Communist Party, putting both of them under FBI surveillance. Jean committed suicide, devastating Oppenheimer. He later died of throat cancer at sixty-one years old.

ERIC BORSUK

Bidders of the Din

FROM *Virginia Quarterly Review*

THE FIRST TIME I heard someone use the term "bid" was my first day in federal prison, just four days before my twenty-first birthday. It was after the intake process, after I was fingerprinted, strip-searched, photographed, given an inmate-ID card, an orange jumpsuit, and a roll of bedding. Before any of this, I'd been instructed by my presentencing probation officer that I could bring "absolutely nothing" with me into the prison. "Just your body," he'd said. So I left my eyeglasses at home, assuming I'd be issued a new pair. I walked blindly through a labyrinth of buzzing steel doors, deeper and deeper into the compound. When I asked about receiving a pair of glasses, one of the guards told me I'd have to wait until next year, since the eye doctor only came around once a year, and he'd just recently visited.

Shuffling down the blurry corridor in my cheap, prison-issued slippers, also known as "Bruce Lees," I was eventually handed off to a nearly identically stout, bald guard at E-Unit. He unlocked the heavy door using an old steel key, like a clichéd prison-movie scene. Everyone stared at me, the fresh meat. As he led me through the unit to my cell, down the bleak concrete hallway, it was hard to fully comprehend that this was my new existence, my home for the next seven years.

Once the guard was gone, a few guys cornered me in my cell and demanded to see my paperwork, the documents new arrivals are given that detail their criminal charges—prison's version of a welcoming party, which shows up mostly just to find out if you're a pedophile. This task is usually carried out by a group of guys from one's hometown, which is easy to learn since the last three dig-its of your ID number indicate which district court handled your case—a kind of proxy for geography—information that, along with your name, is printed on the front of your shirt for everyone to see. The welcome party's request to see your paperwork isn't exactly a friendly one, and of course there's a natural urge to re-sist. But refusing to show it is as good as admitting to being a child molester, so everyone just hands it over. Luckily for me, the crime I'd committed had gotten quite a bit of media coverage, so right off the bat one of the guys recognized me. "Oh, dang, you're one of them art robbers!" he blurted out, chuckling in a high-pitched tone—and just like that, the interrogation was over. I was accepted into the community. In their words, it was because I was famous, but more importantly not a pedophile.

The year before, when I was nineteen, my two best friends and I robbed the Rare Book Room of the Special Collections depart-ment at Transylvania University, in Lexington, Kentucky, where one of them, Spencer, had been attending his first year of college. My other friend, Warren, and I were enrolled as freshmen at the University of Kentucky, which was just down the street. We later enlisted an acquaintance from high school, a guy named Chas, whose family was well-off, to act as both the getaway driver and financier. Among the millions of dollars' worth of stolen artwork and rare manuscripts was a first edition of Charles Darwin's *On the Origin of Species.* The crime made headlines around the world, but it was an especially popular topic of conversation in our home-town of Lexington, about two hours from the prison. "A brazen plot doomed to fail," read the front-page headline in the *Lexington Herald-Leader,* alongside our four mug shots, covering in exhaus-tive detail the case that had quickly been dubbed the "Transy Book Heist."

Most new guys just end up lying in bed on their first day; the bunk becomes a sanctuary, a safe space where they hide from oth-ers, as well as a new reality—as if you could just go to sleep and one day wake up and suddenly everything will be back to normal. After watching me lie in bed all day, my celly, a skinny, middle-aged dude from Detroit, tried to offer some words of encouragement.

"Man, you gotta get a bid," he said.

"What's that?"

"You know—a bid. It's how you do your time."

We went back and forth on the details for a while. It seemed like an arcane term that didn't really make sense until you'd lived in the system for a while. From what I could gather, the word seemed to derive from the noun "bit," pertaining to the length of a prison sentence, much like a "stretch" or a "stint." Something like: "This seven-year bit is a fuckin' bummer."

"Bid" was something entirely different, more like a purpose or raison d'être. It was all about *how* you did your time, like finding a hobby or hustle to get you through your bit. For many guys it was about winning, no matter what the endeavor was. Others just wanted to make money. Some guys used it simply as a way to occupy their minds. For everyone, though, it was all about escaping the slog of captivity. My celly told me he bid off a lot of things, but mostly just gambling—although he did like to dabble in some prison hooch from time to time. He said if I could find this thing— this sense of purpose—it would make all the difference in my life. Without it, he said, my sentence would feel like an endless misery. "Do the time," he said, "don't let the time do you."

All across the compound, there were countless ways of bidding, from gambling to religion, education to gang life, sex, art, and prison jobs (the average prisoner only made about ten to fifty cents per hour). Sports were a popular way to bid. Sometimes nearly the entire compound would come out for basketball games between cell blocks, with stakes high enough that the court would be encircled by guys shouting and cheering and spilling onto the court itself. You rooted for your cell block no matter what, and over time couldn't help but develop an allegiance to it.

Weight lifting seemed to be the most popular form of bidding. All day long you heard grunts and clashing iron coming from a covered corner of the yard, what we called the weight pile. It was a chaotic scene of unchecked alpha where you saw some pretty strange things, such as when one guy got so aroused while bench-pressing that he prematurely ejaculated in his sweatpants. He acted surprised when it happened, moaning in ecstatic bewilderment before slamming down the weight bar and running away in humiliation.

Then there was the annual bodybuilding competition known as the "Peel Off." The name was pretty obvious, as the most muscular guys on the compound would literally peel their clothes off down to their underwear, which was twisted up tightly like a thong.

Standing on top of the softball bleachers, they'd proceed through the standard bodybuilder poses—double biceps, lat spreads, side chest, etc.—flexing, holding, making awkward eye contact with the spectators, while a group of judges analyzed them from the front row. Some guys would starve themselves for weeks before the event so that their muscles would pop. It wasn't clear if anyone actually knew what they were doing, competitors and judges alike, but no doubt every year they would crown a winner, the only prize being bragging rights.

Sometimes, perhaps inevitably, certain bids overlapped, propped up by their own subeconomies. Some guys bid off of gambling on the games—basketball, softball, soccer—while others sold food to the crowd. Cooking homemade (in other words, cell-made) food was probably the most common form of bidding. To do this, the cell chefs would often rely on overpriced commissary items, which they would use to concoct elaborate rice bowls, burritos, even pizzas, using just a microwave and simple ingredients like packaged meats, ramen noodles, and seasoning salt. Even if only momentarily, these meals gave you comfort and escape from the everyday wretchedness of prison life. The lack of acceptable food in the chow hall tended to wear on guys after a while. Slops of meat-mush, dirt-covered beans, rotten potatoes: the list of foul dishes runs on and on. Fajita Fridays turned my stomach the most, consisting of nothing more than a tortilla filled with a rancid dollop of stringy chicken innards.

If you couldn't make it to the commissary, every unit had at least one "store man" to supply your needs, someone who stocked up on commissary items based on demand, then sold the goods for a marked-up price. Since you were allowed to visit the commissary only once a week, having a store man in each unit was essential. The convenience of on-demand goods kept him in business and his bid forever indispensable.

Another side of this equation was the illicit chow-hall food trade, which consisted of things like eggs, meat, spices, dairy, and vegetables. The chow-hall workers would smuggle items out of the kitchen to sell in their units. Since certain ingredients could only be obtained in the chow hall, this trade was a key component of the housing-unit cooking establishment. It also played into another overlapping bid: the prison hooch trade. To make an alcoholic beverage, you needed a steady supply of fruit (or other ingredients like potatoes or tomato paste), plus a great deal of sugar. Guys were constantly getting busted smuggling this stuff out. Time and again, you'd see them being frisked outside the chow hall, pushed up against the wall with their arms and legs spread apart, guards removing hidden bundles of contraband from their clothes, sometimes taped to their bodies. The guys who made it past the guards would hand off their spoils to the bootleggers, who then cooked the ingredients. The process basically consisted of bagging up a concoction of fruit, water, and sugar, then storing it inside cavities carved into a cell's walls, allowing time for the fruit to ferment and the sugar to turn into alcohol. The process usually involved several people, most of whom kept watch.

My own bidding was heavily influenced by being incarcerated with Warren and Spencer. The three of us had been close friends since our early teens, when we started playing club soccer together in Kentucky. From the start, we all just clicked. Even at a young age, Spencer was already a gifted artist, and Warren a well-read thinker with political aspirations. Over the years, we encouraged each other to reject our Southern conservative upbringings for a more subversive approach to life, which may have had something to do with why we all ended up in federal prison together. One day you're reading *Fight Club* and debating the finer points of German idealism, and the next you're robbing a rare-books collection for millions of dollars' worth of artwork and rare manuscripts—a seamless transition.

That said, having friends in prison was a major boon, especially since we were young, and it was our first bit. There was something comforting in knowing that no matter how hard life got, my best friends were right there with me, going through the exact same situation.

The three of us created our own way of bidding. The main principles were self-education, meditation, exercise, and artistic development. We saw it as a way to remake ourselves, stripping away layers of who we were according to how the place we came from had defined us. For me, this meant not so much that I would change through prison, but that, looking back, I hadn't really existed as a real person until prison. The illusory values of my Southern, religious, conservative, materialist culture—and materialism in particular—suddenly faded, like a palimpsest, a ghost of a self. Once we'd shed our old skins and eaten enough chicken gizzards, when our hair and beards were long and tangled, when we were wearing rags for clothes and couldn't care less about appearances or pleasures, when the insatiable, boundless, and obligatory attachment to status and idolization and things was finally gone (all the *things*, never enough *things*)—that's when we could start to rebuild.

To outsiders, our rituals made us seem a little crazy. (*Those three amigos are loco*, they'd say.) We made up words and ways of speaking that only we could understand. Warren, Spencer, and I adopted new names for ourselves—Chip, Din, and Pep, respectively—based loosely on a skit on Adult Swim's *Tim and Eric Awesome Show, Great Job!* We didn't know exactly why the skit seemed central to our new circumstances, but whatever the reason, it went deep, as if the absurdity of the show mirrored the absurdity of our prison lives and life itself.

In time this little madness grew into a philosophy of sorts, an ideal we strived toward that paradoxically only seemed attainable within prison. To do so, we needed to give ourselves up to this thing, this belief, this way of being. No one word could possibly define it, but we had to give it a name. We called it the "din."

Prison is the great equalizer. Everyone plays by the same rules. Although many factors are out of your control, you have to walk a fine line between mettle and modesty to survive, all while trying not to draw too much attention to yourself. In many ways, prison is like a rowdy, high-stakes middle school full of aggressive and confrontational men all constantly and at once seeking to demonstrate masculine superiority, stoked by enough gossip to put a sewing circle to shame. Almost every day you'd hear rumors going around, complete fabrications started for someone's own self-interest or amusement. But it was hearsay with real consequences, and so you had to stay on top of it. We even had a name for the rumor mill: "inmate.com." For example, you'd hear guys start conversations like, "Yo, man, I heard on inmate.com . . ." or "According to inmate.com . . ." followed by some absurd statement that was almost certainly incorrect, like a prison version of the telephone game.

It took a while to accept that my old life was gone, that I'd be a completely different person after this experience. Prison changes you, there's no question about it, but how you let it change you often dictates how you'll bid, and accordingly the direction your life will go.

Due to a lack of rehabilitative outlets, most guys continued their same lifestyle as before prison. Although one's environment may have changed, the hustle did not. To go against this way of life meant to go against a deeply ingrained ideology of survival, one born out of inequity and practiced through self-preservation. In this sense, for many, it was not only unnatural but perilous to go against the long-established prison order—after all, no one wants to be culled from the herd.

Terms like "rehabilitation" were regularly tossed around by prosecutors, judges, probation officers, and prison officials. Year after year, you'd wait for the rehabilitation to take effect, but nothing ever happened. Early into my sentence, it became clear that to make any sort of positive change in your life, you'd have to do it completely on your own, and against all odds.

Since the three of us had been arrested during our freshman year of college, and the prison didn't offer undergraduate degrees, Warren, Spencer, and I set up mock university courses for ourselves, using standard textbooks from core subjects like math, science, history, economics, foreign language, and psychology. Much like a standard course load, our days were divided into different classes, with each of us overseeing the group's progress on a particular subject. We were devoted to a rigorous class schedule. Because we were all housed in different units, we had to meet during open movements in unrestricted areas of the prison such as the library, yard, or gym. At the end of every class, the instructor assigned work due for the following session. Seeing as how self-education was the objective, homework wasn't seen as an inconvenience; rather, it was a privilege, although sometimes it did take some wrangling to get a Spanish assignment turned in on time.

Prison life, especially for anyone new to it, can be a merciless world to navigate. To survive you have to adapt quickly and learn the language. A lot has to go right, and it constantly feels like a precarious balancing act with grim consequences. Sometimes it seemed impossible to go on living another minute in such a hopeless environment. But if you take it one day at a time, eventually it all starts to make some sort of sense. For a first-timer, the shift in lifestyle can be so drastic that it can feel liberating to finally find your own groove, and maybe even your own bid. It gives you a reason to get out of bed, push through to another day. The other thing about prison is that just when you think you're starting to get the hang of it, everything changes in an instant.

I was in line at the commissary, same as every week, holding an empty mesh laundry bag and waiting to slip a folded-up order sheet through a slot in the wall so I could then catch the items as they came flying out of a nearby window. On this particular day, I wasn't there for much, just a few essentials: ramen noodles, deodorant, batteries for my Walkman. My janitorial job only brought in about fifteen dollars a month, so there were never any opportunities to splurge.

Out of nowhere, I spotted two burly prison guards pushing through the crowd and heading my way. I didn't give it much thought—I hadn't done anything wrong—until they were looming over me.

"Borsuk," the larger one muttered. "Come with us."

They walked me back into the compound, down a long corridor with what must have been half a dozen security checkpoints, and eventually to the lieutenant's office. I couldn't figure out what kind of situation I was walking into. I asked the guards if they knew what was going on, but they didn't say a thing. Whatever the reason, it wasn't good. The fact that I hadn't done anything wrong only made it worse. I'd seen guys returning from the lieutenant's office devastated after being informed of some terrible news back home. By the time I walked through the door, I was sure someone I loved had died.

The lieutenant on duty, an exceptionally short, mustached man with a high-and-tight haircut, was wearing his signature camouflage fatigues and Cavalry Stetson. He told me to take a seat, probably just so he could stand over me.

"You're being reclassified," he said.

"Reclassified . . . what does that mean?"

"It means you're being shipped out—relocated."

Relocated didn't make any sense. I'd been at Ashland Federal Correctional Institution for two years with zero disciplinary infractions. For all intents and purposes, I was a model inmate.

I pressed the lieutenant for details, but he cut me off midsentence. "It came from high up," he said, pointing his finger upward. "That's all I can tell you. I've already said too much."

I looked up. *High up? What does that even mean?*

"All right, you're dismissed," the lieutenant said. "Take him to the hole."

Before I could stand, the guards lifted me out of my chair and dragged me down the hall to the Special Housing Unit (SHU), an entire building full of solitary-confinement cells. Once inside, I was handed off to another guard, a freakishly muscular man who always reeked of cheap cologne—I called him Giò, after the Armani stuff. I imagined him getting ready for work every day, posing and flexing his muscles in the mirror, running gel through his hair, before drenching himself in a top-notch gas-station-bought cologne.

Giò shoved me into a damp, dark shower stall, locked the heavy steel-barred door, and told me to take off all of my clothes. Then he disappeared. I was standing there naked, shivering, waiting. Death-metal music blared from somewhere nearby inside the building.

Giò was gone for a long time, but eventually he returned and tossed me an orange jumpsuit (the same kind I'd worn on my first day in prison) before walking me up a flight of stairs to my cell. When he locked the door and turned to leave, I asked if he knew why I was there, but he just walked away.

The day faded, night came on. I lay on the bed and stared up at the ceiling. The hole was much louder than I'd imagined. Guys were shouting from virtually every cell. Most of them weren't even attempting to communicate; they were just shouting, filling the maddening space with voices—a relentless babel that lasted deep into the night.

The next morning, I woke up to the sound of the guards serving breakfast, sliding plastic meal trays through slots in the barred doors. Giò was shouting at an eccentric, self-proclaimed political prisoner with wild, frizzy hair, whom I'll call Rooster. From what I could tell, the argument was over a packet of grape jelly, of all things. I heard someone whispering that Rooster was diabetic and wasn't supposed to receive jelly with his meals. For some reason, Giò was convinced that Rooster was hiding jelly somewhere in his cell, and he was hell-bent on finding it.

The only way to get a glimpse down the hall was to slide your head through the meal-tray slots, a little trick I learned early on. I was skeptical when I first heard about the technique: By the look of it, you'd never expect that an adult's head could possibly fit through such a narrow opening. But turned sideways, with your head parallel to the ground, at just the right angle, your skull slid right through. It was an odd sight to see a row of intermittent, disjoined heads floating along the hallway, but I could see now that the altercation was unfolding just four cells away from mine.

"Hand over the jelly!" Giò shouted.

Rooster fired back: "I don't have any jelly, you fucking psycho!"

They argued, and argued, and finally Giò ordered Rooster to approach the bars and turn around with his hands behind his back. He pulled Rooster's hands through the bars and handcuffed him, so that he was locked to the bars, unable to move. Giò then slipped on a pair of rubber gloves. We all knew where this was headed, Rooster especially, and yet we didn't want to believe it was actually about to happen.

"What are you gonna do with those gloves?" Rooster asked, apprehensive. He was no longer shouting.

Giò pulled down Rooster's pants so that he was naked from the waist down. I didn't see him apply lubricant to the gloves beforehand, but I couldn't say for certain that it wasn't there. Giò jammed his gloved hand upward; Rooster let out a series of high-pitched shrieks and wails, all laced with utter desperation. He writhed violently and tried to get away, but there was nowhere to go.

"Just give me the jelly!" Giò shouted, straight-faced. The absurdity of this statement, as he jammed his presumably dry, rubber fingers deeper into Rooster's rectum, made the whole thing that much more disturbing. It felt like an eternity—the guard's grunting and shouting, Rooster's desperate wails, the clanging of his handcuffs against the steel bars—but it probably lasted no longer than a minute.

Giò finally gave up, stepped back, and then stormed off down the hall, fuming and empty-handed. Rooster, meanwhile, stood there handcuffed naked to the bars.

"You *fucking freak!*" Rooster shouted in his sharp Southern accent, his voice cracking at the end. "I'm gonna sue the shit outta you!" A moment of silence passed—a rarity in the hole—before Rooster continued, "At least pull my pants back up, *you asshole!*"

After hearing that, the entire floor erupted in laughter, which is sometimes the only response to certain horrors. Nearly an hour would pass before another guard came by to help Rooster. The longer I spent in the hole, the more I came to learn that this sort of thing was just part of the routine.

*

The next day, Giò rushed past my cell shouting, "Dog and pony show! Dog and pony show! They'll be here any minute!" He told us to make our cells presentable. "If you make me look bad, I swear to god, I'll fuck you!"

I heard guys shouting, "Warden! Warden!" They all began hollering over each other, airing their grievances. I could hear Rooster shouting about what Giò had done to him, but his voice was mostly drowned out by the roaring chorus and pandemonium.

Eventually, a group of suits, led by the warden, strolled past my cell. They scanned the cell block, stopped and studied me as if I were a creature on display. Unsure of what to do, I stared back at them and waited for someone to say something, but they weren't actually looking at me so much as through me, as if I weren't even there. As they started to leave, I jumped up from my bed.

"Wait!" I shouted.

The strange echo of oxfords and high heels on the concrete floor stopped, and then in eerie unison the group turned and stared back at me with cocked heads. They seemed stunned by the sound of my voice.

"Excuse me, sir, could you tell me why I'm here?" I asked.

The warden, dressed in a pinstripe suit, with black, slicked-back hair, walked over and brought his face up to mine between the bars, uncomfortably close.

"You know exactly what you did," he said, then turned and walked away, his gaggle following. And that concluded the week's administrative tour of the hole, the dog and pony show.

For the rest of the day, I tried to get the guard to let me make a phone call, but all he gave me was a dismissive "fuck off," over and over again. I was desperate to let my family know what was going on. I'd always tried to call them once a week, but if suddenly the phone calls stopped, I knew they'd be worried.

Someone in a nearby cell offered to help. He wrapped a stamped envelope, with a few sheets of notebook paper inside, around a pencil, then cinched it with a string. He made sure the guards weren't looking, and then, like a fly fisherman casting a line, he tossed it down the hall to my cell, close enough for me to reach. Smooth, like he'd done it a thousand times before. I untied the knot, and the string slowly slithered back down the dim corridor to where it had come from. He said I could reimburse him for the stamp another time.

My cell had a desk, a thin slab of steel bolted to the wall. I set out to write my mother a letter. For a long time I just sat there, staring at the paper, trying to think of something to say. My mind was a thick fog I couldn't shake off. Even simple sentences were difficult to put together. I'd been in the hole just a few days, but I was already feeling the effects of solitary confinement. I stared at the page all night, writing down beginnings just to erase them.

Dear Mom, Don't freak out . . .

Dearest Mother, You've probably heard the news by now . . .

Mom, You're not going to believe this . . .

In the morning, a unit manager, who directed my housing unit's operations and security, finally came to see me. He was a bald, portly man with a pinkish hue, known to fly into sudden fits of rage. Nothing good ever came from interacting with him. I usually tried to keep my distance, but this time I couldn't avoid him.

With uncontainable glee, he explained to me that I'd been placed in solitary confinement because of a magazine article that had run a few weeks before. After nearly a year into our sentence, my codefendants and I agreed to an interview with the late journalist John Falk for *Vanity Fair.* We'd communicated over the course of a few months, mostly through letters and telephone calls, and sometimes face-to-face in the visitation room. The article ran in the December 2007 issue, and apparently had infuriated our prosecutor, who used a quote out of context as a pretext to arrange our separation, claiming that we were potentially plotting future crimes. The line comes toward the end, when Warren is quoted saying, "Believe me, you haven't heard the last of us yet." While in isolation that could sound a bit ominous, looking at it in the context of the rest of the paragraph, it's clear that Warren is speaking about a future after incarceration:

> "In a few years we'll be released. We'll all be . . . still young," Warren says. "We will be stronger, better, wiser for going through this together, the three of us. Before, in college, growing up, we were being funneled into this mundane, nickel-and-dime existence. Now we can't ever go back there. Even if we wanted to, they won't let us. That was the point all

along. See, we have no choice now but to create something
new, someplace else. Believe me, you haven't heard the last
of us yet."

After two years of incarceration, one line from a magazine article
was all it took for an assistant US attorney to destroy whatever sense
of normalcy we had left. He had us separated for the remainder of
our sentences—about five more years—prohibiting all communication or contact, even during the probation period after our release,
by registering us in the Central Inmate Monitoring (CIM) system. The
Code of Federal Regulations states that inmates given CIM status
"require a higher level of review . . . to provide protection to all
concerned and to contribute to the safe and orderly operation of
federal institutions." When discussing the different CIM assignment
categories, specifically that of "separation," the regulations state that
"[CIM] assignment may also include inmates from whom there is
no identifiable threat, but who are to be separated from others at
the request of the Federal Judiciary or U.S. Attorneys."

The moment the request was submitted, we were to be moved
immediately from the general population to solitary confinement in the SHU. They even put us on different levels so that we
couldn't communicate with each other, as if we were high-level
national-security threats.

The unit manager, I'd never seen him smile so much (or smile
at all). He handed me a clipboard and said that if I would just
sign the papers, he'd let me out of the hole and make it all go
away. That sounded too easy. I asked him what I'd be signing. Just
standard paperwork, he said. I flipped through the pages. From
what I could tell, it appeared to be an admission of the charges.
It was clear that he really wanted me to sign it, which made me
suspicious. I worried he was trying to get me to sign off on my own
separation from my codefendants. I declined, and his face turned
red. "Sign the fucking papers," he said.

I refused.

We stared at each other, who knows how long, before he grabbed
the clipboard and barreled out of the unit without another word.

The day turned to night again . . . and again . . . and again.
I kept thinking that someone would rectify the problem, the injustice of it, the random, casual cruelty of it all. But nothing ever
happened.

There was always a long waiting list of transportees. Some, like me, were being shipped to other institutions, while others were just entering the federal system. This meant that it would take months before I'd be shipped out, which would be another ordeal altogether. Federal prisoners are required to pass through one of two intake centers, in Georgia or Oklahoma, which meant that for several months I'd be transported around the country on buses and planes, from prison to prison, cage to cage, shackled and corralled, never knowing which institution I was going to or how long it would take to get there. For guys like us who were being transferred out of punishment, there was a popular phrase for the harsh treatment by the Bureau of Prisons (BOP), a division of the Department of Justice and the law-enforcement agency in charge of the federal prison system. They called it "diesel therapy."

While waiting to be shipped out, I'd spend most of my days reading and watching the snow fall outside the little sliver of window that I could see down the hallway. We were allowed one hour of "recreational" time outdoors every day, milling around a small, concrete area completely fenced off and wrapped in barbed wire. The schedule in the hole was twenty-three hours of lockdown, one hour of "rec," which was intended to keep us all from going completely insane. But since it had been snowing on and off for about a week, the guards simply stopped taking us outside, presumably because they could use the inclement weather as an excuse to do less work—I'd always gotten the impression that they didn't feel we deserved even one hour outside—even though the extent of chaperoning was watching us through a window inside the building.

After a week of 24-7 lockdown, we were all getting agitated. We demanded to be taken outdoors. None of us had proper winter clothes, just jumpsuits, slippers, and thin, cotton coats. But it wasn't so much about the fresh air as it was about spiting the guards and making them actually do some work.

The guards gave in, and before long we were all chained up and shuffling toward the doors. For an hour we waddled around in a rotating circle, huddled together like penguins on a sheet of ice while sleet and freezing rain pelted us in a sideways slant. By the end, my fingertips felt like a lost cause; the frozen concrete pierced through my Bruce Lees as if there were no buffer whatsoever between skin and ground. Once you were outside, you had to stay there for the entire hour, but it was the most alive we'd felt in a while. Still, once the doors swung open, every one of us rushed inside as fast as possible. We spent the rest of the day shivering under blankets in our cells.

Every few days, an orderly would come by with a pushcart full of books—mostly Bibles and romance novels, but every now and then, if you searched carefully, you could stumble upon a classic. I was fortunate enough to find Joseph Conrad's *Heart of Darkness* in the pile. I'd lie in bed all day with this book, embarked on a maddening journey up the Congo River, deeper and deeper into delirium. Time slowed and I slept at odd hours of the day. My mind wandered to far-off places only arrived at through isolation. At one point I woke to find my hand clutching a crumpled piece of paper with a quote that I'd jotted down: ". . . you lost your way on that river as you would in a desert, and butted all day long against shoals, trying to find the channel, till you thought yourself bewitched and cut off forever from everything you had known once—somewhere—far away—in another existence perhaps."

Occasionally, I mustered enough focus to write poetry. Thinking back to my time in E-Unit, I remembered waking one spring morning to songbirds, sunlight cutting across my cell. In that moment, or at least as I recalled it, I felt pure contentment. It was strange to be nostalgic for an old prison cell, but I suppose when you're imprisoned within a prison, that's just the reality of the situation. So every day, little by little, I worked on the poem, to get back to that space. When I was satisfied with it, years later back in general population, I sent a copy to *The New Yorker*, accompanied by a pompous, unhinged prison letter detailing the merit of my work and why the poem should be published in the magazine. I never actually expected to hear back from them, but to my surprise, one day I received a brief yet polite rejection letter in the mail, which I taped to the wall like a family photo—a badge of honor, something of a victory in its own right.

After two weeks in the hole, out of nowhere a guard walked up to my cell and unlocked the door. With no explanation, he told me that I was free to go back to my assigned unit. I pried for details. He said that it had all come down to a coin toss, and apparently I'd won. But maybe that's not entirely accurate. We all knew that

Warren would probably be shipped out because the guards just seemed to have it in for him; I'd heard some of them thought he was a smartass. So, it was really down to Spencer and me. Since Spencer had once been caught in possession of a tattoo gun (he was the top tattoo artist on the compound, after all), and I had never received any disciplinary infractions, they decided to let me stay. There was no reason to ship out all three of us. This would still accomplish the intended goal of separation.

Back in general population, and knowing they had no resources down in the hole, I felt an intense responsibility to try to get Warren and Spencer out of solitary. I spent a few weeks studying in the prison's law library about the CIM system and how one goes about appealing a codefendant separation order. Naturally, it's a very convoluted process requiring a great deal of research, and no one is there to help you. On top of that, all the required filing forms must be obtained through the members of one's own "housing unit team"—unit manager, case manager, counselor, etc.—who are oftentimes the very people who put you in the situation to begin with, so they're not exactly cooperative.

The first step is to make an attempt at a vaguely defined "informal resolution." If that fails, it opens the door to filing a formal complaint with the warden. All this must happen within twenty days of the date of the incident or whatever triggered the complaint. Any complaint filed outside that time frame is declared invalid—which is absurd given that you're usually being held in confinement during that time, without any resources, unable to even file the appropriate paperwork. (And if you are able to do so, it's at your own expense—the printed materials, photocopies, envelopes, postage stamps, all of it.) After that, if you're actually able to file a complaint, and you are not satisfied with the warden's response, you can then file an appeal with the BOP regional director, which must be done within twenty days of the signed response from the warden. If you are dissatisfied with the regional response, you can then file a national appeal with the Office of General Counsel in Washington, DC, within thirty days of the date the regional director signed the response. This is the last course of appellate action within the BOP. Multiple copies of each complaint and appeal must be mailed to all involved parties while following the BOP's strict guidelines. If any form is filed improperly, it's considered invalid.

It seemed impossible to find any joy in life—what little of it there was in prison to begin with—at least not while Warren and Spencer were still stuck in the hole, helpless and waiting to be shipped out. All I could do to get my mind off it was to exercise. I'd run outside on the track for hours and hours, wearing a maroon trucker hat that I'd been gifted by a friend who worked in the chow hall that read FCI ASHLAND FOOD SERVICE. My hair and beard were long, and my body turned frail from all the running. Sometimes I'd hear guys yelling at me from somewhere nearby in the yard, "Run, Forrest, run!" There was something in the pain that was reassuring. If Warren and Spencer were in pain, then I also needed to be in pain. I ran and ran and ran because they couldn't.

I eventually contacted John Falk, the journalist from *Vanity Fair*, to inform him of the situation. After learning about what had happened because of his article, he wrote up and signed an affidavit stating that the prosecutor had misconstrued Warren's quote and taken his own written words out of context. Seeing as how he was the one who interviewed us and penned the piece, he wrote in the affidavit, to say otherwise was a deliberate misinterpretation of the facts.

In the hole, the orderlies were the ones who made things happen. The guards would appoint certain well-behaved guys who had been in the hole for a while to become orderlies for the housing unit, meaning they were allowed to leave their cells for a few hours each day to perform cleaning duties. This allowed the orderlies the opportunity to pass "kites" (notes or letters smuggled and hand-delivered) and contraband not only within solitary but also to guys in general population.

Occasionally I'd receive kites from Warren and Spencer. They were usually just telling me about how they were holding up and requesting "care packages"—simple things like toiletries, snacks, and batteries—since guys in the hole didn't have access to most commissary items. Once I'd acquired the items, I'd place them all inside a bag and stealthily toss it over the barbed-wire fence into the yard of the SHU. From there, the orderlies would use a fishing pole–like device to hook the bag and haul it up through a window. Of course, the orderlies would charge a price for their services, especially since it was such a risky undertaking. Luckily, I had a friend who was an orderly in the hole, so he regularly kept me updated on how Warren and Spencer were doing. Through kites, he informed me that Spencer was working on an epic art collage created from pieces of torn magazine pages that took up nearly the entire space of his cell. Apparently, the guards found this amusing, so they allowed him to continue his work. It brought me happiness to know that even in the hole Spencer was able to create art. There was something beautiful in knowing that the piece would exist only in that moment in time. The world would never see this artwork. Once he was shipped out, it would all be destroyed.

One day, the kites stopped coming. I soon got word that, after being held in the hole for months, Warren and Spencer had finally been transferred, although no one knew where. Shortly after, I received notice that my appeals had been rejected.

For weeks, I walked around in a daze, unsure of what to do with myself. In essence, my entire prison identity had been based on my relationship with my codefendants. Now that they were gone, everything felt off. It would be nearly a decade before we'd be able to see or speak to each other again, not until we were all out of prison and off probation. Guys noticed that I was acting strange and kept asking me if I was all right. It was unusual to see one of us alone for very long. Whenever guys would spot one of us without the others, they would always shout out, "Where are the other amigos?" Now, everything felt foreign. I felt vulnerable and exposed, like fresh meat all over again. For a while, I was reluctant to admit it to myself, but I knew what I had to do—I had to find a new bid, my own bid.

I dove back into my studies, hoping the coursework would be enough to carry me through the remaining five years. But right away I found myself oddly uninterested. It felt like something was missing, like I'd overlooked some glaring detail in plain sight. Ever since I was young, I'd always had a passion for writing, but growing up in my area of Lexington, there wasn't much emphasis on the arts. I'd been raised to believe that writing wasn't a real job, it was more like an indulgence or hobby or a profession so far-fetched as to be laughable—like wanting to become an actor, something that other people did, not me. Becoming a writer was the sort of fantasy that could only exist in prison, because in many ways prison was a fantasy world. In confinement, guys created whole new realities for themselves. Prison was a place where you could become a version of yourself free of the judgment of society. And through this awareness, you could ultimately figure out how to bid.

I'd split my days into three parts: exercising, reading, and writing. Exercising and reading kept mind and body in sync, and writing was my main focus. For the first year or so, I researched, studied, and outlined a manuscript. During reading hours, I devoured every book on writing that I could get my hands on: Ray Bradbury's *Zen in the Art of Writing*; *Dreyer's English*; Anne Lamott's *Bird by Bird*; James Scott Bell's *Plot & Structure*; *The Elements of Style*; Stephen King's *On Writing*.

The library actually had a decent selection of books on the study of topics like English literature, grammar, prosody, and prose. Most of the hardback covers had been torn off because guys used them to make pizza-cooking trays for the microwaves. They were dusty old books with titles like *Prosody and Meter: Early Modern to 19th Century*, or *The Origins and Development of the English Language*, or *Sound and Form in Modern Poetry*, or *A Grammar of Present-Day English*. If there was something I didn't understand—like whether it was acceptable to split an infinitive or switch between active and passive voice—I'd set out to learn it. The fact that there was no technology, and only books, seemed to romanticize the learning experience. I read Whitman, Thoreau, Joyce, Lord Byron, Kafka, Dostoyevsky, and Steinbeck. I'd jot down notes in the margins and diagram the architecture of each novel.

At first I was propelled by this idea that my endeavor was somehow profound—as if nothing had ever been written from within a prison cell. The process of shedding this delusion took much time and labor, but along the way, the compulsion to do something original was vital. That compulsion pushes you to endure insecurities and embarrassment and frustration. It makes the work constant. It becomes a pursuit.

By now, I'd moved to working almost exclusively in my cell, unless something needed to be researched in the library. Even though my cell was open during the day, it was the most private place I could find on the compound. Every day, I'd sit on a small, plastic stool, hunched over a roughly single-square-foot piece of steel attached to the wall, a desk of sorts. Using pencil and paper, I'd write, erase, write, erase, write, while shuffling the sooty, graphite-covered pages into order. The way the desk was positioned, I had to write with my back to the door, which took some time to get used to—in prison, you'd almost never leave yourself exposed like that. Even when urinating, you glanced over your shoulder the whole time. But in overcoming this basic fear of sitting at my desk, there were other relentless distractions. My unit was so loud that I had to purchase earplugs from a guy who worked in the factory, which offered a little buffer from the noise but never completely solved the problem. Sometimes I'd cover my eyes with a ski hat in an attempt to find a creative space within the lightless concentration of a makeshift blindfold.

In time, I began writing a memoir. It felt like I'd never be able to write anything else until I got this one story out of my system. I called it *American Animals*, a phrase found in Charles Darwin's *Origin of Species*, one of the books we'd stolen. (The passage referred to cave creatures in Kentucky that stopped evolving eyes because they lived in complete darkness.)

After a while, the very idea of time as something quantifiable faded away. I wrote all day, every day, year after year. I devoted myself entirely to the ideal as if it would not only lead to redemption and forgiveness, but also to a sense of purpose. I owed it to those I'd hurt—the victims, my family—and also to myself.

When I finished writing the memoir, I shelved it and started writing new stories that would purposely never see the light of day or be read by anyone, because in the end it was the devotion that mattered, by living presently and purely in the art as a way of fathoming ourselves. (Many years later, after prison, I'd eventually publish *American Animals*, and the story would go on to be made into a major motion picture of the same name. What a strange sight to see the title I'd spent months agonizing over while reading *Origin of Species* in my prison cell plastered on billboards in major cities around the world.)

After the three of us had been separated, the BOP placed us on a blacklist of flagged inmates, meaning that all of our incoming and outgoing correspondences were read and inspected. Still, every now and then I'd receive letters in the mail from Warren and Spencer, who were residing at different federal institutions around the country. We used our coded language and signed off with names like "Archduke Ferdinand," "Aung San Suu Kyi," and "Ralph Waldo Emerson," just to make things interesting for the prison officials reading our mail. Other times we just signed "Chip," "Din," and "Pep." But names were irrelevant at that point anyway. On sunny days, I would drift outside to the yard after mail call with their letters in hand. Lying in the grass, I'd hold the pages up to the bright blue sky—the same blue sky as everywhere—and run my finger over the deep grooves of their frantic pen strokes, as their words grew sharp on the page in the sunlight. It gave me strength just to hold something that I knew they also had held, as if the pages were a part of their very being, their only lasting physical presence. After all those years, I could still hear their voices in what they'd written. They wrote of prison violence, books they were reading, small joys, and colorful characters they'd met along the way. They wrote of many things, but mostly about the bond we'd created, and how it continued to carry them through the day.

CHRIS DENNIS

We Were Hungry

FROM *Astra*

DEAR MCDONALD'S—

When I called my friend Amy to try to explain why I was writing this letter to you, she asked, "Are you trying to say that a marginal life will always unfold in a marginal place?" To which I responded, "God, Amy, yes." So then I called my friend Heather, who knows more about the design of commercial spaces, and she said, "Have you heard about the third place theory?" She said, "A third place is a place that is not home and not work but still wants us to stay awhile, to feel, even, a sense of belonging while we are there. It can be a library or a coffee shop or a bookstore or even a McDonald's." And I had to ask, "What is a third place when a person has no first or second place?"

McDonald's—when my sister and I were homeless and addicted to methamphetamines and difficult to love, you let us in. Or rather your employees let us in. When we lied and said you'd gotten our order wrong, even though no order had actually been placed, you knew we were lying and fed us anyway. Was this a strategy devised in a boardroom, an attempt at warm brand association? We lied to you over and over, but it was your policy to believe us even when no one else would. You did ask, once, to see a receipt when we wanted too much. You looked at us, exhausted, from behind the black touch screen and said, "We can give you the ten McChickens but not the three Big Mac Meals." You were setting boundaries with love. Is *this* what love looks like? we wondered. Neither of us was able to recognize it. But we felt the truth in our hardly there bodies and said, "Okay." We took the food with desperate gratitude and walked along the highway, passing the paper bag between us. Later, while my sister waited outside with her new boyfriend, I injected drugs in your bathroom. One of your employees came and knocked on the stall door and I said I'd be out soon. "Thank you," he said. "You're welcome," I said. Afterward, too high to even speak, I cupped my hands under the ice machine. The cubes dripped between the gaps of my fingers as I walked—annihilated—out the door into the parking lot, where the sun bounced off the hoods of a dozen Ford Focuses.

We know what it's like to be ignored. To be ugly to everyone, even to you, McDonald's, and to your sad, judgmental customers. But would you die for us? I would never ask you to. But will you say it? When all the other customers have gone and it's just me, nodding off in a booth while Kaylin, the assistant manager, mops the floor, could you whisper it to me? Just say, I'll do anything for you.

What were the chances my sister and I would both end up shooting meth in an abandoned camper at the edge of the Saline River? The chances were high. You must have known that. A little math—location plus sexual orientation plus adjusted gross income—would have told you as much. Yet somehow you loved us before we were even born. Through some deep market research, you named our future desires, you knew our favorite item on the Dollar Menu before we could speak. A brand can draw you toward it, gentle as a drain. The ads work best when we don't know they're working. When we were young, you dressed yourself up like a clown. We longed to crawl inside of that clown, into a place where we could eat and be eaten forever. Where does a craving come from? I needed you, McDonald's. You taught us how to do the clown voice so that when you were gone, we talked to ourselves and pretended we were you. A craving only ever leads to another craving.

You could project with your all-seeing eye: a hologram of my sister and me as young parents, with our heads of matching curly hair, on the front porch of our mother's new mobile home, laughing at our own children, who are playing hide-and-seek just out of frame. Our parents wonder, Where did *that* version of the adult siblings go? Five to seven years later, we would both be sitting in a drug dealer's basement waiting for someone to pass a broken pipe, not knowing or wondering in those feral minutes where our precious children were or who was laying out their clothes for school. How did we even get there? I could say it started in the doctor's office, or when the prescription pain pills weren't enough, or when I started shooting heroin at thirty-five years old, or later when, trembling from opioid withdrawal, I rode with my sister to an apartment building just outside of town to buy meth for the first time, or when we stood in her kitchen afterward, snorting little bumps off the warped countertop. In a room on the second floor of the Economy Inn, high on the horror, my sister and I were like two insects trying to split a grain while our parents turned away from their children's ugly lives, the same way they had turned away from their own.

By the time my sister and I entered high school we were home alone every day for weeks and we fought. I stood at the foot of the stairs and hit her with a hanger. The sound of her cries etched a message onto my muscles and that message was, You are disgusting. I was not her mother or her father. We are two years apart and I remember a time our mother chased me across the yard with a hanger and who was I when my sister needed me? What did we have there in the lonely housing projects, in the quiet apartment? The ability to care for each other, at twelve and fourteen. To watch each other for a signal as we passed a joint on the porch while Larry, the mechanic who lived next door—grinning, his eyes watering with senile delight—showed us a blurry tattoo of a smiley face on the tip of his limp penis. He did it so casually, like he was telling a joke.

There is no such thing as free will. Corporations have wagered the wealth of empires on this idea and won. They read the research on addiction, fished the information from the pockets of a million dead addicts, used it against us so that we would buy more cheeseburgers. We chose you, we chose you, we chose you. We had no idea, in that moment, why we would look at your luminous arches and think, That place. All our longings, in one way or another, were decided for us long ago.

My sister and I stood in the way of so many things that might have damaged the other: car rides with strange men at 3 a.m., drugs from people too eager to sell them, loneliness. My sister stood between me and danger. But the hanger. Such a stupid object. This is how the drugs fill the empty cup of my brain. Where do you carry your own mind when it weighs too much for your neck? To the dealer. To McDonald's. To the bank of the Saline

River. Consciousness is sometimes very inconvenient. I was not her mother or her father. That should not have been the hard part but it was. We were hungry and had been for years, eating or trying to eat everything, trying to find something that would fill us up while we paced the parking lot waiting for the dealer, while the moon rose above the Walmart.

We were two adults with our backpacks full of all we owned and two McChickens each for later, walking down alleys to the garage where we sometimes slept. It was like a dream of childhood. Drugs were a way of pretending we had no body at all, or that we were just a body and nothing else, or that our bodies were a third place where anyone could come and go without paying. My friend Gina once told me that to organize a room, you must first clear everything out of it, then return the most crucial things first, in descending order of importance. Inside the lobby of the Harrisburg McDonald's there is only what is necessary: tables, seating, and so many trash bins. In the end, for you, McDonald's, the trash bins were what mattered most. You can use something and know for certain when it is no longer useful.

Remember the time when my sister and I were little—this was before they tore you down to build a new one in your place—and we sat inside you with our grandfather while he ate a McRib? Tell us how you knew—as my sister and I sat watching the old man who would teach us to drive—that we would become such pathetic adults. That we would beg our grandmother for our grandfather's life insurance money when he finally died, alone and legless in his hospital bed, his skin the color of yellow gold. We would snort the money and shoot it up, sometimes in an apartment in the very same housing projects where we'd lived as teenagers, while our grandmother paced with her walker before the table that held the enamel box of his gray ashes. What little money there was left she used to bail me out of jail a third time.

Homelessness was—at times—such a comfort: walking the streets, living there, like a long hike to nowhere. Was homelessness the opposite of capitalism or the definition of it? The anarchy of drug use was a relief from the meaninglessness of poverty. We could not shrink down small enough—though we tried—to fit inside the old fort we'd cut with scissors through the broom shrub. We could not shrink to fit into the bedroom our mom's boyfriend had painted to look like a chessboard. That was before he stood at the foot of our bed with no clothes on to tell us something unknowable from the Bible. Mostly he wanted us to hear how much he longed to not be an angry drunk. We didn't want to go back to that time, but we wanted to go back to that place. That place where there was still a good life ahead of us.

My sister and I counted once: as children, we lived in eighteen different houses. That's enough houses to fill a McDonald's, if you burn the houses down and pour the soot through a funnel in the roof until all of the air is pressed out of the McDonald's. A McDonald's is not a home. Until it is. Suspend us, McDonald's, in the air above the earth. Lay in our hands a small collectible toy.

I slept in a booth and no one came to wake me or ask me to leave. You looked the other way while I had a quick dream of more drugs after weeks of drugs and no sleep. It is hard, once you have gone into the black room, to stop going into the black room. Who will knock on the bathroom door to say, Is there anyone in there? Are you okay? There's a brother or a sister behind the bathroom door of every McDonald's, dying a little under the directionless light, as they root with a dull needle, as they wash the sweat from their faces in your clean automatic sink. I was hungry long before you. But you were waiting there, near my middle age, to feed me.

Not long after I'd returned from rehab the first time, my sister opened the car door for me. We'd just snorted too much meth and I was sure that inside the vehicle, clinging to the ceiling, were dozens of quivering bats. "There's nothing there, Chris. Look. It's okay." She opened the door and just like that the bats flew up inside themselves. Months later, after I'd started shooting meth and was certain that tiny particles of something were drifting toward me at all times, shredding my cells, she stood next to me, pressed her face against my face, and said, "I can feel it, too. You're not crazy. I can feel it." What is a sibling but proof that you weren't alone through the worst of it? A witness. A fire wall against the gaslight of childhood. "I was there, too," she says.

One time, my sister drove a hundred and fifty miles to pick me up because I was too high. I'd left the hotel room of the guy I was fucking and I was walking the streets. "I'm lost," I told her, "and I don't have a coat and it's sleeting." What else is a sibling but a double you? What else is a McDonald's but a mother or a father, saying, finally, Where are you going, my gay son? Tell me what you need from me, my sensitive child. Wasn't it always the irresistible call of life after death? Or the image of a newly remodeled Mc-Donald's collapsing in on itself, drawing everything in: the cows in the pasture outside of town, the Easter flowers, the rotten tennis shoes, the used needles, the stolen money, the fluttering bats, the eighteen houses, the busted cell phone I used to call my mom for help outside Jojo's Bar, and she said, with so much frustration in her voice, that she was very tired and could we please talk tomorrow. Take me, Harrisburg McDonald's. Show me everything.

What do I want now, in the ghastly radiance of so many gross decisions? To fold a fitted sheet. To wash a dish in a kitchen of my own. To sit with my son in a too-loud movie theater and, even more, to sit with him in the car afterward—eating a ten-piece McNugget while he talks about the film. I want to place my grandmother's pills in their weekly organizer without wanting to eat them all. I want to give back the money I stole and bring her a McDonald's Sausage Burrito that I paid for myself. And I want my sister—still out there in a crater on the moon of chaos—to come back to her seat at our table. I love her. I miss her. I want to stand in the long driveway at night with my friend Gina and stare at the planets nearest to the earth in October while her children, brother and sister, fall asleep inside to the sound of commercials on TV. I listen to those jingles and wonder, Will they shape the future of those siblings? Will the soft Labrador retriever on the couch beside them—wrestling with all of this same hunger—catch the rabbit she's chasing through the overgrown field of her dreams?

Ms. Daylily

FROM *The Iowa Review*

THE CHINESE EMPEROR who died one year before the Common Era began was a man in love with another man named Dong Xian. According to the historical volume *Book of Han*, one morning the emperor awoke to find his sleeve caught under Xian, who was still asleep by his side. Not wanting to disturb Xian's slumbers, the emperor cut his own sleeve so he could get up. Upon recording the anecdote, the ancient historian commented amiably, "such was their love"—a departure in tone from his criticism of the emperor's rule. "Cut sleeve" thus became a synonym for romance between two men. Among many names the Chinese have used for same-sex love, this might be the best known.

That archaic sense of normality regarding queer relationships, however, had been lost on me when I first read the story during my adolescence, my brain already tainted by the mores of the time. In modern literature, such allusions appear in combination with the word "addiction"—"cut-sleeve addiction," for instance. The character 癖—*addiction*—has a semantic component denoting "disease." Emperors being emperors, whatever they did had nothing to do with us ordinary people, or so the teenage me thought in the turbulent 1970s.

My mother began to let me borrow her journals shortly after the new millennium. She'd become rather generous in this; her rapid aging seemed to have freed her from either vanity or obligation. In her seventies, she no longer held her private writing as closely as she used to. Her journals are from 1950 on, five or six decades in the making, each labeled by year. For about a decade, during each of my annual visits to China, I put a few of those into my carry-on bag and brought them back to Boston, where I've made my new home. Those notebooks, full of history, were too precious for checked luggage.

She set no conditions, other than "Don't lose them." I searched in her words for answers to several questions long held in my mind, with little success. A particular one: What exactly had my father done to my mother in 1958, the year of her political disgrace?

My mother's journals are a river of emotions, rarely specifics of events. Again and again the year 1958 leaps out like a slippery fish, only to disappear into the mist. I had almost given up reading—at times, it felt hard for me to keep afloat through so many years of reflection—when a lone bookmark appeared, between the pages she had written around the time I was in middle school.

Actually, the bookmark was just an old piece of paper, about one by two inches, which must have been a corner of something bigger, because the uneven edge on one side showed the trace of scissors work. On this faded and water-stained little piece of paper is printed the picture of an orange-colored daylily.

This daylily picture did not stir me at first, and it would have remained that way if not for what I read on the page: There is a mention of a woman whom my mother refers to as "my forget-worries flower." Because of this woman, my mother wrote, "At this extremely difficult time, I especially find consolation: I am not alone in this world after all."

The woman's name contained a character that means "orange daylily." This plant has several common names in Chinese, one of which is "forget-worries grass." The *Compendium of Materia Medica*, a classical Chinese herbology volume written during the Ming dynasty, has a description of the plant's medicinal use: the soup made from its roots can calm anxiety. Mother, an elementary school principal at the time, apparently exercised her poetic license to substitute the word "flower" for "grass," her romantic self awakening at an inopportune time.

I certainly remember her, *Ms. Daylily*, though I wouldn't have called her that then, not knowing the meaning of her name. She was my mother's colleague, a decorous-looking and even-tempered schoolteacher. Her virtuous demeanor always reminded me of the traditional phrase "loyal wife, devoted mother," an impression readily supported by the love her children, intimate friends of my two older sisters, demonstrated. Living just two blocks from our house, she had been a regular visitor starting from when I was eleven or twelve. As time went by, she became a close aunt to us children. During the Cultural Revolution, when my parents were mired in political troubles and few of their colleagues wanted to associate with us, Ms. Daylily's comforting presence was heartily welcomed by my sisters and me. For a time, while Father was detained and Mother was denied the right to visit him, Ms. Daylily even became a messenger between the two.

A few pages after the daylily bookmark, Mother wrote about Father: "He is an honest man; I can completely understand if he's discontented with our behavior, which does not follow Mao Zedong Thought. But I can also imagine that, if I get into any trouble, he would treat me again just like in 1958. Thinking of this, my heart is filled with extreme darkness."

The veiled words "our behavior"—that is, the relationship between my mother and Ms. Daylily—stuck out upon a second read, though it was "1958" that caught my eye at first.

What my father, a rather timid man, did to my mother in 1958 was something I vaguely knew by rumor. That year, following the stormy 1957, when Mao Zedong launched the Anti-Rightist Campaign against dissident voices, China must have seen a record number of couples divorcing—so many among friends of my parents and parents of my friends had separated then, for fear or for love, especially those with small children. My parents stayed in their marriage, though my mother, a rising star as a woman leader in her late twenties, was demoted and sent down to a rural area for seven years, while my father's position as a Party cadre remained intact; later he was promoted through the ranks until the Cultural Revolution that spared no one. That does not mean everything was fine between them. Nor that everything was wrong—at least as a child I did not sense the discord. They hid it well, thanks to my mother's determination to not burden her young children with parents' problems.

So in the 1960s, for many years of my childhood I lived a consequence that I did not know was a consequence. A child knows only the life she's born into and that is her norm. Mother had been mostly absent since my memory began. (Father was at the supper table every day, but that was pretty much the only time I saw him back then.) If I asked Gaga—my maternal grandma who took care of us—where Mama was, the answer was always "at work." When Mother did come home, on a rusty, clanking bicycle, the visits were often at night and rushed. She'd check our homework, ask Gaga how we'd behaved, and be gone before I opened my eyes in the morning.

There was something about Mama's nightly bike treks that made Gaga worry. It bewildered the small me. I might have been a girl quick at math, but I was slow in understanding the female body. (Several years later I'd take my first period for a wound; I was so frightened by the sudden blood streaming down my leg that I cried.) The opaque conversations between Gaga and Mama—in low voices that pricked my ears—instilled a vague picture in my brain that men posed a particular danger to women under the cover of night. Why? How? I had no clue. I had yet to learn the word "rape."

It took me a long time to see the meaning of those strange evenings under a swaying, fifteen-watt bulb, to understand the vulnerability of a woman's body.

My discovery of the daylily bookmark was not entirely accidental. I was browsing that particular journal more carefully than others because of a puzzling incident from middle school. My memory of that incident always drifts with the missing fragrance of winter-sweet. Wintersweet, orchid, bamboo, and chrysanthemum, as my poetic Chinese ancestors would say, are the four nobles among flowers and plants. And look which is first: the small, light yellow blossoms adorning bare, dark, gnarled branches, their clean fragrance braving the chilly north wind to foretell spring. Each January and February, the fragrance would find its way into our house and gladden my young heart, as my mother kept buying bouquets on the street, no matter the political turmoil.

"*Scattered shadows slant the shallow water / hazy fragrance floats in the moonlit dusk,*" a Song dynasty poet sang of wintersweet.

I did not know the poem then. China was a book-free zone throughout my teens. This is not fiction. It was called the Cultural Revolution. The year was not yet 1984, nor were fire engines repur-posed; nonetheless, books had been seized and burned or locked up. I frantically hunted for books, any book, my eyes open round like an owl searching in the dark. By luck, two friends and I became acquainted with a young teacher who'd hidden away an attic full of forbidden books. We visited Teacher Li's attic once a week, and he let each of us borrow one book at a time. The stealthy visits went on for nearly a semester. I wouldn't tell anyone, especially my mother, a hen fiercely protecting her chicks.

Teacher Li seemed utterly touched by our thirst for reading. "Nowadays where can you find students who want to read books?" he said more than once. As we became closer with Teacher Li and his fiancée, who owned the attic, he told us that, each year, during the Spring Festival in early February, they hiked to the South Mountain and relished the wintersweet perfuming the slopes. "You are invited to go with us next year," he said.

"Really?" I said.

"Really," he smiled.

In retrospect, his invitation would have made for the first literary outing of my life. Only he said it too early, I longed for it too much, and it would never happen.

One day before the summer break I asked Teacher Li for a book I'd heard about, but he did not have it. He said he'd look for it and let me know. My home did not have a phone. I gave him the number of my compound's mail room and asked him to call if he found it. Nothing. After a while I forgot all about the whole thing. I had also forgotten to tell him not to call on weekends because my mother would be home.

That was exactly what he did. When our visits were paused by the summer break, one weekend, someone in our courtyard shouted at my window and said there was a call for me. My mother was in the yard washing clothes. She threw all the laundry in the wash basin and ran to the phone. I was unhurried, not believing anyone would call me. Then I heard my mother demand, "Who are you? Why are you looking for my daughter?"

Bang! My mother hung up. What followed was an interrogation, her yelling and my resentful crying.

I loved my mother, loved her all my life. But that moment stuck with me. She was usually a sympathetic and understanding parent. I just couldn't comprehend where her ferocity toward men came from.

I never visited Teacher Li again. Never had a chance to take the Spring Festival hike I'd so looked forward to, a trip that sounded utterly poetic. All because Teacher Li was a man.

Around that time, one book that I pilfered from a locked and sealed library was *Three Kingdoms*, a classic Chinese novel. It opens, "The empire, long divided, must unite; long united, must divide. Thus it has ever been."* The ebb and flow of conflict survived the emperors and, for my mother, ran from the Japanese invasion of World War II to the Communist takeover of China in late 1949, through the Anti-Rightist Campaign of the late 1950s into the Cultural Revolution of the 1960s to '70s. I witnessed the last as a child, and I grew up with the knowledge that my parents had been "Underground Communists," but decades would pass before I learned the most personal secret of my mother's revolutionary youth.

At the age of nineteen, my mother was teaching at a rural elementary school in Chongqing, the last stronghold of the Nationalist regime. The year was 1948 and, in the north, grand battles between the two political forces were in full swing. The teaching job doubled as a cover for Underground work and a means to make a living. Several of her colleagues were young women her age. From time to time a librarian in another town who had been their teacher came to visit. They spoke highly of him: "erudite," "quick-witted," full of "progressive thoughts." My mother admired those qualities, and she visited him a few times with her new friends. He analyzed the war situation for them with a depth lacking among their peers, and he brought them progressive magazines. Reading between the lines of his words, my mother was pretty sure this teacher was a senior Underground member, though Party discipline prevented any revelation of her own political identity. The shared ideology sped her trust in him. In late 1948, he began to pursue her, threatening to take his own life if she did not agree to be his fiancée. He was ten years older; she had always respected him as an elder and a teacher, and had no intention of changing that relationship.

One early winter day he wrote a letter inviting her to a weekend evening meeting in his library. There were other invitees too,

---

* Quoted from Moss Roberts's English translation of *Three Kingdoms* (Beijing/Los Angeles: Foreign Language Press/University of California Press, 1991).

all comrades in the student movement she had been involved with before. They were going to discuss the war situation, the letter said.

So she went. It took her more than an hour by foot and another hour by bus. She entered the library and its door closed behind her. He was waiting for her, alone.

Then he raped her.

Two years prior, she joined protests against another rape. On Christmas Eve 1946, in Beijing, a nineteen-year-old student named Shen Chung had gone to see a movie. On her way home, two U.S. Marines kidnapped and raped her. Newspapers reported that Shen Chung was so ashamed she wanted to kill herself. International media, including the *New York Times*, reported the "Shen Chung Incident" and the ensuing unrest, which now forms a part of China's modern history. The rape triggered nationwide anti-American protests, and my mother, a seventeen-year-old student at Chongqing Teachers' School at the time, became an outraged student leader in the movement titled "Protesting American Cruelty." The Communists seized the opportunity and covertly sponsored the student movement. They took notice of my mother's bravery and idealism, and they approached her. Thus, one young woman's tragedy led another into a revolution, and my mother thought she had found the path toward women's emancipation.

But when she was raped by a comrade, there would be no mass protests.

For a week following her rape, my mother ate little. She cried through the nights for her lost virginity—she could never have a family, and no man would want to marry her. Shame and desperation overwhelmed her; she told no one of the incident. She even considered marrying her rapist.

She and the man did not have contact for several months, until one day a younger girl friend came to ask her opinion about a suitor. It was the same man. Again he had threatened suicide had the girl not accepted his "love." Outraged, my mother went to her Party superior and exposed his crime. It turned out he had raped seven of his students, all eager to learn "progressive thoughts." But my mother was told that any action, either reporting his acts to the Nationalist police, or seeking his discipline within the Underground, would risk exposing other Underground members. His crime could not be punished. There was nothing to be done.

*

My mother met my father, another Underground member, the following summer, both of them in hiding from Nationalist pursuit. He was attracted by her beauty and country girl's forthright manner, without the pretentious bashfulness he perceived in those pale-faced petty bourgeoisie ladies; she was attracted by his cultured demeanor and timidity, as well as his music teacher's sonorous voice. After being harmed by a "mature" man, my mother must have also found a young man's inexperience with women endearing and safer.

As their relationship developed through shared Underground struggle, my mother was never certain about their future, her heart constantly burdened by her unspeakable secret. In October 1949, after Mao Zedong announced the establishment of New China in Beijing, and while Chongqing, still in the hands of the Nationalists, had started batch executions of captured Communists, she told him all. She had been prepared to die for the revolution.

She told him during a date, after a sudden afternoon thunderstorm poured down on their walk together. She had stumbled and he had held her arm for the first time. She left him calmly after her confession. She'd depart again in the morning, and she slept well that night. The decision was in his hands now.

The next morning, my father saw my mother off at the port, where she was to take the ferry back to her job post in another town.

It was not your fault, my father said. *I don't blame you.*

To my mother, this was the moment that their relationship became certain.

To me, that was such a poignant point in light of his political abandonment of her nine years later—in 1958—in the New China they had successfully fought for. A man who had the vision and courage to brave the patriarchal tradition could not stand up to the Party for his wife.

Nearly five decades after the diary entries, her words surrounding the daylily bookmark are still heart-wrenching to read.

> *August 18, 1971: I never thought that such wild feelings would come to me at this old age* [of forty-two]. *It has never once happened in my life. It crazed me, now writing love letters twice a day . . .*

My mother had written love letters to Ms. Daylily twice a day! How did she deliver them? The mail would've been too risky. They could not afford being found out.

At the time, my mother was away from home, and stuck in a political "workshop" to be criticized and self-criticize daily. As a child I was aware of the first half of the fact but not the second, though I knew other scary circumstances . . .

When the Cultural Revolution began, Mother had finally returned to our family after toiling in the countryside for seven years. She was assigned a new job as an elementary school principal. The school was no more than ten kilometers away, and she usually came home in the evening by bus. If for some reason she needed to stay overnight at school, she'd let Gaga know. But it was only ever one night at a time, until a week in the eleventh year of my life.

When she did not come home for two or three days in a row, no news whatsoever, Gaga became very worried and sent me to find out what was going on. To save money, I did not take the bus; I walked along a riverside trail for about an hour. I had done this many times before.

As I neared Mother's school, I heard gongs striking—the sound of a parade. Pedestrians stopped walking and stepped aside. I stretched my neck excitedly, till I saw the woman who beat the gong in her hand had a dunce cap on her head. With each strike she shouted a curse at herself in the familiar hoarse voice. *Dong!* "I'm a Capitalist Roader!" *Dong!* "I'm a monster and demon!" The escorting crowd, her colleagues and students, all of them wearing red armbands, pushed her along.

I froze, as if a bucket of cold water had been poured over my head on a below-zero day. Nothing in my eleven years had prepared me to see my mother being perp-walked on the street like the lowest animal. The parade marched past me, the striking of my mother's gong and her hoarse shouting getting louder and then fading. The onlookers around me dispersed. I turned and ran away.

The face of the man who led my mother's shame-parade kept following me. I knew that face. He had been a trusted colleague of hers. He had been so flattering to her and so nice to me on my visits before.

When Mother eventually returned home, she was calm, as if everything was business as usual. I never saw her scared by anything.

She never showed us children that side of her. It is me who reads her diary in reflexive fear, long after the fact.

> *August 15, 1971: These two weeks, the feelings between the two of us have rapidly escalated to a scary extent. I can't understand why, I'm scared . . .*

> *August 26: I can't think, my mind a pond of muddy water. If it continues like this, I might really go crazy, I'm scared . . .*

> *August 30: . . . She is scared; it is all because my "political trouble" implicated her. Her depression worries me.*

> *September 10: I heard that Daylily will be sent to labor, substituting for another person. She is a victim completely implicated by my trouble. I feel so guilty. Am very scared too.*

A fortune among all their misfortunes: nobody, with the possible exception of their husbands, knew they were in love. Apparently people, her children included, just thought they were close friends. At the time, two young women walking together and holding hands was smiled upon as a lovely friendship; that would be unacceptable behavior for two men—history retreating from the early civilization of the "cut sleeve" era.

There was a criminal code written in China's law at the time: "offense of hooliganism." What kind of behaviors would be construed as such a crime? Unspecified. But gay men had been arrested, shame-paraded, and spit on, even executed.

> *July 4: I have words but no one to say them to. Mom doesn't understand. Little Third is too naive.*

I am startled by the mention of me, her naive third child. Judging by the date, it was close to my middle school graduation, and certainly long after Teacher Li's doomed call. At fifteen, I was the only one my mother could have talked to. My beloved big sister had drowned three years earlier; Ping, my other older sister, had gone to the countryside to receive "reeducation"; the youngest,

Feng, was only ten years old; seventy-eight-year-old Gaga was fixed in her thinking. Apparently my mother had considered, if only briefly, confiding in me. But being oblivious as I was then, what reactions could I have given if she had?

And I remember this: One day in the last year of my middle school, Ms. Daylily appeared at our door. She usually dressed neatly despite the colorless time, but that day she was somewhat disheveled and looked like she'd just been crying. "He hit you!" Mother said angrily. The two adults talked fiercely in low voices in Mother's bedroom, door closed. I thought I heard Ms. Daylily's sobs. I eavesdropped and heard Mother say, "You shouldn't come here anymore!" When I told Ping about the puzzling incident during one of her visits home, she wasn't surprised. She said Ms. Daylily's husband suspected the two women were in love.

That was the year I'd heard, for the first time, the term "tongxing lian"—*same-sex love*. Those words had a horrible sound. At a time when even heterosexual relationships were shameful, homosexuality was unthinkable.

"He's talking nonsense," Ping had said, referring to the man's suspicion, "she and Mama are just fast friends!" I rarely felt much in common with Ping, but that time we were together against a common enemy, the abominable feudalist man maltreating his wife. I even thought about dumping a chamber pot on him had he chased his wife to our house. But he never did, not wanting to risk making such an affair public.

I recently learned that, in the couple's later years, when Ms. Daylily was falling into dementia and her husband was dying, the old-fashioned man left a will requesting that their four sons and two daughters take care of their mother at home rather than leaving her in a senior care facility, a wish the children dutifully followed. He believed the best care for her could only be provided by her own children. The man who was so concerned about his wife's physical well-being was the same man I knew who once smashed an iron onto her foot to stop her from seeing my mother.

August 27: My forget-worry flower said, "For more than two years I had been in unrequited love with you, even losing sleep, you just don't know!" Yes, it was that onrush, declaring a stubborn, determined, indomitable, loyal love that opened my caged soul; my lifelong

yearning for love is now fulfilled and given every care to. At this
extremely difficult time, I especially find consolation: I'm not alone in
this world after all.

So Ms. Daylily had been pursuing her for two years before my
mother finally accepted her love. That traces the beginning of
their affair back to 1969. In my memory, Ms. Daylily's frequent
visits to our house started in late 1967, so there was a year or two
of friendship before this development. Apparently, it had never
occurred to my mother, who came from a poor rural family, that
she could have such feelings until they were upon her.

Love is more universal than many of us believe. I will never know
what, if any, intimacy the two women achieved in such difficult
times. I can only guess that Ms. Daylily's love must have sprinkled
a timely rain onto my mother's arid heart withered from losses,
betrayal, and unjust punishment.

Then they broke up as lovers, but stayed friends.

My parents hid their 1958 trouble well, until we kids grew up and
they got old and my mother could no longer bear to conceal her
grudge toward my father. Still, she would talk about that time in
general, but nothing specific about him. And we knew better than
to peel the unnamed scab that had never healed.

I did try to find out once, half a century after that history. I was
visiting Hainan, China's southernmost province in the sea, where
spring stays year-round. My younger sister had managed to rent
an "elderly apartment" for our parents' winter escape from frosty
Chongqing. One afternoon during my visit, I saw my father sitting
alone reading a newspaper—my mother must have gone downstairs to take a walk—and the question just rolled out my lips. I
asked what happened between them in 1958.

As soon as he heard it, my father's hands began to tremble, his
face paled, and he couldn't utter a single word. He was shocked
by my question; I was shocked to see just how hard it can be
for a man to face his past wrongs. (The problem with my father,
however, was that he did not know the wrong at the time; as a
loyal Communist who put Party interest ahead of personal, he
thought he was doing the right thing.) I was frightened that I
might be causing him a heart attack. "Okay, okay, you don't have
to answer," I said, raising both palms to calm him, to push away

his panic. My younger sister rushed in to our rescue in the nick of time. She yelled at me half mockingly, "Are you persecuting the old revolutionary?" and she helped our father away to rest. The year was 2008, and by then "persecuting" had become a teasing word for younger people who had never experienced or witnessed it in action.

I never broached that topic with my father again.

In the years following my failed probe of my father, during my annual visits to China, the daily routine was that my sisters and I took our parents for a walk in the sun and talked weather and health, or sang some old songs together, something both of my parents loved to do. There was one song, however, only my mother knew, and she'd sing it with melodious melancholy when she happened to be with me alone:

> *You led me into a dream, but in another one's dream I forgot you*
> *. . .*
> *All day I watered the roses, but let the orchid wither away . . .*

I never heard her sing this song in my father's presence.

Later I'd find out this was a movie song, "My First Love," from the 1930s, and the lyrics were written by the then-renowned poet Dai Wangshu, who pined for another woman throughout his marriage. His wife ended up divorcing him. Feng, my younger sister who lives in Hainan, told me that Mother sang this song all those years when she took walks with her during her winter stays, so much so that Feng had also learned how to sing it.

Three years passed thus. In the spring of 2011, as soon as I crossed customs and connected with my sisters, I heard my eighty-five-year-old father had had an operation to install a pacemaker the day before, following a midnight scare when his heart nearly stopped. I was worried.

But my father surprised me when I saw him in the hospital; apparently there was something other than his heart condition that concerned him even more. He told me he had been deeply depressed lately. This wasn't like him, a jolly, sometimes silly, old man. I asked what was making him depressed. He said, "I keep thinking of the things I did wrong when I was young . . ." He mentioned a number of Party lines that he had believed, including the lies that the big famine of 1959 to 1962 was a "three-year natural disaster" (when in fact it was caused by the government's catastrophic economic policies and prolonged by the subsequent cover-up), and that the "rightists" in 1957 were the enemies of the people and the Party (when in fact the whole ordeal had been started by Mao inviting frank opinions on his Party and then, overwhelmed by mounting criticism, turned around to prosecute those who followed his call to speak up).

The next thing my father said was that he felt sorry about my mother. He did not give specifics, but the year 1958 hovered in the tensing air. I paused, not sure what to say. This was a big change. Last time I saw him, those topics were still unspeakable. Had my probe three years before precipitated his depression?

I looked back at my frail mother, who was staying in the hospital room to accompany my father. I don't know how many times she had dutifully been at his side this way.

My mother did not show much of a reaction to my father's apologetic words. She was about to turn eighty-two. I doubted those words still meant much to her; they certainly came too late. People always say it's never too late to apologize—that may be true for the one who owes an apology, but not for the one owed.

By then I had more or less put the puzzle together: When the Anti-Rightist Campaign began in 1957, my mother was on another assignment away from home, thus fortuitously putting her, a candid person, out of harm's way. When she returned months later, however, she was shocked to see several close friends stripped of everything and about to be sent to labor camps. Her sympathy toward those "rightists" made her a new target. It seems that my father, who believed in the Party more than his wife, spoke against my mother in a series of denunciation meetings, and even analyzed their pillow talk—some quibble about a superior—as politically motivated. My mother, then twenty-nine, was shaken to the core by these actions from the man she loved and trusted. When the Party's decision to punish her was announced, she'd wanted a divorce and my father might have agreed, but a sympathetic superior talked them out of it.

In my mother's silence, I felt I had to say something to the old man. "You didn't know then," I said. This was a filial daughter speaking, not a critically minded writer.

"It's true I didn't know then, but that does not ease my guilt," my father said. His tightly locked eyebrows did not smooth out. His consciousness was torturing itself. My mother still said no words, her expression indifferent.

At the time of my visit in 2011, my parents had just received a puzzling decree from the government demanding a marriage certificate of them, sixty years into their turbulent lives together. Back in the early 1950s, at the nascence of the Communist era, witnesses at a wedding party sufficed to give evidence of a marriage, such as in their case. No paperwork was required then, no photo taken. She was twenty-two and he twenty-five. Why would a certificate suddenly become necessary so late in their lives? My aged mother tittered, as she often did those days at an official nuisance. She also tittered at my father's unquestioning excitement, as he seemed to see it as the chance for a second wedding.

It was not in question that my father would follow the government's request, if only for the fear of unforeseeable consequences. I understood, but I wasn't sure if my mother would be willing to follow through and go obtain a largely meaningless document. A year or two earlier she had threatened to divorce my father— belatedly, after *everything* that had happened to them. Her threat made my sisters and me really worried, for Mother's emotional status and for Father's physical well-being, but my frail mother was the stronger one, as she always had been. My father had been cared for by women in our family—his wife, mother-in-law, and daughters—nearly all his adult life, and he was incapable of doing household chores—no cooking, no laundering. How could he survive a divorce?

It occurred to me though, that the government's request for a marriage certificate presented an ironic dilemma to Mother's threat: to formally divorce is to revoke the marriage certificate. If they didn't have one to begin with, what could she revoke?

To our relief, my mother did not resist—or care about—the idea of getting the redundant marriage certificate. Shortly after Father was out of the hospital, our entire family went to the Marriage Registration Office.

April 12, 2011, was a sunny Tuesday. In the pictures we took that day, my elderly parents hold hands, standing in front of the

Marriage Registration Office. Father's left hand grips a red booklet near his heart; Mother's right hand clutches an identical red booklet by her hip. In the booklets are their marriage certificates—one copy for each. Father's smile is broad and free, Mother's barely discernable and shadowed. Wrinkles like a spider's net surrounding Mother's turbid eyes, she looks a lot older than Father who is actually three years her elder.

Had they a wedding picture from sixty years earlier, I wonder if it would show her belly slightly swollen, her smile fearful or guilt-laden, my big sister growing like an unstoppable weed within her, the consequence of their one impulsive night weighing on her heart like a rock. I wonder if my father's smile would be forced or reluctant, unprepared to marry if not for the need to cover the illicit pregnancy and avoid discipline from the Party.

As we were taking the pictures, behind my hand-holding parents a young couple in their twenties passed by, each with a blue booklet in hand. The woman was crying; the man looked away. The same office also handled divorce, but my parents would never return for that.

My mother's diaries are a mixture of love and resentment toward my father. But as her dementia got worse in her final couple of years, she could only recognize him as a longtime comrade, not her husband.

One day four years after our mother's funeral my sisters and I would bury our father's ashes in the same tomb, as he'd wished. I'd set out to look for Ms. Daylily the next day, only to find she'd died two months before my father did, leaving behind a purse full of my mother's pictures big and small.

The day my mother died, March 8, 2015, was International Women's Day, but that was not the only coincidence.

The Chinese have a saying, "The judgment on one is set when the lid on the coffin is closed." That doesn't apply to my mother. Her funeral was surprisingly deserted and quiet, despite the fact that she had had lots of friends. All I can say is that the farewell ceremony was held in the wrong place at the wrong time, and none of her old friends made it, including those who had a "life and death friendship" with her, as they'd say.

The day after the funeral, a midweek day, my cell phone rang. The phone wasn't mine. Ping, my older sister who still lived in our birth city, had lent me her extra phone because my mobile service was useless in China. I had ignored unrecognized calls thus far, but for some reason I took that call—in my deep disappointment with the funeral, I probably would have vented at any stranger who happened to be bothering me.

But I heard a voice I used to know. "We are going to have a family party for my mother's ninetieth birthday. She wants Principal to come," the caller said without saying hello, just like the olden days. She thought I was Ping.

She still called my mother "Principal" after all these years—all these decades—as if times had not changed, and our mothers still taught at the same elementary school.

"My mom died Sunday," I said.

I heard silence at the other end. Then she said, "Oh."

I identified myself and we greeted each other. I asked how her mom, Ms. Daylily, was doing, and learned that my mother's old love had been suffering from dementia for years. The day before, however, Ms. Daylily had a rare moment of clarity and she wanted to see my mom.

That was the same day I had asked Ping whether she had heard anything about Ms. Daylily. I knew the reason for my question. Ping didn't. She told me she had lost touch with Ms. Daylily's family for ages.

I don't believe in anything supernatural, yet I could not help but wonder what happened internally between Ms. Daylily and my mother at the moment of their eternal parting. Did Ms. Daylily's spirit attend my mother's funeral that no one else from their generation had?

It was early March, and the wintersweet had finished blooming, but when I wandered the residential compound where my mother had lived, here and there the waxy-color petals could still be seen sporadically, and if you pulled a stem close, the faint fragrance would still embrace. By now I have crossed many oceans, and sauntered in many gardens and arboretums, still I have not seen wintersweet anywhere like that in the city of my birth.

SANDRA HAGER ELIASON

The Rough Ride

FROM *West Trade Review*

I'M A DOCTOR.

I was taught to believe I have answers, that people come to me for those answers, and that the answers are correct—scientifically correct and based on proven data. Sometimes, however, what's correct isn't the same as what's right.

Rightness—or not—of my decisions was what came to mind when I saw Serena's name on my schedule. My stomach tightened as our history of mostly difficult appointments replayed itself in my mind. I hadn't seen her since the incident, when she had resumed drinking with near catastrophic results. Now I would have to face her, and the consequences of my actions. I steeled myself for whatever this appointment would bring.

Serena didn't always accept my knowledgeable advice, and I must admit I found caring for her difficult. She could be confrontational and angry, often implying that her problems were the fault of my carelessness or incompetence. Then, I felt my resentment rising and I had to carefully monitor my reactions. The literature reports that doctors find it easier to treat patients who understand their advice and follow it. Conversely, it's easy to dislike patients who reject our advice. I walked on eggshells around Serena, doing my best to like her.

Serena's behavior was often influenced by her drinking. She had tried to stop many times and had been in treatment repeatedly. Her illness was exacerbated by the cocaine she used to self-medicate her bipolar disease. That was typical of the patients I saw. My practice was composed of patients with complicated medical conditions who also had behavioral health problems. Patients like Serena were the norm, and I made it my job to like them all. In my ideal world, I found our common humanity, the spark that made them unique, that attracted me to them. I believed I did not judge, but, of course, I saw the world through my doctor's eyes.

Serena first came to my attention when she burst out of the psychiatrist's office, dashing down the hall tearing off her shirt, screaming, "Get it off of me—get it off of me!"

I looked up startled from where I stood at my wall-mounted table. She had her shirt over her head and was desperately clawing at her bra, her brown hands frantically reaching for the clasp.

Our social worker, Craig, sprung into action to sprint after her, the tail of his polo shirt flapping out of his chinos as he disappeared out the door she exited. I was confident he would guide her safely to the emergency room for evaluation and treatment, as I had seen him do many times with others.

The psychiatrist, Dr. Edwards, followed her out of the room in astonishment.

"Who was that?" I asked him.

"That was Serena," he said, shaking his head, his unruly tufts of white hair floating from side to side. "She's in a manic stage—her medications ran out."

I occasionally caught glimpses of her after that, a dignified middle-aged woman in a crisp blouse and matching pants, every hair in place, medications once again working.

I formally met her when Dr. Edwards referred her to me for a medical evaluation. Although he appeared the absent-minded professor type, with his wild hair and disheveled white lab coat, his knowledge of general medicine was broad. His interest in the medical portions of his patients' conditions complemented my interest in the psychiatric components, and we both acknowledged the overlay of the two.

Serena's high blood pressure was poorly controlled, and he noticed her to have tremors and difficulty rising from a chair. Although those could be medication side effects, he felt in this case they were not related, and asked her to schedule with me.

"Hello, I'm Dr. Eliason," I introduced myself, smiling and holding out my hand.

"I know who you are," she said flatly, glancing my direction, then looking toward the opposite wall.

She sat rigidly beside the desk, arms crossed and lips compressed firmly. Her robin's egg blue blouse tucked into pants a shade darker, and her brown hair swept back in a bun that allowed a few escaping wisps of gray.

She glanced my way again, her eyes sparking, and her face wore a look of apprehension and annoyance.

I stifled a sigh as I seated myself at the computer, trying to remain open. "What brings you in today?" I asked, consciously making my voice pleasant.

"The psychiatrist said you're supposed to look at me," she said, her voice skeptical.

"Yes," I responded, "Dr. Edwards told me about you, and I read his note. He said you have trouble standing up sometimes."

I had reviewed her chart after he talked to me. Multiple admissions for alcohol detoxification and several stints in treatment. A history of multiple medications tried for mania and blood pressure, which worked intermittently, depending on whether she continued them or took them only occasionally. People with mental illness frequently self-medicate with alcohol or other drugs, and that self-medication can turn into addiction. Bipolar treatments, while improving the symptoms and allowing one to feel almost normal, come with significant side effects. A patient can find it difficult to choose whether to continue the medication or look for another, self-administered form of treatment.

Dr. Edwards prescribed the psychiatric medications and saw her as frequently as she would allow for monitoring the possible side effects of Parkinson's-like symptoms or movement disorders, tremor, dizziness, or difficulty walking. He felt her current symptoms were beyond those medication related and wanted me to check for underlying neurological conditions.

I took as complete a history as I could, given her untrusting responses and partial replies.

"When did you first notice these symptoms?"

"I don't know, a while ago."

"Is there anything that makes it worse?"

Shrug.

"Have you found anything that makes it better?"

"Isn't that what I'm here for, for you to tell me that?" She glared at me.

I attempted to retreat to the ideal world I wanted my practice to create, the one where I found a way to build a relationship of trust. Without such a relationship, how could she believe what I said? If she didn't trust me, how could I participate in her healing? I knew healing wouldn't mean her being free of her chronic diseases, but possibly I could help her find increased coping, improved ability to manage, or the tools to get by in the world.

To a doctor, the job always looks like *helping*, imparting the skills, the knowledge, the education the patient lacks. But I can only *help* if I understand what someone is asking for; and I can only hope to understand if I listen deeply to what they mean.

I knew intellectually that it could be difficult for anyone who distrusts the system in general to trust me, a bona fide member of the medical system. And I worked to get myself out of the way— understanding where my skill and education didn't meet another's world. I tried, but Serena did not trust my world, for good reason.

I struggled through her history, keeping my voice even, tone light, and what I hoped was a pleasant expression on my face— wondering where or if we could meet on a level playing field; not realizing such a thing was not possible. The physical exam revealed a slight resting tremor, not worsening with activity, which I suspected might be an obscure medication side effect or drug interaction. The neurological exam did not reveal any asymmetry or weakness. I ordered the expected blood tests, and, not finding anything, referred her to a neurologist to see if there was some underlying condition I was missing. He put a curt note in her chart, stating her condition was not primarily neurological, was due to psychiatric illness and medication side effects, and that she should stop drinking. He referred her back to me for follow-up, saying he had nothing further to offer. I wished he had been more help, provided a solution that gave me more options, to feel I was doing more for her. At least he reaffirmed that I was not missing anything.

Serena came back repeatedly for follow-up, blood pressure checks, medication level evaluations, and treatment of various acute illnesses, though too often after admission for detox or repeat alcohol and drug treatment. At first I had to force myself to be pleasant, to take her rudeness in stride. But as I got to know her, she began to reveal more of her struggle to stay sober, her estrangement from her children, money problems, and interpersonal difficulties. Those vulnerable moments made it easier for me to understand her and feel closer to her, to let down my guard and be authentically pleasant and interested—to care what happened to her. When she had been sober for a while, she could even be sweet, pulling me in. Then, I felt unjudged, and I hoped she did, too.

"Hi, Serena, how are you doing today?" I asked on one such visit.

She looked up with an uncharacteristic smile.

"I think I'm going to be well." She sounded almost hopeful, as though she believed this time she could do it. "My blood pressure's good—I appreciate you working with me; I know you're busy. Thank you for sticking with me."

These visits kept me engaged not only in finding the right medications, but with her as a person, working together to find medications that controlled her blood pressure without interacting or interfering with her antipsychotic medications. At those times, she seemed genuinely interested in finding the right medication. And sometimes, she took it.

More often, however, she would visit her downstairs neighbor to "have coffee." At one visit she let it slip that this neighbor was her cocaine supplier, and when she went for coffee, she was really getting her drugs. While on cocaine, she would stop her prescribed medications, go into a manic episode, and be hospitalized again. From there she sometimes reentered treatment.

After a recent hospitalization, her trust had seemed to erode, and her anger took over.

"Serena, how are you doing?" I asked, entering the room.

She glanced up at me, mouth twisted cynically. "How do you think I'm doing?" She turned toward the wall.

I felt myself tense for a contentious appointment but tried to keep things running smoothly. "I read that you were in the hospital recently. It looks like you had a manic episode, and your electrolytes were not right," I said, opening the computer.

"Yeah," she said, and looked up at me, disgusted. She leaned close, and I could smell her stale breath. "You gave me the wrong medication, and I got messed up."

"Which medication are you thinking caused the problem?" I asked, conscious to hold my face neutral and keep my voice even.

"You prescribed it, you should know," she spat, settling back in the chair, crossing her arms, and staring at me with a satisfied look.

"Let me see if a problematic medication was mentioned in the hospital note," I said.

Reviewing the chart gave me a breather—grounded me in facts, which stopped my emotional reaction, allowing my quickened pulse to slow and my flush to settle so that I could respond rationally.

There was nothing in the hospital note to explain her symptoms, and I wanted to retort, use the same sarcastic tone to point out it was her behavior that caused her problems. But that would help nothing. Resentment, retorts, or one-upmanship wouldn't break down barriers.

It was the disease at fault, and it was still my job to find the medication that worked best, that she could tolerate, and that she was willing to take. We had to be a team, but for her to trust my judgment, I had to respect her feelings and trust her desire to be stable and well.

I tried to talk to her about the drinking and drugs, encourage her to stick with AA, and to support her process. "What would it take for you to stay sober this time?" I asked.

"I don't know, I suppose a doctor who treats me right?"

I stifled another sigh, struggling again with my body and voice, trying not to reveal my frustration. "What can I do to help you?"

"Just find me the right treatment this time."

And we went around, me trying to find ways to be helpful and her trying to push me away.

Then she started drinking again.

I got a report from her county social worker that she stopped paying rent, and was drunk in the hallways of her building, yelling at neighbors and falling against the walls. She was evicted and became homeless. She began living in a shelter, and with the help of the social worker there, found temporary housing. I tried to keep track of her through these transitions, as various social workers sent me reports.

She finally scheduled an appointment where we could reconnect. She didn't show up.

At the end of clinic hours, I tucked myself into my desk to make phone calls, the last one to Serena, to ask her to reschedule. I wanted to connect with her directly, get the relationship back on track. Maybe if I called her personally, asked her to come in, she would follow through. As I dialed, though, I wondered which Serena I would encounter this time.

"Yeah?" she said into my ear.

"Hello, Serena? This is Dr. Eliason."

Silence.

"How are you?"

Silence.

"I saw your name on my schedule today, but you didn't come in. I'd like to get you rescheduled."

"I'm not going to," she said defiantly.

I waited, wondering what to say next.

"You never help me anyway, so what's the point?" Her voice sounded flat, empty of emotion.

I felt my body slump. "Maybe this time will be different," I said hopefully. "I'm concerned about you. I haven't seen you for a while, and in the hospital your blood pressure was too high."

"Who cares . . . Nobody does."

Her words sounded slurred, just enough to make me wonder. I leaned back in my chair with a sigh and looked out the window at the graying sky.

"Serena," I said as calmly as I could, watching the clouds scud by, "have you been drinking?"

"Drinking? Drinking?" Her voice rose, "Yeah, I'm drinking. So what?"

I turned back toward the phone, as though I could see her through the black plastic if I looked hard enough.

"I'm worried about you," I said, seeking a soothing tone, slowing my words. "I'm concerned you may end up in the hospital again, or your blood pressure may be too high, and you could have a stroke."

"Who cares? Who cares?" she yelled. "Let my pressure be bad. There's no point anyway. What's the point of stopping drinking? What's the point of living? I don't care if I live."

My stomach lurched. Her slurring was worsening, and I imagined her in her apartment, weaving, holding on to a counter to stand.

"Serena." I slowed my voice more and lowered the tone, "Are you thinking of hurting yourself?" What did I do if she said yes? I looked to see if Craig was available. He would know what to say. He was sitting at his desk, and I motioned for him to come over as I heard her say, "Maybe—I could." Her voice sounded challenging, like a threat.

I started to sweat. I put my hand over the mouthpiece and looked up helplessly as Craig approached, his blue eyes questioningly meeting mine. "She says she could hurt herself and doesn't care if she lives," I whispered. "What should I do?"

"See if she has a plan." He seemed so calm, normal in his usual polo shirt and chinos, as though this happened every day.

I turned back toward the phone, staring at the numbered buttons with their orderly letters marching in rows, and held out the earpiece so that Craig could hear. "Serena, are you all right? Are you feeling suicidal?"

"I don't want to live," she said, sobbing now. I could hear her rasping breaths catching at the end of each sob.

"What are you planning to do?" I turned back to search Craig's face. It showed the same unflappable calm with which he had once guided her to the emergency room.

"I have a knife," she said, drawing my attention sharply back.

"She's a danger to herself," Craig said. "You're obligated to do a welfare check."

"Serena, don't do anything," I said, heart in my throat, "Can you promise me you won't do anything to hurt yourself?"

"Why?" she yelled. "Why should I promise anything? I have a knife. I could use it."

Things seemed to speed up—my heart, the time—there seemed not to be a second to lose. Craig nodded at me and gestured toward the phone.

"Okay," I said, "I'm sending someone to check on you, to make sure you're safe."

"No. No! You can't send anyone. I won't let anyone in." She sounded panicked, voice rising in fear.

"Can you promise me you'll be safe? That you won't hurt yourself?"

"Why should I promise anything?" She was still yelling. "You don't care anyway. Nobody cares."

"Serena," I said slowly, my words trying to rein in my pounding heart, "I'm sending someone to check on you. I'm concerned, I'm worried about you. I want you to be safe. Tell me you'll be safe."

"No one is coming here! I don't want anyone here!" She sounded hysterical.

I looked back at Craig, who again nodded his encouragement at the phone.

"Then promise me you'll be safe."

The phone went dead. I held the receiver in front of me and stared at it helplessly.

"Call 911!" Craig commanded.

I did.

"What is the nature of your emergency?" the pleasant voice on the phone asked.

I explained the situation, that I had a patient who I believed was suicidal and had a knife, and I needed someone to check on her.

"But it's important that she come to our hospital," I said, naming where I worked. "We know her here. It's important they bring her here."

"All right," the operator said, "I have notified the police, and they are on the way."

"Police?" I heard myself gasp. I didn't know it meant police. My eyes widened in horror. I knew Serena was agitated and could be volatile. The names and faces of Black people shot by police flashed through my mind. "No—not the police," I gasped, then, "Don't let them shoot her!"

The operator was silent.

What had I done? My heart began pounding again.

"Please," I said, "we're waiting for her. Just bring her here."

"The police are arriving at her place now," she said.

I hung up and stared at Craig. His face was unruffled and voice calm as he said, "You didn't have any choice. She was a danger to herself. It's your duty to make sure she's safe."

I felt my muscles loosen as I slumped back in my chair, letting out a long breath. But I didn't feel reassured.

It was five thirty. Past closing time. Instead of leaving for home, I called the emergency room to notify them of Serena's arrival and gave them a brief explanation of her circumstances.

I waited impatiently by the phone, busying myself with reviewing lab results. Everyone else had left, and I was getting hungry, but I couldn't leave until I knew she was safe.

Half an hour passed. The sky was getting darker. No call came.

I phoned the emergency room again. They had not seen her.

I checked back with the 911 operator, who looked up my call.

"Oh yes," she said. "They took her to the county hospital."

"But I specifically told you to bring her here!" I protested, immediately angry.

"That was closer," she said.

I hung up, furious. I jumped up from my chair and began pacing, agitatedly ranting to the walls. I asked for her to come here, I heard myself saying in frustration. How dare they bring her elsewhere? We know her *here*. We care about her *here*. She knows us, we could maybe talk her down. After several revolutions around the office, I began to wind down, realizing there was nothing I could do tonight. I drove home in defeat, sad and worried.

In the following days there was no call from the other hospital, but I got a written history and physical report that discussed her elevated blood pressure, alcohol level, and liver enzymes. There was cocaine in her system, bruises and a cut on her face, and a broken nose.

I gasped. "Craig, look what they did," I wailed, dropping the report on his desk. I was furious, multiple scenarios playing out in my mind. But the report did not state the cause of the injuries.

Now here was her name on my schedule. My anxiety rose as her appointment time approached.

I knocked and hesitantly entered the room. Then stopped in my tracks.

Her nose was crooked, still too swollen to be fixed. Yellow and green bruises sagged along her left cheek, and there were partially healed stitches on her forehead.

She looked at me with the same disgust, but more an "I told you so" twist to her mouth.

"I want you to see what you did to me," she said. "You called the police. I told you not to. I wanted you to see what happened."

The room's fluorescence highlighted her discolored face.

I stood staring, speechless.

"They beat me up," she said. "I didn't want to go with them, so they shoved me against the wall. They twisted my arms behind me and put me in handcuffs. Then they gave me a 'rough ride.'"

I must have looked confused.

"You don't know what that is? They get going really fast and then slam on the brakes so that you fly forward into their cage . . . That's what broke my nose and gave me this cut." She pointed to her forehead. "It's hard to stop yourself when your hands are cuffed behind your back."

I sunk onto my chair with a groan, continuing to stare blankly. I was unable to control my face, which twisted into anger, mixed with helplessness.

"I told you not to call the police," she repeated.

"I—I didn't mean for it to be police," I stuttered. "It was a welfare check. I wanted to make sure you were safe—not hurt you."

She laughed. "Safe? Like the police care if I'm safe?"

"I was worried you would hurt yourself," I muttered.

"Oh, I didn't have to, they did it for me." Her tone emphasized the irony.

My heart sank. "Did you make a complaint?" I naively asked after a pause.

"Of course. I filled out a formal complaint. It's in the system. Do you think it matters? Of course not."

I didn't know what to say. She was right—I had caused this. Not directly, but the chain of events was initiated by me. What could I say? "I'm sorry" didn't seem enough, although I was.

"You know what?" she continued, looking directly into my eyes, "I forgive you. I know you care. I know you were trying."

I looked at her carefully. Was this sarcasm? But her tone sounded sincere, and her face looked serious.

"But don't ever call the police on a Black person," she continued, interrupting my attempt to sort out my feelings.

I looked up at her, mouth open to speak, but I caught myself before blurting out, "I only wanted to help"—because no matter my intent, the outcome had not been helpful. Not all "help" in my world, I realized, was helpful in another's.

I silently turned to the computer, relieved to focus on the rational, the unemotional, the safely known. But I couldn't keep hiding there. I needed to process this situation, revise what I thought I knew, learn what it meant to "help." Where had the system gone so wrong that a plea for someone's safety became a threat? When other "helpers" were not helpful, where did I turn for help? I had prided myself on "understanding" my patients to "meet their needs." But how could I ever understand someone whose world was so different from mine? When help in my world became a vehicle for harm in theirs?

My piece of the system suddenly seemed both larger and smaller than it had before. My actions had consequences far beyond what I imagined, yet I was only a miniscule portion of the system, a cog in the wheel of action and reaction. Awareness washed over me like a wave. Then the undertow tried to pull me back, back to my comfort zone. Where I couldn't stay. I had to rethink my responsibility in this complex system, relearn my role.

I looked back to Serena with new eyes, hoping to start over.

"Where do we go from here, you and I?" I asked.

She gave me a disgusted look, but it melted slightly around the corners of her mouth, and she looked at me evenly.

"Just give me my damn pills," she said with a wry smile.

I had no answers, but I had a start. To truly succeed in understanding my patients, I had to undo the certainty of my knowledge, to become the receiver of information, the listener to my patients' wisdom, trusting their skills.

I began to write the prescription.

GEORGE ESTREICH

Concision: A Sprawl

FROM *AGNI*

> concise, adj.: Of speech, writing, a person, style, etc.; brief but comprehensive in expression.
> —*The New Shorter Oxford English Dictionary*

> Usually, compress what you mean into the fewest words.
> —Joseph M. Williams, *Style: Ten Lessons in Clarity and Grace (3rd ed.)*

IT IS DIFFICULT to be *brief but comprehensive* about an idea so vast in scope.

In his classic text *Style*, Joseph Williams illustrates *concision* by pruning a sample sentence from twenty-four words to six. The shorter sentence is better, but the longer one is, in its way, just as concise: it displays at least four forms of wordiness, including Redundant Pairs, Redundant Modifiers, Meaningless Modifiers, and A Phrase for a Word.

For Williams, wordiness "is like a chronic accumulation of specks and motes that individually seem trivial but together blur what might otherwise be a clear and concise style." Ironically, this is one of Williams's wordier sentences. (Specks *and* motes?) And though I agree with him, I'm after something else: a version of concision relevant to the essay, which is less like a window and more like a gem, or an ice cube, or a tear. A clarity with shape, something that transforms the light it admits. Something to look at, as much as through.

*

Twenty-four words to six. In the qualitative nightmare of revision, concision offers the allure of the quantitative, the mirage of certainty. *Concision,* from CON- + *caedere,* to cut, shares a root with *incision, decision, precision.* It suggests surgery, a healing violence, a line inscribed in the body of the work. But decisions about where and what to cut, about essential and inessential, are always qualitative. They imply value judgments, like elevating concision above other attributes, or caring about essences at all.

For me, concision is almost an article of faith, and like faith, it's functional, whether its object exists or not. It offers rules to police the unruly, the drafts that sprawl like daydreams or sins; it offers the ritual of erasure, deletion as devotional practice; it is rooted in intuition, in visceral reactions to writing both wordy and spare. For this reason, it feels beyond question, which is precisely (PRE- + *caedere*) why I question it.

Concision is a negative virtue. It's subtractive, a removal of specks and motes, and as such its exercise serves (or should) qualities harder to measure, like play, clarity, coherence, honesty, imagination, surprise, instruction, exactitude, voice, delight. It is often equated with brevity, though a long sentence can be concise,a short one wordy. It may, in some cases, be culturally inappropriate. It is likely favored under capitalism, in which work is timed and time is priced, though our attention economy seems more often to produce false concision in the form of slogans and catchphrases that are punchy but empty. In practice, concision has an ethical dimension: we may use more words to signal respect, as in "person-first language," under whose terms my younger daughter is not *a Down syndrome child* but *a person with Down syndrome,* though there are fierce and condition-specific debates about person-first versus identity-first language—*person with a disability* versus *disabled person*—which relate to questions of pride and detachability, endless complications about which it is difficult to be concise, though I prefer, in my daughter's case, to say *Laura.* To ask first whether the category is relevant before discussing how to invoke it.

But I digress. I always digress. Perhaps this is why I believe in concision. It's like magnetic north, an idea of direction in the wilderness. But magnetic north and true north are not the same.

*

In the early nineties, when I was living in Philadelphia and had quit teaching after hating it during graduate school and then gone back to it after hating secretarial work even more, when I was teaching between seventy and ninety students a term at three different colleges and trying and failing to write poems and often found myself faced, on a Monday morning, with the prospect of pushing a boulder the weight of twenty-five students up the mountain of back-to-back fifty-minute classes, I sometimes resorted to worksheets. Often these were about learning to be more concise.

It was a minor amazement to me that someone had written bad sentences on purpose, that someone had deliberately added these problems to the world. That they had been paid to do it. Bleary, wired, and unprepared, I'd stand over the department Xerox machine, reproducing the problems.

I was teaching at what was then the Philadelphia College of Pharmacy and Science, in West Philadelphia. My students were not like the suburban valedictorians in my classes at the University of Pennsylvania, a short walk and a world away. They were often the first from their families to attend college, and in a few years, as licensed pharmacists, they'd be making five times my instructor's salary. I got to like them, but the first semester was difficult. One student told me she had chosen to attend pharmacy school *because* she hated English class. The assignments the students handed in were often short of the required word count, but the end-of-term evaluations were long and detailed. One student printed carefully, "He needs to learn that we are not Edgar Allan Poe."

I eased up. They were not Edgar Allan Poe. They did not even see the point of the humanities requirement. Memorizing lethal drug interactions was relevant to their futures and learning to write elegant sentences was not. I did not want to be a pharmacist, but I envied their practicality. Their brains, somehow, were aligned with the world's incentives. (What's more concise than a pill? It would be years before my first course of SSRIs, but the pills—bitter, but only if you happen to taste them—have helped me edit depression's run-on, its redundant whisper in the inner ear.)

Decades later, I can see how useful the idea of concision was at the time, the work it did for me. It was, for a teacher not much older than his students and insecure in his authority, part of a mechanism of control. It was defensibly gradable. It helped me decide (DE- + *caedere*) which papers were A's, which B's, which C's.

At the same time, it was a connection, however slender, between my unfinished poems and the stacks of papers I graded each week. It was applicable in both worlds, and so it stood for a notional common ground between them, for some future time in which teaching did something besides drain away the impulse and ability and time to write. Some area where work and art were not opposed.

Years later, after Laura came along, I gave up poetry for prose. I began thinking more about who I was writing for and why—about purpose and audience, as I'd once advised my students to do. I'd quit teaching years before to become an at-home dad, but writing and teaching no longer seemed so separate if raising questions counts as teaching, if bearing witness counts. I began thinking about chromosomes, inheritance, disability, belonging. My understandings of *human*, of *family*, of *identity* began to fragment and reassemble and enlarge. I'd always described myself as "half" Japanese, "half" Jewish: what did that mean? Laura's chromosome was "extra," she was "disabled," commonly described—if not to our faces—as "abnormal": What did that mean? What did "normal" mean? What had I believed in and never questioned?

Since aphorisms demand concision, it's no surprise that many are *about* concision. And yet, with each instance, the idea becomes less certain. As if the aphorisms obscure the very idea they illustrate. As if they are both the window and the motes, blurring the view they disclose.

In *Style*, Williams's chapter on concision begins with six aphorisms, such as "Let thy words be few." They vary in tone from judgmental ("loquacity and lying are cousins") to hortatory ("the love of economy is the root of all virtue") to flatly declarative ("less is more") to ironically bemused ("To a snail: if 'compression is the first grace of style,' you have it"). Two are plucked from much longer texts, as if brevity required an equal and opposite prolixity. "Less is more" is extracted from Robert Browning's poem "Andrea del Sarto," whose sprawling monologue is paradoxically concise, its iambic perseverations circling the drain of the speaker's obsession. Ecclesiastes—"For God is in heaven and thou upon earth: therefore let thy words be few" (5:2)—links silence to reverence, to the limits of human knowledge before an all-knowing God. (The same prophet writes in 12:12: "of making many books there is no end, and much study is a weariness of the flesh.")

Concision is never pure. Whenever we talk about it, we are also talking about something else; when we invoke it, we do so for a reason, whether to command humility, teach someone to write, or remind them to be silent. But a recurrent theme is the value of intelligence itself. The same aphorisms that recommend concision concisely are also witty in praise of wit, though this message is typically phrased in the negative: "A fool's voice is known by multitude of words" (Ecclesiastes 5:3). Or Ben Franklin, in *Poor Richard's Almanack*:

> Here comes the orator! With his flood of words and his drop of reason.
>> He that speaks much is much mistaken.
>> Half wits talk much but say little.

And, in a rhymed set of aphorisms:

> Best is the Tongue that feels the rein;
> He that talks much, must talk in vain;
> We from the wordy Torrent fly: Who listens to the chattering Pye?

It's fascinating to me that, in the shortest of all literary prose forms, these writers go out of their way to *characterize*. To praise wit by creating a witless figure, to show that figure as unwelcome in society, to advise readers not to be that figure. The aphorisms are nominally about concision, but their true subject is belonging: to talk too much is to be a half-wit, a fool, an irrational, chattering magpie. To lose status.

Writing essays and having a daughter with an intellectual disability makes for a wilderness of complication. The world of the essay is an intellectual world, from blurbs to publication to prizes to the people in the audience at readings to the universities where readings are held, where intellect's value is simply assumed, the foundation beneath the foundation stones. If I have anything useful to say, it's less about the limits of that entire structure and more about the tensions of resisting a problematic faith, one I cannot entirely abandon.

The clearest equation of concision and intellect comes to us from Shakespeare: "Brevity is the soul of wit," which has floated free of *Hamlet* to sound like unironic advice. In context, the words convict their speaker of being a half-wit, a fool, a chattering magpie. Addressing Claudius and Gertrude, Polonius is anything but brief: he takes foreffingever to deliver, at most, three pieces of actionable information. Metadiscourse—a key source of wordiness, according to Williams—is the cause of the holdup. Instead of delivering the news, Polonius lectures endlessly about *how* to deliver news. He is both painfully self-conscious and totally unaware, his speech halting and droning. Gertrude cuts him off decisively (DE- + *caedere*) with a single, cutting aphorism of her own: "More matter, less art." He keeps talking, though. Later he is stabbed to death. He literally dies because he can't shut up: Spying on Hamlet and Gertrude from behind a curtain, he lets out a cry of surprise. Hamlet, a talker himself, runs him through, then goes back to haranguing his mom.

The writing I love has listening at its heart, and the writing I love most listens to silence. Kobayashi Issa:

> On a branch
> floating downriver
> a cricket, singing.
> > (tr. Jane Hirshfield)

> In this world
> We walk on the roof of hell
> Gazing at flowers
> > (tr. Robert Hass)

These poems are economical, but they trade in economies of transcendence. They are alchemical, turning plain words into gold. They burn impermanence into the page.

I don't think the American reader gets the least fraction of what's in a haiku. Still, when I read Issa, or Bashō, I have a vague quasi-genetic sense of inheritance, of strangeness-in-familiarity. When I was nineteen, I went to Japan to meet my relatives and see the country my mom had left behind. I traveled from city to city with my backpack and my Japan Rail Pass, lugging a telephone-book-sized compendium of train schedules. My uncle Kazu had pressed it on me, presumably to keep me from getting lost. Eventually I

discovered that I could just show up on a platform and a train
would come along. Most people could speak some English: I didn't
understand the place, but the place understood me. I did and did
not belong there, like home in a dream.

It is a category error to say that a haiku is "concise." It is not like
a bigger, wordier poem that has been boiled down to one image,
some concentrate or demi-glace of a landscape. It is more like a
tiny, 300,000,000-volt thundercloud. Or the reader is the cloud,
electric with potential, and the haiku is the single tree on a hill.
What happens between is the flash I live for: not the epiphany
reaching skyward, but the shortest path to ground. Which is, nonetheless, forked.

I grew up with the silences of another tongue. I understood
them better than any word, but I could not translate them into
clear American. I knew only a few words in Japanese but used
them every day: *mother, good morning, I'll be back later.*

Concision is a defining idea for nonliterary prose, less so for
poems or essays. And yet even as I understand that an emailed
announcement of the link for an upcoming Zoom reading is cat-
egorically different from a poem by Emily Dickinson, I know that
an oceanic gray area exists between them: literature can argue and
inform; memos can be unnecessarily well written; a given piece of
criticism can be more imaginative, more ambitious and inventive,
than a given poem; an essay avails itself of any and all approaches
to meaning, refusing nothing. You cannot simply cut "literary"
from "nonliterary" with precision (PRE- + *caedere*), nor would you
want to. This has two practical implications for the writer. The first
is that concision, in its ordinary sense, is useful: ordinary tools can
be used for extraordinary ends. The second is that an ordinary
sense of concision is not enough. A different version is needed,
one as open-ended as the essay itself, one less subtractive and pro-
scriptive. Something more than a negative command.

Do we expect sentences to be individually concise—to get to
the point—even as we expect essays to wander? Do we want them
to wander, but efficiently, purposefully, tracing a songline if not a
superhighway?

Probably the most famous description of literary concision comes
from Hemingway:

> If a writer of prose knows enough about what he is writing
> about he may omit things that he knows and the reader, if
> the writer is writing truly enough, will have a feeling of those
> things as strongly as though the writer had stated them. The
> dignity of movement of an ice-berg is due to only one-eighth
> of it being above water.

But what if the problem with the unspoken is precisely that it *is* unspoken?

In the new world I lived in after Laura's arrival, the least word could be the tip of an iceberg. Beneath a comedian's use of *retard*, or a friend's, was a mass of underwater assumptions about intellect and belonging, ancient typologies of status, ideas about how people might be classified, the classes ranked. Beneath the open stares, or the shining eyes of those who gazed through Laura to some imaginary angel, beneath every word and glance and gesture was something heavy and frozen and white. Or, less metaphorically: As a writer, I could not depend on a shared context of understanding. Most of what I had come to learn about Down syndrome and disability was not common knowledge, and what *was* commonly believed was often false and/or poisonous, which meant that omission was not a viable strategy. I had, somehow, to talk. To teach.

I could not omit things I knew and expect the reader to feel them. It was not only that I knew things most readers did not, or that parenting a child with a disability, not to mention disability itself, was commonly misunderstood. It was that the same misunderstandings entangled me, and I was trying to free myself, and freedom came only in proportion to the ability to accurately name the error. To understand, in a new light, the old phrase *what goes without saying*. To say it aloud. To pronounce my own unspoken misconceptions and what it felt like to be suddenly, guiltily aware of them, and the way they began to evaporate in Laura's presence, like puddles in the sun. To say what was left, what was changed, what was still changing. If I had anything to teach, it was what this process felt like: a dramatized *coming to terms*, a phrase that usually connotes closure, but which I choose to read as open-ended. I came to terms with the fact of Laura's Down syndrome long ago; I will always be coming to terms.

Hemingway's declaration is itself an iceberg, and part of its massive subtext—the underwater fraction he didn't need to point to, or explain—is an idea of the reader (pretty clearly white and male) and an idea about what "he" and the writer share, including a certain level of capability, of competence, however defined. I'd like to think I'm free of these confusions, but to critique an error is one thing and to be free of it is another.

And in one sense, Hemingway isn't wrong. What can you do but have faith in the reader? What can you do but trust them to hear the same silence you do? Despite everything, I love the paradox in Hemingway's framing: if you write truly enough, the unseen becomes visible, the unspoken audible. What is most essential is conjured, in the reader, by omission. As if writer and reader were entangled particles, aligned across space and time.

In the preface to *Style*, Williams writes that he has tested his precepts "with a good many adult writers in government, the professions, and business." His book was directed, in part, to administrators in the American white-collar world my father inhabited and I do not, where time is money and clarity matters and men (mostly men) in government and business manage the systems that sustain or help or entrap us all. Speaking to that audience about writing, Williams might as well be speaking of fatherhood. He laments "the lack of a common language": "If you are responsible for the writing of others and find it unacceptable, you have to communicate to those writers more than your displeasure." And yet "[n]either the administrator nor the subordinate has a vocabulary to express what either sees as the source of the difficulty."

I would've liked to talk about concision with my father. It's been twenty-five years since his death from lung cancer, and anything related to my being a writer was a tricky subject between us. Still, I can imagine concision as common ground. It would have appealed to his mechanical engineer's practicality, which I sort of have, even if I apply it to impractical things. I'd love to have had that conversation as I'd love for him to have known my daughters, to get over the concern and maybe skepticism about Laura he never got to feel, to have his doubts be displaced by her, to be charmed by her, to love her for who she is. I long for that alternate timeline in the way I long for a lost idea of clarity, or for my former naïve belief in its possibility, in the way I long for a mythical understanding in which engineering squares tidily with poetry, math with metaphor. A synthesis in a single line. But I digress.

*

To think about concision is to think about readers. Readers of memos don't *want* to read memos; they read to extract information, like gold or coal, which is then spent or burned. For readers of texts like these, concision is unambiguously useful.

But readers of essays have different goals. We want to get something from the essay, but the something is less extractable. *Re: grief, Re: injustice, Re: transcendence*—we turn and return to essays for instances of the inexhaustible. We want to experience the language, not mine it. What we get is a chance to waste time, or to experience time and usefulness in a different way, or to inhabit time in a way not governed by use. The essay says, Take a minute, look at this landscape, what can you get from it without destroying it?

Even as I write this, I think: Shit. I've lived too long in Oregon. This argument is *so* Pacific Northwest—too easy, too sentimental, too tidy an alignment of literary and environmental virtues. Writers do violence to experience, and readers do violence to essays. We are not preservationists of our own wildernesses. We *mine our experience*, as the saying goes. Or, to reverse the metaphor: We—writers and readers both—are mined *by* the essay. We are the landscape, and the essay discovers value in us, something heavy and lumpy and pure, something we recognize instantly but could not have found or named on our own.

Writing in 1866, John Langdon Down—whose name Laura repeats when she says, *I am Down syndrome*—published a paper about a new condition he called "Mongolian idiocy." The people he described, he believed, had "degenerated" in the womb, acquiring features of a lower ethnic type. In 1883, Francis Galton, Charles Darwin's cousin, invented the word *eugenics*. He and his twentieth-century successors, genetic determinists obsessed with intellect, hoped that those they called "feeble-minded" (subtypes: *moron, imbecile, idiot*) could, with time, be cut precisely (PRE- + *caedere*) from the social body. They thought they could breed, sterilize, incarcerate, and police their way toward what David Starr Jordan, the first president of Stanford, called an "aristocracy of genius." Their writings are monstrous but, just as often, clear and concise. An essentialist worldview lends itself to concision, as does a faith untroubled by doubt.

After Laura was born—or, more precisely, after she was first diagnosed—I began, in my haphazard way, to study genetics. Her "extra" chromosome seemed the essence to which our lives had been stripped, so it seemed essential to learn more about it. This was a mistake, if an understandable one. Focusing on the chromosome—as if experience could be reduced, concisely, to biology—only expressed my faith in certainty, in a home beyond complication, in a true north beyond the wilderness in which I found myself. That faith was misplaced. Uncertainty was inescapable. There was no true north, and the wilderness was my home now; maybe it always had been. The chromosome was no more essential than recent developments in heart surgery, or the existence of early intervention, or the mistaken belief that the molecular was more essential than the social, or that an understanding of human chromosomes could be pure of human concerns. Nothing was solid, and nothing ever had been. It all mattered, context mattered from the molecule on up, and little was certain, and in that lack of certainty was possibility and hope.

Revelation at the Food Bank

FROM *The Sewanee Review*

"DID YOU EVER have sex with another woman?" I asked my husband when he was eighty-five and we had been married for sixty-two years.

I could see he was dumbstruck. I was angry about something, maybe about everything, the stupidity of everyone, the mistakes that were made every day by careless, indifferent idiots.

My husband had ordered new glasses—just ordinary glasses, a regular pair and a pair of sunglasses—and when the optician's office called to say, "Your glasses are ready," he drove ten miles to pick them up only to learn that only one of the two pairs was ready. Was this not ultimate stupidity? Why wouldn't I be angry? My husband rarely gets angry, so I have to be angry for him.

Another time we went to In-N-Out and ordered two burgers, two fries, and extra ketchup. A girl handed me the bag through our car window. When we got home, we found she had given us three fries and ketchup, but no burgers. Of course, I tried to call when we got home, but you can't call the place where you bought the food—only the corporate offices in some other state. We ate every one of the fries.

I never used to say "fuck." But lately, I say it more frequently because our old house is so crowded with fifty years' worth of stuff, and things keep falling down on me—books tumble out of bookcases, clothes stream out of closets, and pills crash out of medicine cabinets. Now these cabinets are also full of face masks, and latex gloves to be worn while taking in the mail.

At the start of the pandemic, my cleaning lady, who worried about us because we are so old, suggested I go to the food bank because it was safer than going grocery shopping. Why would I go to a food bank when I hadn't lost my job, wasn't homeless, and could pay for my groceries? She insisted that I would be less likely to catch COVID-19. I'd have no contact with people and could stay sealed in my car. She gave me directions to a church, told me they were the kindest, nicest folks, and that they gave away free turkeys every Thanksgiving. I so desired a free turkey for once in my life. After our last Thanksgiving, my husband said we should no longer buy a turkey for the holiday—it was too heavy for him to handle, too hard for him to carve now that he had a tremor, too much leftover food for just two people. Who of our children would even come to spend Thanksgiving with us? All our daughters were grown, lived far away, and not one would be interested in the little chocolate turkeys I used to buy them at See's Candies.

I drove the two miles to the food bank at the church—really just one left turn from our street onto the road that goes from our house to the magnificent golden cross at the church's entrance. WELCOME—YOU MUST WEAR A MASK, the sign read, and I joined the orderly line of supplicants winding their way through the parking lot in a colorful parade of cars. Among them I noted a BMW, a red Mercedes, and a Humvee. A pretty woman at a table greeted each car, one by one. She talked briefly to every driver, and typed something into a small computer. When I got to her, she took my name but didn't ask me if I were poor or homeless, and placed on my windshield a little card that read ONE SPECIAL ITEM FIRST VISIT.

"Have a great day," she told me, "and God bless."

When I arrived at a temporary stop sign, an older man bent toward me and kindly asked, "How many families and where do you want the food? Back seat or trunk?" I told him one family, trunk. He wrote *1-T* on my windshield in white marker. I drove forward and noticed a swarm of volunteers wearing bright orange vests hurrying to the open trunk of the car ahead of me, each person carrying a carton, or a gallon jug of milk, or a bag of vegetables (some celery stalks sticking out the top), or a lumpy, foil-wrapped object, shaped, I thought, like a frozen chicken. One female volunteer was smiling as she deposited a bag into the car ahead. A young man with powerful arms was loading a large sealed box into the trunk. On its side was printed LOS ANGELES REGIONAL FOOD BANK and under it the words FIGHTING HUNGER. GIVING HOPE.

My turn now. I stopped, I felt vibrations behind me as my trunk door was raised, and a series of thumps shook my car. The trunk was gently closed; the man wiped the white letters off my windshield, gave me a thumbs-up, and I drove off, only to stop at one more station. A woman about my age came to my open car window and said, "How can I help you? Baby diapers? Wet wipes? Formula? Hand sanitizer? Masks? Dog food?"

"I don't have a dog." She looked at me closely. "Maxi pads? At my age I have to use them, maybe you can use some too." Then she astonished me by extending her closed fist through the open window toward me, and I automatically extended mine, and we fist-bumped. "Friends!" she announced. She handed me some carefully wrapped portions of maxi pads. "See you next week, my friend," she said. I drove home, somewhat stunned but aware that I was smiling.

When I opened my trunk in the garage, I felt a rare excitement—a kind of delight that a surprise awaited me, as on a special birthday. I carried a bag of potatoes into the house and asked my husband to help with the rest. The gallon of milk was too heavy for me. The carton, also. We put all the food on the kitchen table.

A beautiful chocolate layer cake, which I guessed was my special first visit item, showed an expiration date of two days ago, but I was certain it was perfect. Someone had also placed in my trunk an orchid plant in a red plastic pot. It was mostly wilted, but it still had a few floppy purple flowers hanging off a stem. How kind someone was to do this for me. Even imperfect beauty raised my spirits. In the big carton were bags of rice and beans, a box of spaghetti, cans of tuna, chicken and soup, jars of peanut butter. We unpacked the various bags and found a bottle of cooking oil, a pound of butter, apples, walnuts, carrots, onions. Other gifts I discovered included a can labeled LIQUID DEATH, a bottle of dark-truffle ketchup, a six-pack of caramel-pumpkin yogurt, and a package of wild sardines in hot jalapeño sauce.

"Do we really need all this?" my husband asked.

"Do we need to eat?" I replied.

*

Whatever roused my anger toward my husband had been percolating in me for years. He was such a caring and thoughtful man, yet common annoyances surfaced. Why does he put so much cream cheese on his bagel? Or leave lights on in every room of the house? How come he tries to open the front door after our walk before he thinks to put his key in the lock?

At one trip to the food bank, I was given a five-pound bag of frozen diced ham, packaged in a long cylindrical tube. Baffled by how to store this inconvenient shape, I'd stuffed it way back in the refrigerator. That night, considering what to cook for dinner, I pulled out the tube. The sealed end split open and five pounds of freezing ham shards shot out and struck my body everywhere, ham juice soaking my pants and running down my legs into my shoes.

"Fuck," I yelled. But wouldn't anyone?

My husband would not. Such words do not abide in him. The anger that comes over me around mealtimes is because I have to make all the meals. We married young, when men were not house husbands, cooks, or babysitters. The man had the job. My husband was a professor, he worked many hours and graded many papers. That was the arrangement. The challenge of every meal belonged to me—three times a day, year after year. I *also* had a job—I wrote stories and books. But *I* did my work at home, where all the other work, including the care of our children, awaited me.

I must have long ago been resourceful and creative about food. I once had a professional deli-meat slicer, a bread-making machine, a blender, a toaster oven, and a pressure cooker—along with a cake mixer, waffle iron, popcorn popper, tortilla press, and everything you would need to core, peel, or shred an apple. Most of those gadgets still crowding my counters and stuffed in my kitchen cabinets have died by now—parts having failed or gone missing, their instructions booklets vanished. I still had one beloved Jewish cookbook that contained my favorite banana bread recipe, and I'd written hundreds of dates up and down that single page over the years, the days on which I baked that one perfect bread.

Since I was now stocking up at the food bank, certain foods never showed up at our dinner table. An eggplant, for example. Chicken livers, never. Lox, of course not. Cream cheese, croissants, blintzes, chocolate bars. Whenever I needed something essential, I simply—like everyone else—ordered it from Amazon. One day my husband said he'd lost his nail clipper, so I ordered six of them for $6.99 from Amazon. A big truck came the next day, with a bearded driver in it, to deliver the tiny nail clippers with a key chain attached to each one of them. Another day, a soft envelope turned up in my mailbox from Nordstrom, where I never shop. It was addressed to a woman named Linda Black at an address exactly one block to the south of my house. I could feel that whatever was in the envelope was silky and soft, perhaps a nightgown or a blouse. I could imagine it on my body. Who would ever know if I kept it? I could slit that package open and be the owner of whatever was in it.

However, when my husband saw me bringing in the mail, I told him that a package had been misdelivered. He said we should take a walk and bring it to its rightful owner. I considered telling him I'd do it myself later. He'd never know I'd kept it. Why is it I've never confided to him the truth about certain lowlife instincts I harbor? Does marriage require these kinds of confessions? Does he conceal such thoughts from me? I doubt he has them. But I often wonder how his truths differ from mine and how much we hide from each other.

We walked to the neighbor's house, rang the bell. The man who lived there opened the door. We didn't know him, though we'd lived in our house over fifty years and passed his house nearly every day on our walks. In truth, we lived in an indifferent and chilly neighborhood. Taking the package from me, he appeared to recognize, as I had, that the object inside was soft and flexible. He held up a forefinger as if he had just remembered something—and then told us that his wife had died two weeks ago. Of breast cancer. He shook his head sadly at the package. A little dog appeared at his feet; as we stood at the door, he bent to pat it gently. Then he thanked us and wished us a good day. Whatever expensive garment had arrived would never be worn, almost certainly would never be returned to the store, and, after all, could have been mine.

Some days later, as we sat outside our front door admiring the oak trees that largely concealed the slope of mountain to the north, we saw the bereaved husband walking his little dog. He waved and was, in fact, coming to see us. He held out our bank statement that had been misdelivered by the mailman to his house. We all agreed heartily that United States postal workers ought to notice that streets have different names, even if some of the house numbers are the same. *Learn how to read, folks,* I thought.

Now that we seemed to have made a local friend, I was distressed when, shortly thereafter, a FOR SALE sign went up in our neighbor's yard. On our next walk, we stopped to pay attention to the garden that he had long ago planted in front of his house—a design of shapely stones, large boulders, and colorful drought-resistant plants. Almost overnight, it seemed, one of those desert-like plants had shot forth a great, phallic stalk. Within days, it sprouted layer upon layer of smaller phallic stalks. With my cell phone, I took a picture of the odd creation. An app identified the plant as *Nepenthes,* which brings forth growths that look exactly like the human penis. A garden of penises—amazing. Having had only a sister, I never really saw one of them until my wedding night.

The house sold quickly, and whoever bought it proceeded to destroy the stone garden and tear out all the beautiful drought-resistant plants. I felt a pang to see those handsome phalluses cut down, but I also realized that the widower's house had a much better view of the mountains than ours. He no doubt sold his house for a lot more money than we would ever get for ours. Thoughts like this convince me that I am unlucky, though my husband often tells me how lucky we are.

There are ever-present, recurring reasons to be distressed, to be furious. I seem to contain a switch that, once flipped, destroys whatever peace I might have briefly achieved. My husband has affectionate advice for me all the time. He takes my hand when he sees me getting agitated and begs me: "Please, just relax." What kind of advice is that? He certainly has experience in relaxing, as it is my job to write all the complaint letters, call the banks when they make mistakes, schedule appointments with the tax man, the doctors and dentists, write the checks to the housekeeper and the gardener and pool guy and notify—when our credit card has to be updated—the twenty places that bill us every month for whatever we have to pay endlessly for.

At the food bank, my fist-bumping lady friend looks forward to my weekly arrival. She seems thrilled to dispense unusual non-edible materials that for some reason are donated, or have expired in some unique way. Bars of soap made out of sugar. Bamboo toothbrushes—the lightest handles with the softest bristles. A glass mug engraved with the words: ENJOY THE MAGIC OF CHRISTMAS! One day she handed me a three-by-five index card on which she had personally written these words:

> I can tell you are a worrier. Throw all your anxiety onto Him, because He cares about you. Cast your burden on the LORD—He will support you! Don't be anxious about anything; rather, bring up all your requests to God in your prayers and petitions along with giving thanks. Then the peace of GOD that exceeds all understanding will keep your heart and mind safe in Christ Jesus.

Of course, I thanked her. Clearly the people at this church want me to enjoy life. They give me gifts, they welcome me, they wear masks to protect me from the pandemic, they invite me back, they bless me and bless me. Who else does this? Who else wants me to have happiness? I'm a Jewish girl, but I've never known the rewards of religion. Is it too late?

Unquestionably, my age presents challenges, though the internet tells me I have a good chance of living to ninety. But the road ahead is filled with so many medical tests. My doctor, who doesn't actually see her patients now but instead communicates only by video call or email, ordered a series of blood tests for me. Since my breast cancer surgery ten years ago, she requires me to have a CEA test, which tracks a particular cancer marker. She called to inform me that my recent test results were concerning; my antigens were elevated. She duly ordered another and, after I had my blood drawn at the lab (both the tech and I wearing our masks), she called to inform me they'd risen further. Duty bound, she then referred me to an oncologist, who, without ever seeing me clinically, ordered yet another test, a CT/PET scan.

Though the date for this scan was set, the day for a previously ordered test, my colonoscopy, was also approaching. Before I could have the colonoscopy, I was required to take a COVID-19 test. To do this, I had to pay a visit to the clinic, whose drive-through line wrapped several times around the parking lot.

While slowly inching forward, I sneezed. When I leaned sideways to grab the handkerchief on the passenger seat, my foot briefly slipped off the brake and I hit the car in front of me. The impact was very soft, but it was a bump. The woman ahead leapt out of her car and strode furiously toward me. She was baring her teeth. I turned off my ignition and got out of my car. I checked her bumper. Not a scratch. The line ahead was now moving forward, and the cars behind us began to honk.

"You crazy bitch, you fucking bitch!" She stood close to me, wearing a nurse's badge. "You hit me! I'll sue you!"

"I'm sorry," I said. "But there's no damage."

"The whole fucking world is damaged," she yelled.

She *hmphed* away, shaking her fist. I returned to my car, started the engine. Moved forward. Stopped. Another nurse at a table stuck a long Q-tip up each of my nostrils, and jabbed another one into the back of my throat.

COVID-negative, my reward was to drink the ten gallons of lemon-flavored liquid in preparation for my colonoscopy. In the pre-op room, I could hardly wait for the anesthetist's infusion of propofol. I remembered the same moment before previous procedures—for my gallbladder surgery, for my hysterectomy, for my breast cancer surgery, for my knee replacement. Why not just get put out for good and be done with it all! With the tests to come and the waiting for results and the fear, followed by even more tests! We all will fail the ultimate test, so why keep going? Can't an old woman get some propofol for at-home, domestic use?

For the CT/PET scan, I would be injected with a radioactive material and have to wait an hour for it to circulate through my body. My husband drove me to the imaging complex that did MRIs, CTs, ultrasounds, digital mammography, nuclear medicine, fluoroscopy, and guided biopsies. As he drove, I took a picture of his profile. I always have my camera ready in case something amazing passes us by, but my husband is often the only subject available. I've acquired hundreds of these photos of him driving us to supermarkets and medical appointments, but also through the Tuscan hills outside Florence where he once taught for a term, and through the moors in England when we spent his sabbatical in Oxford, and on Highway 101 through California where the ocean breeze ruffled our hair through the car's sunroof. His handsome profile had changed considerably since the last time I took pictures of him driving—his cheeks now were visibly sunken, his hair had thinned, his beard's stubble was completely white. His beautifully shaped lips seemed narrowed into a tight line. What was happening to him? And though I meant to take only photos of the subject in front of my camera lens, I sometimes accidentally took a selfie and realized that whatever was happening to my husband was also happening to me.

The CT tech, a middle-aged man who introduced himself as Jimmy, called me into his office. He asked me to leave all my belongings with my husband and told me to follow him down the hall. "I'd like to take my phone," I told him, "so I can read if I have to wait an hour."

"Take nothing with you. You are going to just have to relax while you wait."

Relax again? While waiting for radioactive material to light up places in my body where cancer might be growing? My husband threw me a pitying glance and took out his copy of *The New Yorker*.

Just as I was about to recline on a soft chair, Jimmy came in and whispered: "Don't worry about getting through this hour. In a few minutes I'll be back, and I'll tell you my life story."

I wondered how to pass the time. I tried to meditate, which lately I had been practicing with a Zoom class. The key to successful meditation was to choose an anchor, ideally your own breath going in and out, and hang on to the anchor no matter how wildly your thoughts might flit about. In meditation, we were encouraged to accept ourselves in whatever state we were in at the present moment. To be at peace without criticizing ourselves was the way to enter a transformative process. I was just getting into the rhythm of it—my breath going out like a little death and then coming in as a blessing, over and over again—when Jimmy returned and said, "Now I can tell you how I got this job, how I always wanted to be a jet pilot, how I came to this country from Lebanon and found the most beautiful woman in the world to marry." I pretended to listen while still focusing on my breath. Finally, I begged to know if the radioactive stuff was now sufficiently distributed through my body and could we please have the scan?

Jimmy ushered me into the room, which he said had to be kept very cold since the multimillion-dollar scanner was temperamental and easily overheated. It looked like a cylindrical refrigerator laid on its side, into which I had to be strapped. Jimmy's narration of his life story had ended happily with a double wedding at which both he and his brother married the two most beautiful women, who were, like the brothers, also from Lebanon. He told me to hold still, he was about to start the scan. He turned out the light in the room and closed the door. A motor turned on and I could feel something whizzing above my head. I lost the anchor of my breath at once, since meditating in a dark freezing tube was like meditating in a coffin. I hated being in this situation but I tried to accept myself and appreciate my hatred.

Fury sits in a pouch inside you somewhere and shoots out suddenly when you least expect it. It's a crack on the skull with a hatchet. It can strike while you're putting on your socks, or as you catch a glimpse of cable news. Fury seems a reasonable reaction to the delivery of a big cardboard box from Walmart with only a single jar of jelly in it, but the wrong flavor. To a mistaken letter from the IRS informing me that I owe the government four thousand dollars. To a robocall that insists I've been charged by Amazon for a new iPhone and I need to press 1 to cancel the charges. To news that my truck warranty has expired and I need to renew it. To a scam call from a guy pretending to be my grandson: "Hello Grandma, you may not recognize my voice since I have a cold, but I've been in a car accident and I need your help."

Old traumas also rise up, painful enough to bring tears to my eyes—my husband's mother, who hated my guts because she thought I was too thin and not rich enough for her son. Who, with her husband, tried to throw me down the stairs when we told them we were engaged. Who, when I finally married my husband, looked at my delicate, gold wedding band and said, "Such a skinny ring! What's the matter, are you ashamed of being married?"

Fury at the bastard who reviewed my first novel, published when I was in my twenties, that told the story of my father's tortured death by leukemia at the age of fifty-five. I got the exciting news from my publisher that *TIME* magazine was to review my book. The magazine sent a photographer to my home to take pictures of me sitting at my typewriter, holding my baby daughter in my arms, and standing beside my handsome husband. For once I felt lucky. A review in *TIME* could make my name. The photographer stayed all day. He asked me to change my clothes three times; he asked me to pose in the backyard sitting on the swing and holding a flower; he asked if I could make him a tuna-fish sandwich.

When, a week later, I read the review, I nearly fell to my knees:

> Abram Goldman is a robust and endearing antique dealer with an imaginative zest for life. When he begins to suffer from leukemia, he is treated with the inevitable escalation of drugs, yet his condition deteriorates. His Jewish-mother-type wife and his daughters—one, the narrator, married with two daughters; the other, the novel's problem child, unmarried and with one foot in the Beat scene—observe his gallant but losing battle.
>
> Such a tale is, of course, depressing. But Author Merrill Joan Gerber makes it even more so by coating it with sentimentality. A short-story writer who has published in *Redbook* and *Mademoiselle*, she seems glued to the traditional women's magazine faith—the world is blackest just before a rose-tinted dawn. After Abram's death, the problem sister marries her beatnik lover. The other sister decides that she will bear a son with her father's name—"It was all I could do in this world—all I could hope to do." Almost any death has a quantum of emotion, but because Author Gerber writes from a self-pitying, self-absorbed point of view, she grabs most of it for herself.

Fury! "Jewish-mother-type wife?" The man misunderstood every word in my book. A moron! A woman hater! An asshole! And *TIME* magazine printed not one single picture. My old age has brought on anger. Let's look at it full in the face, the face that now has become a wreckage of my former smooth cheeks, lovely lips, delicate neck, blue eyes, flawless earlobes, chestnut-colored hair. And below, my once gracefully shaped body, with a dancer's arms and legs, adorable breasts, firm bottom—what's become of it now? An elephant in a nightgown! And inside? The uterus gone, a breast disfigured, a knee missing, a bladder that leaks, a heart that bursts into tachycardia without warning, and my God, the horrifying whiskers on my chin.

What is this punishment for? Punishment is for being bad, of course. My grandmother told me to be a good girl all the time because God would know when I was bad and would punish me. When I was five and in kindergarten, I was instructed by my teacher to go up the stairs to the principal's office at P.S. 238 in Brooklyn—the place where only bad children were sent. I went up those stairs shaking with terror I could feel in every cell of my body. When I entered the principal's office, he handed me a snapshot of myself in the schoolyard wearing a little hankie pinned to my coat as I stood with two other children playing a game and said, "Hello dear little girl, the school photographer took this photo, and here is a copy for you and your family."

There's a picture of my husband and me taken in Miami Beach outside our high school's theater at an evening concert where my husband was an usher. As a volunteer, he got to attend concerts for free, and on this night, our first real date, he planned to let me in a side door so we could both watch a famous pianist perform. He was wearing the required white jacket and looked so astonishingly handsome that when I saw him, I felt an actual weakness in my knees. I was newly sixteen, I was thin, with curly brown hair, and I wore a gold four-leaf clover necklace (a gift from my father) in the square-cut neckline of my dress.

Studying that picture in later years, I think my husband looks a bit like Elvis Presley or Tony Curtis, but on that night, he was just my gorgeous new boyfriend. As I sat beside him in the dark row of the concert hall, he slowly slid his arm along the back of my chair and touched my shoulder with his fingers. I gasped.

After the concert, but a half hour before my father was to pick me up in front of the theater, my boyfriend and I walked down to the beach and sat in the moonlight by the ocean. He reached for something on my neckline (I thought my four-leaf clover), and he said, "Mine?"

Thinking he meant the necklace, I said, "No!" But what he was really saying was "Mind?"—did I mind him touching me there, where my small breasts were blooming? My saying *no* gave him permission to touch them gently, first one, then the other. I knew then that he must touch them forever.

My husband and I keep visiting retirement communities. My God, I don't want to live in two rooms, my husband in the next room with his piano, or in the room with me. I don't want to attend lectures, exercise classes, or learn origami. I don't want to eat every meal surrounded by other old folks. Although it's true I am so very tired of cooking all our meals, I can't see that paying ten thousand dollars a month to be rescued from that chore is worth the cost.

When my husband and I visit these various retirement communities, we briefly forget that at home we have a ten-room house filled from one end to the other with the essential objects from our fifty-odd years of living there. We sometimes talk about the practical benefits of moving into one of these expensive retirement units, packing only a few articles of clothing, a couple of books, even a bathing suit (all these places have pools), and moving into a totally neat room or two, with the promise of having whatever color of paint on our walls that we choose, and having them install any color carpet that we want.

The concept is deliberately, intentionally inviting—just us, a few necessary things, and excellent meals prepared for us every day. A new, inviting social world, maid service, entertainment, instruction, a personal gym, a beauty shop, as well as promises of emotional tranquility, safety and protection, transportation to medical care if necessary, and a subtext that it's likely we will be so much healthier in this supportive, welcoming community, that we'll never be sick.

Sometimes I imagine that our entire house has vaporized—not a thing left, as happens when a plane crashes into a home. Not a single photo album remaining, not an obsolete pile of computers, no tax records, medical bills, vinyl records, videotapes, cassette tapes, reel-to-reel movies, CDs, or eight tracks. Gone would be our stacks of *The New Yorker*, the *New York Review of Books*, *The Sewanee Review*, the *Atlantic Monthly*.

Lost sock drawers would be dispatched, never to be sorted through again. Closets of extension cords, hammers and pliers, miscellaneous bulbs, plugs, rolls of duct tape—vanished! Let me out of here with just the clothes on my back. Immigrants have faced such a bleak landscape for centuries. Our grandparents did it, why not us? With our bare bones, why not venture into a new life?

But once we get home after such a visit, once we enter our cluttered, familiar, messy place, we begin to cherish our space, in which we can wander, fortunate as we are: my husband to his music room, where his grand piano sits and his pile of precious volumes of Bach's music, me to my sewing room (where I have not sewed in forty years), where my mother's sewing box sits with its red tomato pincushion, its container of unique buttons, its seam-ripper, and her silver thimble pocked with tiny dots. Even her black wooden darning egg with which she showed me how to darn the holes in my father's socks is in there. A skill to remember, she told me.

Our house: container of all memories, events, emergencies, place of all meals, of our thousands of nights of falling asleep together in our bed, of telling our daughters their bedtime stories, of standing, grateful, under the showerhead to be washed clean of the day's stains, real and imagined.

What? Move to a retirement place where the old who preceded you in that clean, repainted apartment are dead? Might have actually died in there?

The real terror is this. Which of us will die first? (It stands to reason he will.) Which of us will be able to survive in this house all alone? Who will open the jar of blueberry jam? (Me needing him.) Who, when the pipe bursts under the sink, will have the presence of mind to go outside and find that green wheel and turn off the water? (Him needing me.)

But I also know that we are isolated, losing interest in all things, even each other, and that we almost never see another human being in a social context. We are not joiners. We are Jews without a Jewish community. We don't believe in God, or heaven, or an afterlife, or even in having funerals. Who are these people who have two hundred guests at their funerals? They seem to be rich guys who traveled the world, flew their own planes, invented the zipper, gave their wives diamonds, and have brilliant, successful children. And who are we? No one.

Not really no one. We, too, have lived long, interesting lives, we have had children (but where are they?), and we did a few important things: like work, and teach, and write a book, and be nice to some people, and help a few to achieve some goal or other, but still, who would come to the funeral of either of us? Why would we want anyone to come?

My husband's parents' ashes are in the back of a closet at his sister's house. She keeps intending to scatter them somewhere, sometime, and though she could now add her husband's ashes to the mix as well, she still never gets around to it. Her husband shot himself in the head in their backyard when he realized he was becoming helpless. He knew how to use a gun; he'd been in the Korean War. He told his wife what he was planning. She knew it. She knew what he was going to do the day he went out into the backyard in his bathrobe with his gun. He was suffering three fatal diseases at once, and he was aware he was a few days short of total dependence on others. She waited for the sound of the gunshot. And she waited. Then she heard him calling her name. Oh, she knew he might not do it, and that would mean total servitude to him for the rest of her life. She was terrified he would do it and also feared he might not. And when he called her name, she went to the garden door to ask him what he wanted. He said, "I can't find the bullets." She said, "Look in your bathrobe pocket." He looked and said, "Oh yes, thank you." And then she went inside, and she heard the gunshot. The police checked her hands for gunpowder just in case.

My husband and I don't want funerals, though he once said he wished his parents had graves somewhere that he could visit if he wanted to. Since their graves are still in his sister's closet, he decided we should buy funeral plots even if we don't want funerals. In fact, we already own four graves for the two of us. We bought two expensive plots in the Jewish cemetery in Hollywood Hills when my mother died and was buried beside my father, and then we bought two more cheap plots in the little graveyard—the Pioneer Cemetery in our small town, established in 1881—a block down the road from our house. It spans two acres and features magnificent oak trees. We walk through that cemetery very often. We breathe the same air in our house that gently blows over the graves in that cemetery. The oak trees are so tall that they nearly block our view of the mountains that rise just to the north. We appreciate our little cemetery because it has no gift and flower shop, no piped music, no rules about embalming or having a cement enclosure for each coffin. It has no worker collecting little printed cards signed by funeral guests as they exit a fancy chapel in time to see a coffin containing a body being slid into a shiny black hearse for the trip to the gravesite.

In fact, our cemetery overlooks a park where little kids ride on swings, and where families picnic, and where dog lovers play with their dogs. It hardly reeks of death at all. At Christmas we see poinsettias decorating the graves, and on the Fourth of July, the city parade passes right by the buried dead, music blasting from big speakers as the owners of old Fords and Pontiacs wave to the people lining the street, the search and rescue team marches by with their sweet, slavering dogs, and the fire trucks shoot darts of water at the onlookers on what is usually a very hot day. For a cemetery, it's really a cheerful place. Sometimes, when there's a burial, the sounds of bagpipes come floating down the street toward our house. It's a pleasant place, and seems it would be homelike for us to be buried there.

Sometimes I wonder if, in our old age and loneliness, we decide to join a synagogue, and we get to have a rabbi. Will we have to then be buried in the Jewish cemetery alongside my parents? Will someone have to say the kaddish for the dead over our graves? Should we learn the words of the kaddish ourselves so that one of us can say kaddish for the other? I looked up the translation of the kaddish prayer itself. How could it be that it never mentions dying?

> Glorified and sanctified be God's great name throughout the world which He has created according to His will.
> May He establish His kingdom in your lifetime and during your days, and within the life of the entire House of Israel, speedily and soon; and say, Amen.
> May His great name be blessed forever and to all eternity.
> Blessed and praised, glorified and exalted, extolled and honored, adored and lauded be the name of the Holy One, blessed be He, beyond all the blessings and hymns, praises and consolations that are ever spoken in the world; and say, Amen.

The kaddish for the dead is asking quite a bit. Should we be required to bless and praise, glorify and exalt, extol and honor the Holy One, especially since the Holy One has just allowed our beloved person to die?

What if one of us falls? I've had one very serious fall. It happened on a day I was planning to go to my therapy group at the medical clinic. Our therapist had confessed to me a love of lemons. She was in her late fifties, about the age of my oldest daughter, unmarried, good-looking, with dyed red hair that fell in a strange pointy cut on either side of her face. We had a lemon tree in our backyard, and I decided to bring her several lemons. She counseled five depressed patients, including me, who met with her each week. Every one of us was dealing with some form of mental illness: PTSD, bipolar disorder, an eating disorder, a panic disorder, suicidal thoughts. I personally had considered drowning myself in our pool for no clear reason that I could recall. My husband thought my depression might be due to my car accident, which occurred on a day I was on my way to the Cancer Support Center for my painting class. By that time, my chemo was over, my radiation completed, and a fairly large part of my left breast had been removed. During my recovery, I continued to drive to the support center for a healing art class.

The art teacher showed us wonderful ways to paint palm fronds, but I painted only images from my family photo album—my grandmother as a girl after arriving in America from Poland, wearing a black lace dress pulled tight at her waist. My mother in her eighth-grade graduation dress in a photographer's studio in Brooklyn, a diploma in her hands, and on her breast a small, gold pin inscribed with her name and the words ACADEMIC EXCELLENCE AWARD. My beloved, died-too-soon father, wheeling me in a carriage on the Coney Island boardwalk, he smoking his pipe, and I teething on another of his pipes' stems—an actual white wooden pipe of his in my tiny mouth. My mother and father with me at the Bronx Zoo, the three of us in front of a cage of wild animals, while in my gloved hand I hold a box of Cracker Jacks.

Driving to my painting class one day, my car was suddenly hit from behind by a truck and sent spinning around to face oncoming traffic. I felt myself sailing through the air, I spun around to see trucks speeding toward me, and then one of them smashed into my car, then another. I felt the windshield glass crumble into my lap.

I was transported from the car to an ambulance and then to a hospital. I was injured but not badly. But the accident unmoored me. I had just survived cancer and then—when the truck smashed into me—I found myself having to face death again.

I began to think I had lived long enough. I wandered the edge of our pool, wondering how long it would take to drown. I counted all my pills saved over the years from my many surgeries—phenobarbitals, Vicodins, Valiums, tramadols, Norcos, Ativans. When my husband saw me reading my old copy of *Final Exit*, published by the Hemlock Society, he convinced me to see a psychiatrist. She encouraged me to join my therapy group, which was the reason that on the day of my fall I was going into my backyard to pick lemons from our tree to give to my therapist.

A lovely, large lemon on the back side of the tree caught my attention. I pulled on the fruit, but it would not release into my hand. I pulled even harder. The branch of the tree shook, but the lemon held on. I used all my strength. The lemon snapped free, sending me backward so fast that I fell over a brick planter and landed on my back in the dirt, smashing my head against the wall of the house behind it.

My husband, hearing me yell, came out and at first could not find me, invisible as I was behind the tree and hidden in the weeds of the planter. He tried to pick me up but he could not; only his fingers remained strong from so many years of playing the piano.

I told him to call our nephew, a very tall young man. Though I had to lie there in the planter for another hour, my nephew arrived, all six-foot-four of him, and lifted me up in the blink of an eye. I did not get to my therapy group that day with a lemon for my therapist because I had broken a vertebra. Man proposes, God disposes.

My friend at the food bank began to worry about my health when I told her I had to have a biopsy of my thyroid. The scan results had announced the following:

> Conclusion: Hypodense right thyroid lobe suspicious for hypermetabolic neoplastic pathology and thyroid carcinoma. There is intense tracer activity in the region of the urinary bladder.

When I emailed my oncologist, she sent me a happy-face emoji. All that tracer activity in the urinary bladder was simply the radioactive material being peed away. As for the thyroid—well, yes, tracer activity there might mean cancer. She advised another biopsy in three months. If it was cancer, we'd deal with it. Forget it for now.

Forget it?

I wish my husband would remember to take out the garbage. To change a light bulb. To put a new water filter in the ice maker. To clean up the bear poop.

One morning we found the garbage can knocked over and the remains of a week's worth of trash littering the front yard. Bears have been coming down from the mountains where there's been no rain and food is scarce. Neighbors' security cameras catch them climbing into their pools and up their avocado trees. On the day our trash was strewn everywhere, I noticed what looked like an enormous turd on our lawn. I studied this huge, segmented thing and wondered if I should take a photo of it with my cell phone, maybe examine it through the lens app to confirm it was actually produced by a bear. When I told my husband I wanted to take a photo of it, he looked at me with his eyebrows raised. I knew he disapproved of the idea. It was unseemly to him. I was always willing to cross lines he would not venture past.

I indicated to my husband that we had to get rid of it; or, more specifically, *he* had to get rid of it. He agreed. I thought it should be done right away. A week later, the thing was still on the lawn. When my husband and I went out to take our walk, I pulled a long twig from a tree and knocked the pieces of shit, over and over, until I got them all the way to the curb, where on Monday the street cleaning truck would swoop them up with a big brush and take them away. But when I saw my husband watching me, when I saw the puzzlement and dismay on his face, I wondered if our marriage was finally coming to an end.

My husband has allowed me to cut his hair every month for the last fifty years. This shows some trust, I think. I learned how to cut hair when I was five, in my aunt's little beauty shop, which was in a bedroom in our Brooklyn house, where she served the neighborhood ladies. My aunt dedicated herself to the wartime efforts in Brooklyn; she sold war bonds, rolled bandages for the soldiers, marched with the Red Cross women in parades on Avenue P, all of them dressed in white, like angels. From her customers she collected little trinkets—beads, pearls, costume jewelry—which would be distributed to pilots in case their planes crashed on a mountaintop in New Guinea and it was necessary to trade with natives for food. My aunt and her customers talked incessantly about their husbands or sons who were off fighting, the food rationing, the latest news from various fronts, all the while my aunt's scissors dancing around the heads of these worried women. As a child, I listened to their stories, I bent fallen hairpins into the shapes of animals, and I learned enough to cut my own hair and the hair of my future husband ever after.

Now, once a month, I roll a kitchen chair into our little bathroom, and my husband removes most of his clothes and sits before me while I cut his hair with a pair of antique scissors rescued from my aunt's beauty shop. I proceed from the tender back of his neck to the edges of his ears, to the top of his head (now with barely a hair upon it), and finally to the front of his face, where I trim his eyebrows, carefully, with a much smaller pair of scissors. With a little electric clipper, I shape his sideburns. Sometimes, when I am this close to him, he leans forward and kisses me wherever his lips land. Sometimes he lifts my shirt and he kisses my breast. I kiss the top of his head and hold it against me. We are so lucky to be together, alive, and at this old age, still taking care of one another. I want us to live together forever. Or even better, maybe die at the same time.

I am struck with an idea for a new business. I will finally become an entrepreneur. I will call my company The End of the Road, and it will be a service for newly bereaved widows or widowers who want to skip the horrors of being the one left behind with all the crap to take care of, with all the financial details to sort out, the one who has to call the mortuary, order the coffin, throw out her husband's old shoes and give away his shirts and hats, the one who has to call tax lawyers, realtors, trust fund managers. My new business will simply be a kind of gentle transition—not the kind that hands off the grieving mate to a retirement community and arranges for the furniture to be laid out in her new one-room life but will provide a much-needed service for painless self-deliverance, the kind of end a sick, well-cared-for dog enjoys. My company will provide fast and guaranteed death while at the same time contracting to take charge of all the requirements of ordering the death certificates, remodeling the run-down house, and selling it for a big profit, assuring that all its contents will be sold to the highest bidder and that one's heirs will get their rightful shares.

My new business will allow those who sign up to skip all the end-of-life horrors. Even better, my "premium" level of service could be chosen by both mates at the same time. On a selected date, together they'd check into a spa-like, cozy place, together, with Baroque music playing, they'd clasp hands as a stream of propofol would be sweetly, painlessly administered to each, followed by a boost of fentanyl—and poof, all things unpleasant would vanish, especially the horror of protracted dying. Nothing left, nothing to it, just sweet nothings now and forever.

My kind friend at the food bank has new gifts to press upon me. A bag of modern, brightly colored, silicon soup ladles, with price labels attached: *$18.95*. Each! "What am I supposed to do with so many?" I asked her. "Be a good neighbor," she suggested. She handed through my window a supersize container of laundry detergent. "Listen to this," she said, and read to me from the label: "The uplifting scent of orange essential oil blended with essence of grapefruit and notes of lemon and exotic citrus bursting with sunshine will brighten your mood. Smile and take on the day with your refreshingly clean laundry. So concentrated only an eighth of a cup will do a large load of clothes!"

"It almost makes me want to do the laundry," I laughed. As I was about to drive away, she said, "Wait! One more gift!" and put into my hand a small, leather-bound book titled *And He Walks With Me: 365 Daily Reminders of Jesus's Love.*

"I want you to keep this," she said. "I've underlined the most important parts on every page. Read a page every day. If you're sad, my friend, or scared, just remember, those who know Jesus as their friend are never alone. You will always have a friend in Jesus. And a friend in me." "But what if you need it?" I asked her. "Don't worry. I have the whole Bible!" she assured me, and we fist-bumped one more time.

I keep my laundry in my pink and yellow seersucker laundry bag from college, on a hook in my sewing room; my husband keeps his in his Air Force duffel bag that hangs on a hook in his closet.

When I was aware that we probably both had no clean clothes left to wear, I normally would ask him to bring his laundry bag into the laundry room (where I assumed he would put his clothes into the washer). Though he seemed to hear me ask this, he also seemed to forget my request immediately. In the most recent enactment, I began asking him on Sunday to bring in his laundry. I usually make my request while we are eating a meal together, the time when we're most likely to exchange information. I asked him again on Tuesday if he would bring in the laundry so I could do a wash. He agreed. He didn't do it. I wondered if I would need to lead him by the hand to the hook in his closet. What was it about this simple request that made it so hard for him to process? Of course, I could easily have done it myself, delivered both his laundry and mine into the washing machine, but I didn't. I thought he should bring in his own dirty laundry. By Friday, I asked him, with some impatience, if he would now, this minute, bring in the laundry, that I was totally out of clean clothes and had to do a wash. "I've asked you several times," I reminded him, "so do it right now, will you?" "I will." He nodded, and then I watched him walk down the hall to practice the piano.

There are limits, even in a marriage of sixty-two years, that can be breached. How many times do Bach's French Suites need to be played, no matter how beautifully and artistically and precisely, when a family's underwear needs to be washed, dried, and folded? How much patience toward a partner, how much kindness and understanding of his needs, tolerance of his basic nature, acceptance of his human faults, even in view of one's adoration of his solid psyche, marvelous strong chin line, masculine handsomeness, sexual prowess—how much can a wife tolerate, finally? Not enough, apparently. Which brought me, at last, to throw at him the question growing ever more insistently in my bosom since I first met him one day before my sixteenth birthday. The question, shaped like a snake, came shooting out of my mouth when he came into the kitchen to take his heart and blood-pressure pills. "I have to know something. I've thought about this from the day I met you. Did you ever have sex with another woman? Did you do sexual things with some girl before me?"

He blanched. I never knew what that was until I saw it happen. Holding on to his pill bottle, he said, "Why are you asking me this now?"

"Because if I should have cancer again, I want to know the answer before I die. When you married me, I was pure as the fallen snow. I never, never, never—"

"Of course," he said. "I know that." He made a move toward me, as though he might pat me reassuringly, even tenderly, on my shoulder, but I jumped back.

"I wasn't even sixteen but you . . . you were eighteen! Older. More experienced. Please tell me! *Did* you have sex with some girl before me?"

I watched his eyes, the tilt of his head, as he thought about his reply. He appeared to think I had gone crazy. I understood his hesitancy: many men of eighty-five—even of fifty-five or thirty-five—have had multiple, maybe dozens, maybe hundreds of women, girlfriends, lovers, wives, and here I wanted a total confession, one that might un-man him and his right to his own secrets, his own private knowledge of his intimate history. He had a right to his secrets, didn't he? At that moment I didn't think so. From this man, to whom I had given myself in utter innocence, I wanted a pledge of his total loyalty and purity as well. We never would have gotten to this moment if only he had brought in the fucking laundry.

The look of anguish on his face revealed his unspoken reaction: That's enough. I can't do this. I can't listen any longer. As he turned to walk away, I knew I'd lost my final opportunity.

"From now on do your own laundry!" I cried out, helplessly, in tears. "I won't ever ask you again." I heard for one instant the pure madness in my voice.

"Oh, please, please," he pled, even as he turned to walk away from me, as he shuffled down the hall, as he struggled to get to his music room. "Please, can't you just relax," he said, talking to me over his shoulder while escaping from me. "You have been the love of my life. You have been my sweetheart forever." His head was shaking with the tremor from which he suffered so badly. "Please don't do this to us now," he said, "when there is so little time left for us to be happy."

Siri Tells a Joke

FROM *The Sun*

ONE DAY WHEN I was driving around, I asked Siri to tell me a joke. She gave me this:

Three men are stranded on a desert island when one finds a bottle, and out of that bottle a genie emerges to grant each man a single wish. The first begs to go home and is dispatched. The second, too, wishes for home and disappears. The third hesitates for a moment, then says, "I miss my friends. I wish they were here."

After my husband died on Christmas Day, I walked the streets near our rental house and wished him back. He needed to come back. I wanted him to return here, to the house where we'd set up camp after a forest fire had rendered our own home uninhabitable. I missed his presence, his malty smell and whiskery face, his grouchy edge. His ability to recognize my edge. I walked up and down the rainsoaked hills looking for him, wherever he'd landed above the Oregon clouds that sagged like old pillows. I reminded him that I couldn't manage what he'd left for me. Didn't he know that? The glaring absence of the man I'd shared my life with. Our property largely done in by wildfire. Attorneys and adjusters and morticians asking mind-bending questions. Even this body of mine that seemed compelled to remain in motion, as if I'd been charged with wearing a hole in the neighborhood rug.

My agitation had to do with what felt unfinished. I still had things to work out with him: the last tensions between us, the ones that tend to collect and congregate in a long relationship like a few sour droplets clinging to a bowl. If he showed up again, we could find peace with each other, I was sure of it, and I might cook one more meal for him. We might make a last visit to the river, where he would point out the dorsal fin of a salmon just under the surface or spot a heron tucked into the brush. But mostly, on these post-death walks, I sent out the apologies that hadn't been issued before he was gone: My irritation over the cat-food cans he left in the sink. I'm sorry. The way I fidgeted in the passenger seat when he drove like an old man on the freeway. How I shut myself off after our arguments. I'm sorry. I'm sorry. It turned out the only person who could soothe me through the death of my husband was my husband, and if he'd only boomerang in again, I could show I was a kinder woman than the one he'd left. Look how nice I am now! The pettiness of my quotidian complaints fuzzed in me like rotting fruit.

Up the hills, down the hills, until I at last stepped into an over-heated house that was not mine, not ours, to tuck myself into a bed that was bereft of him.

My husband had been sick long enough, a string of years, that I'd begun to think of his diagnosis as a rumor. He was interminably terminally ill. Until he wasn't. Until he was on a hospital bed with skin as pale as the sheets, except for a few age spots floating on the surface of his forehead like smooth boulders. His jaws were un-locked to suck in air, and I stared into the cave of that mouth: the tinge of decomposition. The trembling tongue. And underneath it, the gone-black lingual frenulum, as if it were designated first to die.

I was with my husband, holding his hand, when he took his last breath. Two days later I stood by while the mortician nailed the lid onto his coffin and our daughters shoved it into the furnace. And yet I still managed to believe—for half a second—that he could return. I awoke on winter mornings and rolled to the right, away from his side, as was my habit. I didn't move—no shudder or flinch. I stared at the wall so I could let myself believe he was on the other side of me, his back to mine. If my faith was mighty enough, he would soon reach out to put his hand on my shoulder, pulling me toward him. A man made whole.

I once discovered a brochure from the 1840s that advertised lush agricultural land in Oregon's Willamette Valley, distributed free by the government, forty acres at a time. A bounty beyond imagination,

the ad promised, while also claiming that a man who'd fallen dead
in the dirt had stood up again in minutes, restored by the nutri-
ents in the soil.

Shortly before his death, my husband knelt into a mound of ash
at our property in the mountains above the Willamette Valley. He
stood up again to rake through the devastation of the wildfire that
had raged down the corridor where we lived together, where he'd
lived for fifty years, a fire that miraculously had not reached our
house and yet had burned nearly everything around it for miles.
Our region's long drought had made perfect, crisp-dry conditions
for fire, and yet the smoke and flames had seemed to come out
of nowhere, jarring us from bed in the middle of the night to run
for our lives.

The day I'm remembering was weeks after that, when we were
finally let back in to discover what was left and what was gone for
good. The air was thick with smoke that lodged in my throat. Trees
I had considered our sentries, well over a hundred years old, were
reduced to black pillars that would peel from the ground in the
season's first windstorm, crashing into splinters. My husband's
gloved hands were wrapped around the handle of a rake, his boots
powdered gray, his pants, face, and hair spiky with particulates.
He was sifting through the remains of the building where he'd
stored five decades of his work, hunting for anything recognizable,
a remnant of what had been decimated in a single night of howling wind and flame. I noticed his body jolt, a slight whip of the
shoulders and a quiet gasp from his mouth. A few minutes later
it happened again. That's when I realized his metal tool had hit a
live wire snaking through the ash. "Put it down," I said. He ignored
me. Another jolt, and I stood up to take the rake. "Stop," I said.
"That's enough."

I thought of those small shocks two months later as I rubbed
ointment on his back, burned by defibrillator shocks administered
in the ER. One dull and cold Sunday morning at the rental house,
my husband's heart had decided not to beat on. An ambulance
had transported him to a hospital, where doctors had startled his
heart into continued service. I remember thinking of Mary Shelley's dead frog, its legs reanimated with pricks of electricity for
purposes of entertainment and curiosity, not to give the frog a
chance to jump, to safely land again. After a few days we returned

to our temporary home, my reawakened husband and I. There I spent the next few weeks watching the life drain out of him.

By the time Siri told me her joke, it was late spring, maybe summer, and my husband had been gone for half a year. Still, I hadn't given up. In my own interior I conjured a genie's bottle made of the thinnest glass, which I rubbed once a day, twice if my mood was indulgent. I kept on making wishes for his return, imagining them swirling through the air like maple-tree samaras, landing on his shoulder or in the tangle of his hair. I waited for his response. A red-tailed hawk parked in the highest branches of a poplar tree. *Is that you?* The wad of twenty-dollar bills I found in the pocket of his jeans—a reassurance that I'd be okay? A wineglass that shattered in my hand. A folded note in his handwriting in the bottom of my purse. A sudden, familiar creak of his desk chair upstairs.

I might stand outside studying the hawk until the rain drove me in, or allow the blood to drip from my palm into the sink in the shape of a cuneiform inscription, but in the end I couldn't decipher these tidbits, these crumbs. Genie, was my wish not clear? I asked for the whole man to come home, as he was before, free of the illness that overtook him and the fire that crippled his spirit. A man, I hoped, who'd be glad to be reunited with me.

I guess we laugh at Siri's joke because the first two men have no choice: they're about to be snatched away from their dearest places and redeposited on the sand. They're helpless to do otherwise because another man has opted for himself. Does the third man believe the others will be the same people who left him? That's impossible. All three will be altered, whatever relationship they'd once had now in shambles.

I decided, a few weeks after hearing it, that Siri's joke was a retelling of the Lazarus story, in that the dead man from the Bible was returned to life because others willed it to happen. Lazarus had no say in the matter. I picture the stunned Lazarus, suddenly not dead, hobbling into his small house. Here the familiar sweat-soaked blankets on his bed, there the half-eaten broth congealing on the table, his spine tingling with confusion while new blood pushes out the dried-to-dust blood in his veins. The Book of John describes the stink as Lazarus blinked his way out of the tomb four days after he'd been laid away, yanking off the strips of cloth he'd been wrapped in, onlookers folding into the shadows to avoid the stench of death.

I wondered how the sisters, Mary and Martha, had whipped up the temerity to ask Jesus to bring their brother back: a big request. But then a friend—a pastor, steeped in Scripture—told me that Martha went out and met Jesus on the road not to ask for a miracle but to complain. Jesus had failed to answer their urgent message of a day or two earlier, insisting that he rush to his old friend's side and save him before it was too late, and Martha meant to give him what for about it. She might have wished, as I do, for her loved one to be alive again, but she wouldn't have asked Jesus for such a thing. Would she? At most she might have raised her voice in frustration: *Where were you?*

"Jesus wept." It's the celebrated shortest sentence in the Bible, and Jesus's reaction to the news of his friend's passing. He wept, and then he went to the sealed tomb and, surprising everyone, called to Lazarus to rise again. And Lazarus did.

The risen man has stuck like a burr in the human psyche, explored in songs and poems and films, a story of particular interest to those of us left behind when a loved one dies. What would it take, exactly, to get them back? Whatever it is, we'd like to be let in on the deal.

The sisters had to be overjoyed at their brother's return, if bewildered and somewhat undone. But what about Lazarus? What did he get out of it? He suddenly had time—thirty years, says the Bible—if time is what he longed for. Except that he had slipped inside the ultimate mystery, a gauntlet he must have pondered every day for three decades, aching for or else dreading its final tap.

Jesus returned to the village a few weeks after Lazarus's rebirth and sat with his friend for a meal. What passed between them? Did Lazarus thank Jesus for the gift of another shot at life, or did he lean in with a reproach? *How dare you—you who claim to love me—rob me of my peace.*

At least a year before my husband's death, before the fire, he flew to Alaska to attend a memorial service for a longtime friend, and he returned with a mug. It was a simple green mug with an image of a raven on one side. My husband had asked the dead friend's family if he could take it as a memento, a clean and unchipped remnant from a life that had become progressively more worri-some and disheveled.

When he went upstairs to take a nap, I set the mug in the sink along with a couple of bowls and various cutlery. I turned on the water, dribbled in soap, and was preparing to wash when I smacked the edge of a dish, and a perfect wedge popped clean from the mug. Just like that, the vessel my husband had carried home in his hands from Fairbanks to Western Oregon was broken.

I didn't admit what I'd done right away. He found the cup and its wedge sitting by the sink. For a second I hoped he would decide that a settling of the house or a wind through the window had caused the break, but he knew it was me. He picked up the pieces and held them out. Not toward me, exactly, but toward any force that might stanch the confusion rising in his guts.

It sounds simple now (though, for reasons I'm still sorting out, it was not simple then): I'd step up and apologize, steeling myself against his disappointment, and we'd soon put the episode to rest. But I didn't do that. I decided his disappointment was more than I could bear. I said instead that I'd make the cup right again. Good as new! I talked too much and too fast about how I'd find a person capable of fixing it. I didn't give my husband a chance to growl and spout, to eventually cool off, to reach the point where he could say, *It was just a cup*, and learn to live without it.

If he did say those words, I suppose I refused to hear him.

The ceramicist I found in Portland turned the mug over in his hands, then pointed out that it was likely a cheap souvenir from a gas station or café. If the mug was as important as I'd claimed, he suggested the Japanese technique of *kintsugi*: a delicate line of gold, riverine and subtle, acting as seam between the broken pieces. "Embrace the flaw," this man told me. "Make it into art."

But when I returned to retrieve the cup, I found the opposite of art. It looked as if a child with a glitter-glue gun had stuck the pieces back together with zero finesse. I paid the $150 and rushed outside, holding the mug and its bejeweled globs above the wet pavement, tempted to throw it down and smash it into shards that I could then cart home: *Here you go, Husband: evidence of my folly.* But I put it in the passenger seat and drove the three hours to our house, disgusted by my habit of dragging things out. At home my husband pressed the mug, remembrance of a beloved friend, into the far corner of a cupboard. We never spoke of it again.

*

The three-men-on-a-desert-island joke is the only one I've heard from Siri. My request that day was random, a whim. Still, I can't help but believe it was meant to be: that particular one laid on my doorstep as if it had been waiting to land there, a brown-paper package that I have unwrapped and rewrapped, a gift that arrived overloaded with expectation. It's the joke that prompted me to read up on Lazarus; the Sylvia Plath poem ("Ash, ash— / You poke and stir") and, better yet, Anne Sexton imagines Lazarus in heaven, "as dead as a pear / and the very same light green color." The joke reignited the memory of the broken cup, unfinished business that rattles like a loose window in the middle of the night. All that reading and thinking over a period of months: I figure now that I was shaping one of those juicy life lessons about moving on, about release and liberation. Or maybe I was writing a fable for myself about cup shards spun into false gold, a story whose last line insisted that accepting brokenness is the only way to peace.

Except no wisdom of this sort emerged to serve me on the last day I spent on our property. I was alone that afternoon. The contractors who'd repaired the damaged house were finished, their trucks packed up and gone. A logger had carted off the charred and fallen trees, while the remaining forest detritus had been bull-dozed into a massive pile to be dealt with later. It was early November, a year and two months after the fire and more than ten months since my husband's death. A time without time, though I recall details of that day: How I packed a final box, mopped the kitchen floor, inhaled the pungent air of our home (which had a smell like no other dwelling), locked the front door, and left the key for the new owners. How I tied on my boots and walked into our dark woods.

Once, when we were far into the Oregon wilderness, my husband taught me the word *preternatural*. That's what this final afternoon in the woods dished up: A preternatural ending. A preternatural quiet. The deeper I went in—climbing over burned trunks and limbs until my shoes and pants and hands were covered in soot, stepping over tendrils of green ferns and tangled blackberry vines, taking care with this fresh growth—the more the quiet fell over me. Not even a soft breeze through the trees that had survived: the Douglas fir, the cedar and hemlock, the alder and maple, missing their disappeared companions, which were part of the sky and the soil now.

The path was one I'd walked most days before the fire, when ospreys had circled overhead and pileated woodpeckers had drummed on cedar trunks, but on this day all signs of the former trail were burned up, the old way hardly recognizable. No birds. No raptor calls or songs from a Swainson's thrush. No elk droppings or faint scent of cat musk. I made my way to the creek, which babbled at the lowest decibel, as if adhering to the day's code of silence. The log I sat on gave way under me, so that I was suddenly slung in a hammock of rotting wood. I stayed there for a good beat, waiting for what might unfold on this final afternoon at my home. The moment teetered on the verge of unbearable.

And though I knew better, though I was clear that it could not possibly happen, and clear on the disturbance it would cause if it did—that is, if I convinced Jesus or the universe or whoever was in charge to bend time and space—and though I'd read the part about how Lazarus never smiled again after this savior pulled him from the tomb, I couldn't help myself. I sent out yet another wish. This one as fervent as all the ones before, as if I'd learned nothing.

Husband, please return. Not for thirty years, not even for one year, but for this day. For this one hour. Land here beside me and give me a single, silent hour together in our woods. No one will see you, and I promise I will never tell.

This was my invocation, which sailed into the remaining canopy of our once-lush forest, into the green and gold of autumn, into the hillsides slashed by fire, into the tumbling river that ran through the life we'd once made in this very place. *I miss my friend. I wish he would come back.*

EDWARD HOAGLAND

On Aging

FROM *The American Scholar*

AGING IS SLIPPAGE. Wax, then wane, toward humble pie, another day, another dollar. I was born a month after Franklin Roosevelt was elected president. So I clean my plate at meals and follow that famous bit of fatherly advice, Neither a borrower nor a lender be. Wry but spry, I never mortgaged my future and though I pee more often now, my wallet, at least, is tumid. When dressing, I may forget my second shoe; I wear long underwear for half the year. Sightlessness has various effects. If you've driven for almost seventy years, shouldn't that be enough? So many worries hitch a ride on your car. Oil change, check the tires. The BBC will give you world news when you can't read the *Times*. Exercise cautiously, not to slip or pull a ligament. Tamp down one's crabby self. The luxury of shedding a rigid daily schedule should be solace enough. In a free country we each have written our own script for decades, and patience is a craft we ought to have mastered long ago. Pop-up memories produce the names of five girls from my eighth-grade class. God bless them if they're okay. A lot has changed for girls since 1945, and for someone headed for the writing game as well. My first agent and my best publisher were handling William Faulkner at the same time as me. That is, it was possible then to *be* William Faulkner—a towering genius in a now-eclipsed field. I didn't know him but did meet two other Nobel winners: Steinbeck and Bellow, whose careers would seem miniaturized nowadays.

Dale Somebody was the first real cowpoke I ever knew; Trevor Bale and Mabel Stark, the first tiger rasslers. Eric Robbins, *Time*'s man in Africa, introduced me to that fabled continent. Old age generates a jumbo screen inside your brain on which fitful memories vividly flit. Himalayan rope bridges; Rome in the sixties versus 2013; the Matisse Chapel in Vence shown to me by the beauteous Countess Karolyi of Hungary—an intimate friend of Bertrand Russell's—and her houseguest Ralph Hotere, the Māori painter. Big Apple scenes on Delancey Street and Yogi Berra's first at bat in Yankee Stadium. Joey Giardello, the middleweight champ, on First Avenue, and Jessica Lange tending bar on Christopher Street. Being a downtown person, I didn't know a lot of fame hounds but did have neighbors like Grace Paley, Philip Glass, Donald Barthelme, and Seymour Krim.

In Iowa's Amish country, I lunched with the faithful, in San Francisco with the Beats. I never had a bad romantic relationship, so no street anywhere would be painful to revisit except in the sense of a comrade gone. But loss becomes ubiquitous as the years wane—friends of both sexes and more than just the human species. My setter, Flash, at Taggart's Pond; my chums Tom Hunt and Jimmy Dunn at our school-bus stop; then Rutger Smith, another classmate, bloated with cancer in middle age. Gone is the me who used to walk fifty blocks for a lunch date in New York, and the journalist who shouted at the president of South Sudan back when he was just a murderous warlord in 1993. I've boarded ships near Nome and Ushuaia, loved the Nile and the Nulhegan, and watched my daughter's birth in New York Hospital, so groping for a curbstone with my cane feels less like a comedown than a phase. White hair isn't ugly, nor a hobbled knee. Your posture may resemble another animal's on occasion, like a spider or a goat, as you age. Emergency and commonsense responses kick in.

Absent pain, the passage to death is often quite benign at the end, in my experience as a diener in a morgue sixty years ago. The bodies tended to wear that dawning smile I'd seen on Etruscan statuary. I expect my mouth will be the same. It's the living who weep.

Old age is a slippery slope, but if you enjoyed sledding as a kid and improvising ever since, it shouldn't be degrading. A pile of books-on-tape or unread magazines, a dog learning that its once-wise owner, huffing and puffing, has become worryingly fallible. No more "bearding the lion," so to speak; we're in survival mode, our eyes with crow's-feet around them from squinting. Old age is not for sissies, the saying goes, though sissies undergo it.

Passively, however, there are rewards, like no alarm clocks and the precedence given when traveling. Young folk feign curiosity asking about family history. Dozing off is forgiven and often a pleasure, and bores aren't insulted. Yet, our wide-screen memory enriches our dreams. Movies and bus fares get discounted, and the genders intermingle without fuss or sexual innuendo. Forgetting to put your teeth in, looking tously and slipshod with scratchy beard, pallid, a scruffy'jama guy, is okay. If you shoplift, claim senility. I haven't had many friends slide off the deep end—no incorrigible crooks or drunks—just a few who died too soon from dropping a hair dryer in the bathtub or jumping off the Mystic River Bridge.

"Cat got your tongue?" we'll ask a sulky grandchild, as our grandparents asked us, but provoke hilarity because it's another era. Or, "Have you got a frog in your throat?" We may refer to "single-wing" football or a "three-bagger" in baseball as "the cat's meow." Grandparents, if lucky though, bear a tincture of grandeur. We get command performances on guitar or piano, without the eon of practice. Money and equanimity help, unless the dribbling away of energy has sapped our panache. Do mothers still question their daughters about "petting"? Mickey Mantle was a newbie to me: no Joltin' Joe DiMaggio, my hero. And who could top Jack Benny and Fred Allen? Or Roosevelt? Talk about greatness in politics.

I know the old days seem always the best days to oldsters. My father, after his death sentence at sixty-three from a cancer doctor, tried to comfort himself by telling me history only repeats, so he must have already witnessed whatever was going to happen. Mentally, of course, I demurred but now, half a century later, need to resist similar fallacies. *His* grandfather had fought at Shiloh and marched through Georgia. Around my own fiftieth birthday, I returned to New York's Museum of Natural History to delightedly confirm I'd visited all of the scenery—from cheetah veldt to caribou taiga—I'd pined to see when I was ten or so. I hope my grandsons will manage the same. As for my father, his legal work took him to all the NATO capitals in Europe, which for him was like my wish to span taiga and veldt.

So we have our big-screen memories of the Seine or whatever. That's geezerdom, plus old friends from twenty settings who drift to mind. Ordinary lives, ordinary guys, and women generally a little nicer than the men. I trust everyone a little, few a lot. I've never known someone I would cross the street to avoid, never been beaten up. Have I lived too sheltered a life? I think we sculpt our own lives. A "ladies' man" grooms himself to play around, or smokes if he wants to cough, drives fast if life without accidents is a bore. I didn't want recriminations, accidents, dangerous living.

Aging gracefully is the watchword. Don't wet your pants. Only nominally are your opinions of interest. Will the cost of eldercare exceed your assets? We want our oldsters mildly colorful, as if they've been around the block but picked up no social diseases. Despite that shrinking of the radius we live within, death isn't scary, and it's important to convey this to your survivors, young or old. Gracefully means not in rebellion but with salty serenity or stoical agnosticism.

Aging involves constructing a new persona, as one did in adolescence. We invent new attitudes, less quarrelsome, perhaps, even cultivating sympathy and patience. Tempos change. Naps intersperse the quietude of clean-slate days. You decide whether to mark Valentine's Day, for instance, as well as holidays with children and grandchildren, and whether to keep paying attention to new movie stars or the phases of the sky. Do you become gentler, more accessible as old friends die, reaching out for new ones, or consolidate your affection in memories? There's no longer such incitement to read or inform oneself competitively. How you want to be remembered is not germane, partly because you won't be, or insofar as you are, those actions are indelibly recorded already from your behavior thirty years ago. If you "blotted your copybook," as the English say, it's done; too late now.

Aging is a skid, and as in driving, when you turn in the direction of the slide, don't wrench the wheel toward being a youngster again. Old cars are comfy, though, and so is old age on a good day. I like old dogs, old houses, old trees, and so on. Old houses creak, old cars cough, and old dogs sleep a lot, and we love 'em. Marching music still turns me on, and phoebes twitching their tails, or a cardinal red as the Vatican variety, and Kermit the green frog. You say goodbye to tooth after tooth but still like to see a well-heaved fastball or pigskin, remember the Brooklyn and George Washington bridges, South Street Seaport, and Morton Street Pier. Old Saint Patrick's Church south of Houston, the Cherry Lane Theatre, the Lion's Head bar, the Sullivan building at Bleecker and Lafayette, the Dutch Reformed church on Second Avenue. Trumpet and sax I'll miss, and saucy oysters, sweet corn.

Old age is shrink-wrapped; it's hard to get at things. I think of all the kitchen counters I've known, from Bennington to Bank Street. Or my friend Gene, a fireman's son who thrived at Harvard, taught school in Turkey, but penniless in Miami with Parkinson's, found a friendly doctor to assist him to an easy end. I remember a man my mother loved, Chauncey, who died alone because even at eighty she thought it improper to go to his apartment unchaperoned. Another friend, who grew marijuana for a living, so his check from the government is minimal, survives on the grudging charity of an ex-girlfriend who cracks the whip, making him shovel snow despite a heart condition. Love affairs I'm grateful for, and resting in an overstuffed chair. I preferred women to men as friends once I was out of college and the army. But aging is a banana peel. Don't slip. Keep your arms out but not to snap a wrist. I sometimes tell people who help me with my footing that I'll mention them to Saint Peter when I get to his gate. I like the notion of Saint Peter at a gate, having few serious regrets to prompt a reckoning. But being in actuality a pantheist, I like still more my alternative: dissolving organically into the elements that fuel all life in the soil, a stream, a lake and river, and then the swaying oceans, mother of us all. Even before Peter, there was an ambitious salamander.

"Applaud, my friends, the comedy is over," as Beethoven was said to quoth on his deathbed. And if larder and shelter are secure, a good deal of life is comedic, even its stress. Silly as a goose or Chicken Little, we worry about our feathers before a party. TV ads warn us against "mouth breathing" or being "underinsured." Will the IRS audit your deductions? How about "erectile dysfunction"? Will global warming veer a hurricane our way? When you're aging and lose your balance, is it an early sign of stroke? Or did your heart stutter a bit? You deal with the genes you've got, cancerous or not. The human comedy has more traction as a label than its opposite would. Babies and superannuated folk in "a second childhood" are equally comic, though we try not to laugh at the latter. "Let me check out. I don't want to be a burden," an old guy might tell his offspring, refraining from complaining that he feels neglected because he knows how seldom he phoned his own parents in their infirmity. And what do we know, for all our years? Not to quarrel gratuitously. God must not intend old age to be a breeze or He'd schedule it differently. Go reluctantly seems to be the message.

Don't lie, don't steal, don't gamble as an avocation, we learn early on, not just from conventional hectoring but because lies require a chain of remembrance, which becomes a drag, and stealing turns dangerous. A candy store proprietor probably won't call the cops, but the shop owner next door may want to nip you in the bud. Gambling eventually could involve a panicky response. To throw yourself on the mercy of a cop or casino owner offends one's sense of selfhood. Drinking yourself silly, too, is not productive. If we've taken up killing things for fun with rocks or a .22, we also tend to outgrow that (I don't squash bugs or bite the ears off chocolate bunnies), tennis or gardening being less destructive. Inevitably we'll vegetate ourselves, before joining the vegetable kingdom through the roots of cemetery plantings.

We learn as children that if we hit other people, they will hit us; if we hurt their feelings, they'll retaliate. Soon sympathy develops, for a friend or a hungry goldfish. That fellow feeling expands to classmates who aren't buddies or a lonely local character. In school, teachers speak of kindness, and it registers. We'll actually do favors by and by—having experienced inklings of empathy and developed into the adults we become. In old age as our energies shrivel, so do selfless impulses. We do feel twinges of compassion, but less so, more fatalism. That's the way the world works. We swallow pills. One guy dies in his sleep, another suffers gruesomely in organs we don't want to know about. It's too late to be an idealist, we think. We'll vote, but that's it, or write a check. Yet you keep being the kind of person you were. The same balance of selfishness and charity, the same temperamental bent toward anxiety or equanimity. You've had your shot; you've shot your bolt. You're on an angled glide path. Your shelf life has expired.

Vitiated of virility, we do smile, remembering romantic friendships or nebulous flirtations that almost gelled. There seems no niche for us in the current cultural splatter. Mainstream churches are in retreat as technological velocity and scientific perspectives alter our mentality. One soul's salve seems gobbledygook to another. Democracy demands tolerance, however, but can we pray with that old sense of unison? Laws are passed to enforce basic ethics but not the commonality of values a civilization thrives on. Islam is wracked by schism, while Western Christendom seems flaccid in the face of current catastrophes, despite an inspiring pope. Where is God? People used to think they knew, and built cathedrals. Can you imagine building Chartres now? Yet I'm genuinely pleased when people tell me, all too rarely, they include me in their prayers. Quivery flesh, vulnerable senses, we're here today, gone tomorrow.

Wax and wane. Did you burn the candle at both ends, or hide your light under a basket? The carousel swings up and down. Whatever goes around comes around. As to health, leave well enough alone. Heaven is on earth, Emerson believed. I'd love to be a passenger on trains again, ambling down the corridors toward the bubble car to chum with strangers while the scenery rises and falls. I'd rejoice in gazing out, crossing a continent with the random souls chance has thrown my way.

LAURA KIPNIS

Gender: A Melee

FROM *Liberties*

The king was pregnant.
— Ursula K. Le Guin,
The Left Hand of Darkness

IT TURNS OUT the supply-side cheerleader George Gilder was more correct than not when he forecast, in the poignantly titled *Sexual Suicide* in 1973, that women playing at being men would spell the collapse of Western civilization and probably the social order itself. What he meant by sexual suicide was "the abolition of biological differences between men and women"—in his day, feminists demanding paychecks and forcing men to do housework, and thereby selfishly violating the pact they were supposed to be upholding with nature. Nature had endowed humankind with different sorts of bodies, from which different social roles followed: motherhood for some, breadwinning for others. Nature did not intend men to clean toilets! Or women to go to work, needless to say. It wasn't just child-bearing that society required from women; as the morally superior gender we were also meant to dragoon reluctant men into playing *patres familias*, according to Gilder, luring them into domestic cages like lion tamers at the circus, civilizing their beastly sex drives into socially productive ones. If we shirk the task, everything falls apart. Gay liberation was thus another sore spot in Gilder's catalog of contemporary woe, a world where women's charms held no sway and male carnality thus ran amuck.

How vulnerable the "primacy of the biological realm" would turn out to be, how tenuous its hold on the species if each of us had to pledge fealty to the gender binary to keep civilization afloat. How confident can nature's defenders really be in the sell-ing power of this story? After all, alarm bells aplenty have rung over the last half century yet have thus far failed to herd those renegade female factions back into their kitchens.

And look around now! Gender is more of a clusterfuck than ever, and yes, civilization's destruction indeed looms nearer: birthrates have dropped below replacement rates around the globe, down four percent in the United States in 2020 alone. Male breadwinner families are on the extinction watch list. And the damned libera-tionists still aren't happy. Today's gender vanguards—trans activists, the "genderqueer"—want to sever the link between biology and gender entirely, letting men become women and women men, sur-gically acquiring penises and cooches, rebranding important body parts with gender neutral language ("front hole" for vagina), not to mention poisoning innocent children with cross-sex hormones and puberty blockers. (Far more patriotic to mow them down with as-sault weapons, at least according to the child welfare experts of the GOP.) Some members of the younger generation want to abolish gender entirely, demanding the whole English language be revised to accommodate them and their impossible-to-remember pronoun preferences.

Where gender distinctions blur, monsters seem to lurk, like those snarling creatures at the edge of the world on sixteenth-century maps warning sailors away from the abyss. I was thinking about the monster problem recently while reading an interesting history tracing the relation between the invention of endocrinol-ogy and the growing demand for gender reassignment treatments. Called *Changing Sex: Transsexualism, Technology, and the Idea of Gen-der*, from 1995, it opens with the author, Bernice L. Hausman, a mostly lucid writer, confessing in the book's preface that she'd been pregnant while revising the manuscript, and was "perhaps one of few expectant mothers who worry they will give birth to a hermaphrodite." I was therefore not surprised when the book takes an anxious anti-trans swerve in its epilogue, though prior chapters provide fascinating facts about the discovery of glandular therapies in the late nineteenth century. This includes the story of a researcher named Charles-Édouard Brown-Séquard, who in 1889 found, by injecting himself with canine (or possibly monkey) testicular tissue, that what would later be called testosterone had sexually rejuvenating effects in men. Thousands of men were soon arranging to have themselves likewise injected, though whatever rejuvenation followed was later thought to be a placebo effect—the testes don't actually store testosterone, it turns out.

If commentators as disparate as Gilder and Hausman are, in their different ways, a little panicky about the gender system collapsing, if both envision nature-defying creatures (feminists, hermaphrodites) snapping at them from the abyss, then we're in the realm of what the fairy tale expert Marina Warner calls the monstrous imagination. Aroused by scenes of chaos and emergence, it mirrors our lack of understanding back to us in the form of menacing hybrids, typically depicted as scary inhabitants of dark underworlds. Among the chaotic emergent things no one much understands (especially these days) is gender, despite everyone supposedly having one. Yet what is it, where does it come from? Certainties abound, yet somehow they keep changing. With Western civilization itself a rickety boat navigating these tumultuous waters, perpetually about to sail over the edge into some posthuman future, no wonder the conversation gets a little shrill.

Revolutions are threatening, and what Hausman calls the "new forms of being human" that emerged in the twentieth century *were* revolutionary, especially once "hormones"—so named in 1905—were extracted (from glands) and then synthesized, leading eventually to new possibilities in gender reassignment procedures. Oddly—though maybe this is just the usual blinkers of an academic with nose pressed to his own research subject (in this case, transsexualism)—Hausman fails to mention that the ability to synthetize hormones also led to the development of birth control pills, first marketed in the United States in 1960, which prevent ovulation in women. It strikes me as weird that Hausman doesn't see that far more widely implemented gender-altering technology as part of the same story, also ushering in new ways of "being human" for roughly a hundred million women worldwide. (Estrogen both figures in hormonal contraception and feminizes men who wish to change sex.) Maybe her pregnancy made her less attuned to this aspect of the narrative, but it's hard to think of anything more consequential for natal females than the ability to effectively control fertility, which radically contested the existing gender regime, not to mention fundamentally transforming the experience of heterosexual sex. (See under: Sexual Revolution, The.)

But how did the old regime manage to uphold itself in the first place when it disadvantaged so many? Conservatives will tell you that gender comes from nature and sits firmly on top of biological sex; these sexual differences are imagined to be binary. But this binary was always rather imaginary—the incidence of intersex babies was always higher than was generally acknowledged. Doctors made capricious medical decisions and interventions to assign those babies to one sex or the other, precisely because gender ideology dictated that binary gender had to be preserved. (Apparently intersexed babies are as common as red hair.)

In other words, a certain bad faith seems to come with this territory, by which I mean a refusal to know what you know. Look at Gilder, famous for touting the very economic policies which crushed the single-paycheck family that *Sexual Suicide* was trying to corral America back into. The signature program of these guys (*The Bell Curve* author Charles Murray was another of the big guns)—suppressing wages and cutting taxes for the rich, shifting income shares from workers to capital—was a program so successful we're still living with the consequences. Everyone's seen the stats about upward redistribution of wealth in the last half century, and the gap keeps widening. As Gilder must know, it wasn't feminism that catapulted women into the labor market in the 1970s, it was stagnant male wages, post-industrialism, and the expansion of the service sector; and then came the economic hits of Reaganomics. When labor was winning, as it had been before 1973 (a bad year, between an oil crisis and a recession), a middle-class household *could* survive on one income, not the two or more that are now the norm for vast swathes of the country, often sans benefits.

But why not finger-point at feminists, those sexual gargoyles, chewing up men and spitting them out, though between the union busting and the job exports, capitalists were doing a lot more chewing and spitting than women ever managed, not that we wouldn't have enjoyed it. Oh, and the declining birthrates? The majority of those recently surveyed in the United States cite childcare costs as the foremost reason not to procreate, along with climate change, another of free market capitalism's great accomplishments. (France, the EU country with the highest birthrate, also funds eighty percent of childcare.) Obviously blaming women, homosexuals, and pornographers for macroeconomic shifts is a better yarn. Behind the monstering process lies an appetite for thrilling perversity, Marina Warner observes, for "lurid scenes of other people's sins"—titillating even while they purport to condemn. (Speaking of titillation: along with feminists Gilder has a peculiar animus about sexologists, who come up frequently, though they can, admittedly, be creepy.)

What if we were to put it as a question instead of an answer: Why *has* the traditional gender order lost so many adherents these days? A less hysterical version of Gilder's laments may be found in Francis Fukuyama's account in *The Great Disruption*: in his telling, late capitalism no longer required gender differentiation for the technology and knowledge-based jobs that a post-industrial economy needed to fill. Women didn't suddenly rise up and demand economic independence—Fukuyama goes so far as to call feminism an epiphenomenon of the information society, a symptom of social disruption and not its driver. The explosion of late twentieth-century liberation movements—the sexual revolution, second wave feminism, gay liberation—that freed individuals from the tethers of traditional norms and morals were likewise sparked by the transition to a post-industrial society.

Capitalism smashes things while ushering into existence all sorts of new human freedoms (economic equality unfortunately not among them). If the male-female binary is losing its grip on the human psyche as a social organizing principle, and the premise that gender roles are rooted in nature has been crumbling for the last century, the causes are obviously multiple: an increasing focus on personal fulfillment, the decline of patriarchal authority that accompanied men's declining economic fortunes and women's economic independence, and resulting changes in the family structure. Or go back further: as Eli Zaretsky points out in *Capitalism, the Family, and Personal Life*, the gender order has been breaking down since Freud unwittingly hastened its demise by undoing the "knot that tied the sexual instincts to the difference between the sexes."

My point is that maybe feminism and transgenderism aren't separate stories. Maybe the rising reports of gender dysphoria and plummeting birthrates aren't separate stories either. There have always been people who did not fit easily into normative categories but were herded in by threat and force, and who are increasingly breaking loose. Because yes, the old structures are ever more enfeebled, unable to demand fealty. Conformity to their dictates is waning. For some that spells catastrophe, for others it's a circus of possibility. Paul B. Preciado, author of *Countersexual Manifesto* and *Testo Junkie*, billed by *Vice* as a "punk trans philosopher," says that "we're transitioning from being a society which is organized by sexual difference." We're moving from a binary gender and sexuality regime "to a new and different regime that has yet to be named." In other words: if endocrinology makes bodies malleable, and families instill (slightly) less repression this century than in previous ones, why not explore those possibilities instead of bemoaning the situation? Preciado suggests regarding gender disobedience as a model for social transformation. Why not start implementing "A Day Without Gender" in schools, hospitals, homes, museums and see what happens?

Gilder obviously wasn't wrong that paychecks and the sexual revolution gave women more access to what had traditionally been male prerogatives. (As to whether these were or are "freedoms" is a more complicated discussion.) But the question that Gilder and followers never get around to is this: If capitalism no longer requires gender differences (and soon will barely require workers at all, except for really shitty or "public-facing" jobs), why is it up to the rest of us to keep upholding these differences? What's in it for us?

That the snarling creatures at the edge of the gender abyss were once feminists now sounds quaint, since for today's gender liberationists (trans activists, "enbys," intersectionalists) the feminists are toothless and mainstream, also complicit in monstrous historical crimes. At least four books with "white feminism" in the title were published in 2021 alone; the term is not used with approbation. In the updated version of the story, white women are the ones responsible for electing Donald Trump—even those who voted or worked for Bernie—and will forever be saddled with the humiliating label "Karen" as payback.

In another twist, weirdly it's now feminists—well, a certain breed of feminist, mostly the dreaded white ones—wielding the "nature" card, demanding that the old binaries be kowtowed to, otherwise monsters will get us. In Gilder's iconography of gender catastrophe, the monsters were women in pants; in the updated version they're wearing skirts, but disaster still beckons. J. K. Rowling has been mounting alarms about the monsters in skirts—that is, trans women (assigned male at birth but who identify and live as women), who are supposedly haunting women's bathrooms and changing rooms, intent on sexually assaulting natal females. None of this has been great for her brand, but she seems undaunted. Among Rowling's fears are that if gender self-identification laws go into effect in the United Kingdom, trans people will be allowed to change the gender on their birth certificates without going through the previous gauntlet of psychiatric diagnosis and permission, and then any man who says he identifies as a woman would be able to get a Gender Recognition Certificate and state sanctioned access to gender-segregated facilities.

To inject a bit of reality into this anxious morass, the fact is that no one is stationed at the changing room entrances and public bathrooms checking birth or gender certificates now, so how would banning gender self-identification keep trans people out of non-state-run segregated spaces? There are, to be sure, no shortage of vigorous informal policing mechanisms not infrequently inflicted on trans people who don't sufficiently pass muster (are "clocked" as the wrong sex) in civic spaces, gender-segregated and not. Among the pernicious things about Rowling's statements is the likelihood of them empowering other women to make scenes when in proximity to anyone whose gender presentation is not to their standards, people who just needed somewhere to urinate when out for the day.

In a statement articulating these anxieties, Rowling revealed that she was herself a survivor of domestic abuse and sexual assault, citing this history as a reason for opposing gender reforms. She regards herself as a vulnerable party in the emerging gender order. Yet she doesn't appear to have been assaulted by a trans woman or a man masquerading as a woman. Then why shift responsibility for male violence against women onto trans people who, it is widely acknowledged, are disproportionately victims of violence and harassment themselves, especially when forced into facilities that don't align with their chosen gender? Rowling did acknowledge that the majority of trans-identified people pose no threat to anyone, yet the gender self-recognition movement was still "offering cover to predators like few before it."

Are there really legions of roving trans women predators out there attacking other women, aside from "problematic" Brian De Palma homages to Hitchcock? (*Dressed to Kill* is the locus classicus—

spoiler alert: the psychiatrist did it.) Like Rowling, the feminist philosopher Kathleen Stock seems to think so. Until recently a professor at University of Sussex, Stock voluntarily resigned her post in 2021, saying that she had been subject to bullying and harassment because of her views on transgender identity, and indeed, there had been a student campaign calling for her dismissal. Even her receipt of an OBE—Officer of the Order of the British Empire—was protested by over six hundred fellow philosophers, though a counterpetition signed by two hundred philosophers supported her, or at least supported her academic freedom to say what she wanted about gender.

Reading Stock's essay, "Ignoring Differences Between Men and Women Is the Wrong Way to Address Gender Dysphoria," from 2019, it's easy to see why she is controversial. Things start out reasonably enough, with Stock delineating the difference between what she calls "sex eliminationists"—those who argue there's no difference between biological women and trans women because biological sex isn't a meaningful category—and "gender eliminationists," who hold that distinctions between men and women aren't meaningful, and we should treat all humans the same. From there things become, to my mind, exceedingly fuzzy. Stock argues that because "there will always be some social stereotypes about the sexes that remain programmed in our minds, if only because they correspond to statistically recurrent empirical truths about biological men and women," then the most we can reasonably hope for, when it comes to damaging social stereotypes, is to be "gender critical"— "consciously critical of the particularly damaging social stereotypes we collectively uphold, aiming to replace them over time with better and more socially useful ones."

This slides rather fast from social stereotypes to empirical truths. I find myself wondering how Stock, a lesbian active in LGB organizations, can speak so confidently about the empirical realities of gender, while mysteriously oblivious about how recently so-called experts defined a reality in which homosexuality was a pathology— psychological in origin and thus, notoriously, "fixable." Or one where women were unsuited to the professions. Nothing is less stable (or empirical) than social stereotypes about gender, as anyone who reads a work of history or anthropology knows. The traits associated with one or another gender bounce around and reverse over the centuries and between cultures: sometimes men are the more sentimental ones, elsewhere women; men are the lustier ones, no, actually, it's women (amoral and multi-orgasmic); and so on.

Where I have some sympathy for Rowling and Stock is that the political interests of sexual minorities (gay people), gender minorities (trans people), and feminists (Stock and Rowling are both speaking as feminists) do not always align. While you might be a trans lesbian-feminist, some trans-identified people are also quite attached to the kinds of binary gender distinctions that some feminists would like to abolish. Natal women and trans women have different health and reproductive issues. I don't think natal women need to hold on to some proprietary definition of woman-hood, but there are political reasons, in the current political climate and with abortion rights under threat, to acknowledge that bio-logical womanhood disadvantages biological women in ways that will always defeat equality if not addressed. (Trans men, too, can get pregnant and require abortions.) In any case, no one has to be monstered. Nor does cisgender (not being trans) need to be a slur, or "cishet" a synonym for clueless, nor "older generation," though no doubt these disagreements are generationally inflected. But even lumping "cis" women (a term I don't love) into one pile overlooks a lot—for instance, pro- and anti-abortion cis women see their interests very differently. Race complicates things even more.

Trans men and trans women are also not always allies. In fact, the age-old war between the sexes has lately been transposed to intra-trans disputes, with trans women calling out trans men for transmisogyny on Twitter. A trans man I know recently accused certain trans women in our circle of being "hard-core bros until like a year ago" and moving through the world expecting the same privileges while moaning about being victims of institutional sex-ism. The intra-trans tensions broke into the public sphere in 2020 in the academic journal *Transgender Studies Quarterly*, when trans theorist Jack Halberstam reviewed trans theorist Andrea Long Chu's book *Females: A Concern* (in a piece funnily titled "Nice Tran-nies") and accused her of being the Allan Bloom of trans studies, while having "a deep antipathy" to trans men and butches. (Chu was recently appointed book critic at *New York Magazine*.)

Personally I'm more interested in political alliances than in gender- or identity-based ones. Clearly identity doesn't in itself predict anyone's political affiliations or savvy. A surprisingly high percentage of trans people surveyed—thirty-six percent—were

Trump supporters in 2016, according to a peer-reviewed study a year later in the journal *Politics, Groups, and Identities*, to choose one of many available examples. Trying to make sense of this, the study's authors explain that one of the unifying themes in Trump support was anti-feminism; a big way that the GOP has attracted adherents is by signaling that rejecting feminist positions is part of what it means to be a Republican.

The trans versus feminist tensions are hardly new: open warfare was long ago declared between the brand of feminist some label TERFs ("trans exclusionary radical feminists") and the trans community. (Stock and others regard TERF as a slur and insist on "gender critical" as the correct label.) This often unpleasant standoff commenced with a vicious little tract published in 1979 by the radical feminist Janice Raymond titled *The Transsexual Empire: The Making of the She-Male*, which argued that trans women are closet patriarchs who want to colonize women's bodies by parading all the worst stereotypes about them. In the decades since, trans women were often excluded, in not particularly kind ways, from feminist spaces, because feminists such as Rowling declared themselves vulnerable parties, at risk of assault by trans women, who came equipped with inborn male aggression despite presenting as women.

Natal men may indeed perpetrate the majority of the violence in the world (though it's been argued that female violence takes more hidden forms, for instance violence against children), but the majority of men are *not* violent. It's men, in fact, not women, who are far more often the victims of violence. The week that everyone was talking about the Gabby Petito murder case (the missing travel blogger who turned out to have been killed by her fiancée) and the grim prevalence of missing women, the FBI annual murder statistics for the previous year were released, according to which roughly four times more men were murdered than women (14,146 men, 3,573 women, 35 gender unknown). Obviously women are subject to violence by men, frequently their husbands, boyfriends, and exes, but men are vulnerable to violence by men, too. (As are trans women, especially sex workers, assaulted by straight men who can't own up to attractions that might make them, in their minds, "gay.") Somehow we prefer telling stories about endangered cis women.

Stock, along with Rowling, also seems bent on shunting blame for male violence onto trans women. Stock offers the case of a preoperative trans woman named Karen White who sexually assaulted two female inmates while housed in a British woman's prison. Described by her neighbors to *The Guardian* as "volatile and violent," White was also a convicted pedophile on remand for grievous bodily harm, burglary, multiple rapes, and other sexual offenses. Does Stock think White is a typical trans woman? Is this even typical cisgender male behavior? Stock seems to think yes. Arguing against those who say that excluding trans women from women-only spaces is analogous to excluding lesbians from women-only spaces, Stock counters that there's no "analogous pattern" of lesbian aggression comparable to patterns of male violence. In other words: Trans women *are* men and must shoulder the blame for male violence. And one violent trans woman is a pattern.

Is this intellectually honest? I don't think so. As someone pithily tweeted about the sorts of fears circulated by Rowling and Stock, "The reason predatory men aren't becoming trans to prey on women? It's a lot easier to become a cop." In other words, we panic selectively. Reports not infrequently surface about mothers doing violence to, sometimes even murdering, their children. To date there are no attempts to ban motherhood. We see those episodes as anomalies, though non-anomalous enough that there are laws and (generally understaffed) child protection agencies, and of course a thriving memoir subgenre devoted to abusive mothers. But motherhood is also supposed to be the "natural" condition of things, thus maternal abuse, no matter how many cases a year surface, is always an exception. Whereas an isolated case of a violent trans women is a pattern.

Let me press a little harder on the maternity analogy. Both Rowling and Stock worry that transness is contagious, and young girls will get the idea that changing genders is a good solution to the inherent problems of being female. But *all* our ideas about gender are contagious—that's how culture works—including deep-seated ideas such as "maternal instinct." Except that it's not an instinct, it's a concept that arises at a particular point in history, circa the Industrial Revolution, just as the new industrial-era sexual division of labor was being negotiated, the one where men go to work and women stay home raising kids. (Before that everyone worked at home.) A new story arose to justify the new arrangements: that these roles were handed down by nature. As family historians tell us, it was only when children's actual economic value declined, because they were no longer necessary additions to the household labor force, that they became the priceless little treasures we know them as today. The romance of the child didn't get underway for the middle classes until the mid–nineteenth century (it was well into the twentieth that child labor laws went into effect). It also took a decline in infant-mortality rates for mothers to start regarding their offspring with much maternal affection. When infant deaths were high, maternal attachment ran low. It was only as families began getting smaller—birthrates declined steeply in the nineteenth century—that the emotional value of each child increased, which is where we find the origin of contemporary ideas about maternal instincts and fulfillments.

All I'm saying is that what we're calling a "biological" instinct is a historical artifact and a culturally specific development, not a fact of nature. An invented instinct can feel entirely real. I'm sure it can feel profound. As can the kinds of fears and vulnerabilities that Stock and Rowling are leveraging. But if we're getting empirical, let's acknowledge that childbirth has killed far more women than murderous trans women ever did, though I suppose the sentimental premise is that all those dead mothers died fulfilling their gender destiny, not defying it. The point is that a lot of behind-the-scenes conceptual labor goes into establishing the "naturalness" of gender, not to mention the vulnerability of gender critical feminists.

As far as nature goes, the reverence for it is pretty selective. We're happy to take cholesterol blockers, mood elevators, and erection enhancers as needed without worrying whether it's what nature intended. The other day a pig kidney was transplanted into a human. Technological possibilities on the horizon include uterine transplants for sterile women, which raises the possibility of uterine transplants for trans women—maybe eventually for cisgender men too. Why not? Humans have always made it their business to conquer, alter, and repurpose nature—and then to invent monsters lurking at the crossroads.

Not surprisingly, Rowling's and Stock's brand of panic-mongering soon became fodder for the fringe right in America. In July 2021, QAnon followers staged two weekends of violent protests in Los Angeles after a customer at a Koreatown spa (Instagram handle: "Cubana Angel") filmed herself complaining vociferously to the manager about a trans woman supposedly using the Jacuzzi in the woman's area of the spa. "He's a pervert," shouts Cubana, "waving his penis and testicles around!" The sight was traumatizing for her. "His dick is out!" says Cubana's friend, voice trembling. "His dick is swinging left and right!" She repeated the word "swinging" so many times it led me to wonder if these were rehearsed lines. "What about women's rights?" shrieks Cubana, as the manager patiently tries to explain that California's Civil Code prohibits businesses from discriminating against anyone on the basis of gender identity or expression. "We're concerned about women's safety," yells Cubana. "We're gonna take it worldwide!"

Which is exactly what happened: The video went viral. Tucker Carlson aired a segment about it, the first of seven on Fox over a week. Antifa showed up to protest the QAnon protesters, evangelicals and the Proud Boys showed up, a reporter was clubbed, protestors threw smoke bombs at cops and pepper sprayed each other, riot cops fired projectiles and beanbag rounds into the crowd. Amidst all this, reports appeared in *Slate*, *The Guardian*, the *LA Times*, and other liberal outlets suggesting that the report about a trans woman in the spa was likely a hoax, and according to a spa employee there had been no trans patrons with appointments that day.

But the story turned out to be more complicated. According to the journalist Jason McGahan, who tried to untangle it five months later in *Los Angeles Magazine*, there actually was a (possibly) trans person in the spa that day. Police issued a warrant for fifty-two-year-old Darren Merager for indecent exposure; Merager does have a penis and is a convicted sex offender. But is Merager actually trans? It's unclear—he or she seems to have a female driver's license, though until recently was identifying as male, according to acquaintances, and McGahan isn't sure which pronouns he or she uses. Is Merager a predator? He/she has a criminal record for theft, but it appears that his/her previous sex crime arrests were for exhibitionism, which, according to the psychoanalytic view, typically does entail wanting to be caught. (Robert Stoller calls these scenarios "scripts" in *Observing the Erotic Imagination*.) In this view, exhibitionism is a pathology of gender identity, not a sexual behavior. The motive is courting humiliation and punishment, not getting off sexually. It's a (not very successful) remedy for gender dysphoria, not predation.

Still, there it was, a penis in the woman's pool. Did this put natal women at risk? It is the case that many (or most, or lots of) cis women have been socialized in ways that can make the sight of an exposed penis in non-private settings feel alarming. Perhaps that will someday change, though I don't imagine such feelings are exactly voluntary—any more than gender dysphoria or compulsive exhibitionism is voluntary. But once again, to what extent is it possible to be intellectually honest about the distinction between an anomaly and a pattern? Perhaps it's not, especially when there are competing interests and clashing vulnerabilities at stake. Especially when titillating monsters hover—and Merager made a wonderfully convenient one—feeding the "appetite for thrilling perversity."

Why *is* gender such a melee? Can't it be a comedy instead of a tragedy, a playground and not a police state, with room for experiments and transformations? You don't have to be some sort of pomo-structuralist to think that no one knows what gender is or where it comes from. Clearly all we have are stories about gender and sexual difference, which shift with the winds, the centuries, and political-economic contingencies. Why not see gender the way we do other human variables—personality, for instance, capacious enough for thousands of permutations and infinite mutability?

"Smash the family!" feminists used to declare. Look around: it's smashed. As far as who done it, it's not that big a mystery—could Gilder and cohort not see its demise up ahead when they tanked wages and trashed the safety nets? They were so caught up in their deregulatory zeal that they couldn't imagine the S&L crisis, the housing bubble and evictions, Enron, and the opioid epidemic. No, the only thing they wanted to regulate was gender!

Yes, capitalism breaks things while ushering in all sorts of great new personal liberties—expressive individuality, your very own idiosyncratic unconscious, unisex clothes. It brings whatever you want right to your door at all hours (if you're among the lucky "haves"). Shopping for things, including identities, is the great modern consolation. Is having a gender identity—another recent development in the annals of modern selfhood—a trap or a freedom? Yes.

To those who fear trans women in the ladies' room: make sure to pee before you leave the house. Those immutable laws of nature you're attempting to enforce today will be dust tomorrow, and soon enough so will you.

PHILLIP LOPATE

An Archaeological Inquest

FROM *The Threepenny Review*

I HAVE IN my possession a copy of an old *Partisan Review*, Winter 1960, Number 1, price $1.00, which was given to me by a student who knew of my interest in American postwar nonfiction. It is an astonishing object, like one of those time capsules buried with the hope they will amuse our descendants. Perfect-bound, 190 pages, with a modernist graphic cover design, probably by Alvin Lustig or one of his imitators: the words "Partisan Review" appear in dark blue against an olive square; below, another olive box promises its interior contents—a short story by Alberto Moravia; essays by Leslie Fiedler, Elizabeth Hardwick, Richard Wollheim, Max Hayward, Harold Rosenberg, F. W. Dupee, and Lionel Abel; criticism by A. Alvarez, Richard Chase, Irving Howe, Lewis Coser, Frank Kermode, Howard Nemerov, among others; and poems by W. S. Merwin, Kenneth Koch, James Merrill, Robert Penn Warren . . . In its utter differentiation from the literary scene of today, it may as well have been the nineteenth-century *London Magazine* featuring William Hazlitt and Charles Lamb, or one of those fat Russian periodicals that included chunks of novels by Tolstoy and Turgenev.

The back cover contains a full-page ad for Edmund Wilson's *Memoirs of Hecate County*: "Here is the book that became a *cause célèbre* when it was first published thirteen years ago . . . Now Edmund Wilson has polished and perfected this devastating portrayal of the waspish women of suburbia." Well, times have changed. You have to hand it to that publisher, though, who knew well the aspirational readership of *Partisan Review*. Before diving into the issue's meaty essays, I pause with curiosity at the ads inside: a four-page spread (!)

devoted to Robert Lowell's *Life Studies*, with blurbs from Alfred Ka-
zin, Stephen Spender, Elizabeth Bishop, F. W. Dupee, A. Alvarez;
announcements for other periodicals—*Encounter* (its contributors
listed as, among others, F. W. Dupee, Harold Rosenberg, Dwight
Macdonald, C. P. Snow), *Dissent* (its editor Irving Howe proudly
announcing a fifteen-thousand-word document "On Socialist Realism"), and *Midstream* (a "Quarterly Jewish Review," featuring Irving
Howe, Leslie Fiedler, I. Bashevis Singer, Lewis Coser . . .). How
amazingly unified the literary class of that period looks! We might
characterize it in shorthand as the New York Intellectuals, with an
Anglophile back office in London.

Perhaps our review periodicals today (*The New York Times Book
Review*, the *New York Review of Books*, the *TLS*, the *LRB*, *Bookforum*,
Harper's, *The New Yorker*) are not that dissimilar, featuring as they
still do the flavor of the month (Sheila Heti, Elena Ferrante, Karl
Ove Knausgaard), and more or less sharing an overall outlook (a
respectful nod to diversity and political correctness). But our critics reviewing the latest topical products haven't the same preening
self-importance as did that gang featured on the cover of my old
copy of *Partisan Review*. Those dinosaurs effortlessly and unapol-
ogetically monopolized the cultivated reading public's attention,
while seemingly in constant, if bickering, communication with each
other.

It is not just that the same names keep popping up, but that
they share a rhetorical level of gravitas, an agreement about the
sound of serious prose, regardless of their location on the political
spectrum. To be sure, that commanding tone was a performance
having more to do with willed, imaginative mimicking of authority
than actual sovereignty. As Irving Howe noted in a witty essay, "The
New York Intellectuals," analyzing his tribe:

> Few of the New York intellectuals made much money on
> books and articles. Few reached audiences beyond the little
> magazines. Few approached any centers of power, and pre-
> cisely the buzz of gossip attending the one or two sometimes
> invited to a party beyond the well-surveyed limits of the West
> Side showed how confined their life still was . . . For all their
> gloss of sophistication, they had not really moved very far into
> the world. The immigrant milk was still on their lips.

The year 1960 was probably the high point of their influence, which had been building all through the fifties; soon it would decline, and by the late sixties they already seemed a throwback, supplanted by the more demotic voices of pop culture and youthful rebellion. But what a display while it lasted! In perusing the essays in my *Partisan Review* copy, I am awed and impressed by their self-assurance, their ex cathedra opinions, their standards of maturity, worldliness, and wisdom—their confident belief that there even *was* such a thing as wisdom—and at the same time disconcerted by their narrow provinciality. Were I still the young cub I was in 1960, entering college, who might have picked up that just-printed copy of *Partisan Review*, I'm fairly sure I would have taken their views as gospel, secretly embarrassed that I'd not already come to the same conclusions. But since I am now an oldster, with a long literary career behind me, I feel freer to quarrel with their assertions—respectfully, mind you, in a filially indebted spirit.

For instance, Leslie Fiedler's essay "The Novel and America" takes the position that the American writer

> is forever *beginning*, saying for the first time (without real tra-dition there can never be a second time) what it is like to stand before nature, or in a city as appallingly lonely as any virgin forest. He faces, moreover, another problem, which has resulted in a failure of feeling and imagination perceptible at the heart of even our most notable works. Our great nov-elists, though experts on indignity and assault, on loneliness and terror, tend to avoid the passionate encounter of a man and a woman, which we expect at the center of a novel. In-deed, they rather shy away from permitting in their fictions the presence of any full-fledged, mature women, giving us in-stead monsters of virtue or bitchery, symbols of the rejection or fear of sexuality.

All this sounds merely an extension of D. H. Lawrence's pioneer-ing *Studies in Classic American Literature*, which had the additional advantage of its boldness and wackiness. But where is Willa Cather, Zora Neale Hurston, Edith Wharton, Henry James, Kate Chopin, Nella Larsen, Ellen Glasgow, William Dean Howells? Of the last-mentioned (one of my favorite American authors, it so happens),

Fiedler sneers at "historians who have been pleased to speak of 'The Rise of Realism' or 'The Triumph of Realism,' as if the experiments of Hawthorne or Poe or Melville were half-misguided fumblings toward the final excellence of William Dean Howells!" Fiedler could have benefited from consulting Lionel Trilling's more measured essay, "William Dean Howells and the Roots of Modern Taste," which appreciated what Howells had to offer while acknowledging his lack of ferocity. Fiedler seems to want to have it both ways: castigating American fiction for its supposedly adolescent lack of mature women, while ignoring actual women writers and sympathetic male authors as somehow too genteel to be taken seriously.

Lionel Abel, who wrote hilariously in his memoir *The Intellectual Follies* about the posturing of the New York Intellectuals meeting to figure out what their stance should be toward the Soviet banning of Boris Pasternak's novel *Doctor Zhivago*, is represented here by "Not Everyone Is in the Fix," a critical response to Jack Gelber's off-Broadway play, *The Connection*, about heroin addicts waiting for their dealer to show up. Significantly, Abel doesn't mention by name the jazz musicians (led by saxophonist Jackie McLean) who brought such life to that production, nor any of the skilled actors, nor even the director. Nor does he bother to place the play in the larger context of experimental theater or, for that matter, American drama in general (say, *The Iceman Cometh*). Instead, he takes a lofty position above the fray, saying, "You are bored stiff by the junkies on the stage; they are bored stiff too, with each other and with themselves." But he defends the play because it forces us to consider what, if anything, are our "high experiences." Abel's graybeard detachment toward the cultural scene he is examining shows why Susan Sontag's pieces a few years later, about Jack Smith's *Flaming Creatures* and rock 'n' roll, created such a stir. The *Partisan Review* crowd desperately needed a Sontag who could bring them more informed reports on the downtown scene.

Richard Wollheim's "Orwell Reconsidered" argues sniffily that *The Road to Wigan Pier*—to my mind an endlessly evocative, stimulating, if tortured account of English miners—is nothing but "dated journalism." Perhaps Wollheim's efforts to downgrade Orwell before he'd been accepted as a major figure in the canon were excusable. Still, the whole notion of "datedness" is so rank and

debatable, as is the blurry line between high journalism and literature, that Wollheim's essay itself looks wrongheaded in retrospect.

Of course, it would be unfair to judge these critical pieces by
hindsight. How would Irving Howe have known, in his intelligent
assessment of Norman Mailer's *Advertisements for Myself*, that it
would be the hybrid form of that book, more than its contents,
which would so inspire future writers? Howe commends Mailer for
his verve, his "bravado and good humor," while properly registering skepticism about his romanticizing of the hipster: "Hunting
for an emblem of energy in the hipster, he seems at one rather
shocking point in 'The White Negro' to be praising the violence
of a hoodlum who beats up an old shopkeeper. Even if one puts
aside the ethical question, which certainly should not be done for
long, this kind of thing can be very dangerous to writers." We can
be grateful that Howe issued this caveat, even if he was silent about
the problem today's critics would unpack: Mailer's presumptuous
categorizing of Blacks as amoral hipsters.

Elizabeth Hardwick's "Living in Italy: Reflections on Bernard
Berenson," a reminiscence about her personal encounters with
the great art scholar, manages to invoke gossipy dirt about him
without settling the central issue one way or another. "Was Berenson shady, crooked?" she asks. "Did he make his fortune with the
help of willfully false as well as genuine attributions?" It is a classic
Hardwick performance: sparklingly written and a little catty. F. W.
Dupee contributes a thoughtful piece about Dickens. Max Hay-
wood offers his expertise on the state of Soviet literature. Lewis
Coser takes C. Wright Mills to task for his simplistic, self-serving
book, *The Sociological Imagination*. Harold Rosenberg pugnaciously
asks if the reproductions in art books are replacing our need to
see paintings in person. Frank Kermode mildly critiques a series
of American poetry collections, and Howard Nemerov does what
he can with a group of forgettable novels. No matter: what counts
is the attempt to cover all areas of artistic, literary, and intellectual
endeavor.

And then there are the poems by W. S. Merwin and Robert
Penn Warren, James Merrill's masterpiece "An Urban Convales-
cence," and Kenneth Koch's pricelessly cheeky "Variations on a
Theme by William Carlos Williams." The short story by Alberto
Moravia, "The Woman From Mexico," is about a guy who leaves
his house overdressed in the summer heat and gets suckered into

a sordid erotic adventure. Moravia was riding high at this point: his stock had not yet taken a nosedive, shortly to be deemed unfashionably realistic, replaced by the more playfully postmodernist Italo Calvino. I was a big Moravia fan at the time, and was puzzled when he went from stardom to patronized near-oblivion. So I can forgive the editors of *Partisan Review* for placing their bet on the wrong horse, hoping for a little worldly international glitz.

What lingers in the mind is the sense of an intellectual caste that regards itself as superior to the culture it is judging. They are not afraid to show off, to sprinkle quotations in German without bothering to translate. Whence this self-confidence? Is it a good thing or a bad thing? Let us say for the moment that in some ways it is a good thing, at least compared to our present critical discourse, which trembles at the accusation of elitism. How much of it is the function of a past educational system—or of a social set, with its bonds of friendship and competitiveness—rather than an agreed-upon agenda? I am not saying I prefer the old manner, nor am I waxing nostalgic for the Good Old Days. I am simply pointing out how strange it looks from our current perspective. I would hate to see a return to that secular rabbinate, which was undoubtedly so hard to crack, but I can't help admiring its rock-solid certainty. A lost world, in any case.

CELESTE MARCUS

A Thousand Gentle Smotherings

FROM *Salmagundi*

—For my mother

I

SHE WAS LITHE, slim, and so pale that when her cheeks flushed the pink seemed almost painted in watercolor onto her iridescent white skin. Thick blond hair spilled over her shoulders and down her back, and her wide, sapphire-blue eyes gave her an aura of innocence and delight. This small, lovely creature embodied fully the clean goodness of our shared religious universe. In the ceremonies and the services that the congregation came together to perform, she flowed effortlessly into the spirit of collective holiness to which every other participant was, to varying degrees, failing to give themselves over. Quiet, modest, tiny, and sweet, she was a model member of our community—a chosen one among God's chosen people. In the knee-length skirts and simple long-sleeved blouses that we were required to wear at our Modern Orthodox Jewish high school, she was wholly comfortable and naturally pure—so far above and worlds away from anything crude or even complicated. It was mesmerizing, the way those clothes wrapped her body, the way her little hip bones gently punctuated the folds of her skirt and her shoulder blades were just barely visible beneath the flowing fabric. She was sublimely delicate. For four years I adored her, and the adoration flickered into an obsession, not because I wanted *her* but because I wanted to be like her, and if I could not be like her—as I was later to discover, brutally, I could not—I would be near her, study her, and admire her.

We met first when I had just become what I would always remain within that world—an outsider, thrown into and enamored of the peculiar energy of Modern Orthodox Judaism, and especially of Modern Orthodox Jewish women. It seemed to me that all of the many laws governing the temperaments, the orientations, and the actions of Modern Orthodox Jewesses were designed to create a girl just like her. There are so many rules and restrictions, so many carefully delineated categories. Consider only the room, the "sanctuary," of a Modern Orthodox Jewish synagogue. Through it runs a *mechitzah*, or partition, which divides the men from the women. In the men's section is the closet or "ark" which contains the Torah, toward which the congregation faces; and the *bimah*, or stage, on which stands the *shulchan*, or table, from which the Torah is read; and near it the *amud*, or podium, from which the *shaliach tzibur*, or "messenger of the congregation," leads the service. From their seats in the women's section, the women watch the ritual and liturgical action of the men, except in those synagogues in which they cannot adequately see it—there they merely listen. Men can be rabbis and women cannot, and this, coupled with the centrality of the male section of the sanctuary, conditions women to be comfortable as quiet spectators. (We were often told that men need to be bribed with positions of leadership to convince them to participate in rituals, whereas women, naturally holier, are inclined independently to worship.)

Men and women who are not related to one another are forbidden any form of physical touch, and even husbands and wives are forbidden from touching while the woman has her period because menstruation renders her impure, a condition that can be remedied by her immersion in a *mikvah*, or ritual bath when her period ends. A woman must at all times be *tznuah*, or modest. The practices of *tznius* vary from community to community, but broadly they require that when in public a woman's skirts must cover the knees, shirts must cover the collarbone and the elbows, and married women must cover their hair.

These are all facets of Orthodox Jewish life which are the products of concrete and time-honored laws, which, with the proper training or guidance, one can look up and read for oneself. All of these statutes, and the cultural etiquettes and norms—the *min-hagim* or customs—that are more powerful for not being written down, conjure an image of femininity entirely fulfilled by that tiny blonde's chaste, cherubic smile.

II

I make people think of sex. Among the long-skirted mothers who kept watch over the sacred plot of earth surrounding our synagogue, there developed the suspicion that something filthy had been smuggled in and let loose. The women intuited this, they detected it, long before I knew what that thing was. Since I was a little girl, a creature in me—the highest, dirtiest iteration of me—has emanated a kind of intense awareness, an energy that induces others to feel like they are being seduced and stripped. I wanted to excise this sexed thing who robbed me of any pretensions to modesty, sweetness, innocence, and purity—the certified conditions of proper girlhood. She is discomfiting, this daemon of mine. People, especially other girls, don't like women at a high pitch. (Judging from the insecurities and the prejudices of the women I have encountered in adulthood, I gather that this initiation into girlhood is near-universal.) "Softer, gentler, calmer, please," girls think, silently tensing their fragile bodies. When we are still toddlers, girls are taught to suspect womanly intensity, to fear it and abort it. "They can smell it on her," one rabbi told my father when I was still in high school. I was a pathogen.

Purification is always an act of violence. Eventually, when all else failed, I tried to kill her. I began to associate the sensation of my ribs and knee sockets jutting into the underside of my skin with goodness, with sisterhood. They would like me this way. A ferocious need for acceptance sustained me while I sat in my seat, pinching and twisting excess skin on my arms and hands to distract from the buzz in my ears. I so badly wanted them to like me. If I starved her down to a fidgeting, senseless slip, the inner vixen would be neutralized and I would be clean. The girls in my class would not be repelled by me. I could stop hunting their mothers' faces for side glances and pursed lips, listening for the steel in their voices. I would be like them: blunted, muted, small, and supremely innocuous.

I became a girl who starves herself the way a riverbed erodes—steadily, irreversibly, after a thousand gentle smotherings. Years of grating my sex against their purity sanded me into that peculiar self. Circumstance is always messy. Within the experience, it was difficult to interpret accurately what was happening, how I incited the responses and made the choices I did. Now I will try. From this vantage point, with the clarity of hindsight and a full stomach, I will plot the strange trajectory out of childhood into that hospital bed.

III

Even in middle school, my sex inspired different responses in men. Some were wary of it and kept their distance. Others interpreted my dirtiness (even now, reflexively, I accept that descriptor) as proof that I fell within the jurisdiction of their desires and appetites. Those who indulged the impulse considered me their thing. I was for them. When I was young this sort of man—fathers of classmates, teachers, religious leaders, parents' friends—manifested their sense of possession through paternalism. It was a guiltless expression of ownership, a legitimate way to assert an illegitimate claim. They didn't touch me, they just protected me from corruptions beyond my ken. They imagined the sins for me and sometimes they even described them to me.

An early memory is particularly illustrative. In a synagogue parking lot after a bat mitzvah party, I hoisted up a sequined JCPenney cocktail dress that shimmied downward while I walked toward our car. A few paces behind me, Solomon Goldberg, whom I still associate with beer, football games, and too-tight polo shirts snug over an expanding gut, whispered to my father, "Your daughter's a fox." My dad relayed the message, probably to justify his disapproval of sequined cocktail dresses. At the time I was relieved that this man had been honest or grotesque enough to say it out loud, to put words to the suspicions I so often had that there was something transgressive and unjustifiable about me. "They *do* see it," I thought. And simultaneously I recognized that my relief was a vile response to his prurience, and I was ashamed of that, too.

In the years between bat mitzvahs and twelfth grade, my family became rapidly more religious. Whereas in elementary and middle school I attended Conservative day schools, I transferred into the Orthodox high school in ninth grade, and the Orthodox bubble into which I had only ventured with my father for synagogue on Saturday mornings became my entire world. It felt like being thrown without warning into a dance for which everyone else had been learning the choreography since infanthood. The steps were unfamiliar to me. Diligently, almost obsessively, I studied the etiquettes and behaviors of my new peers, convinced that if I could only learn enough, if I could only become proficient in their vernacular, this marrow-deep alienation would dissipate. Over time as I came increasingly to love it, I nonetheless realized that there was something essential about me that would always be at odds with the texture of that place.

I was not the only one to notice this. One afternoon just before the start of senior year, a rabbi from school visited my house. Apparently, he had asked my father for permission to warn me about the evils that were awaiting me in the big world beyond our bubble. ("Your father told me I could have this conversation with you.") Standing in the middle of my backyard armed with his iPad, he navigated to the Aéropostale website, and held the screen out to me for inspection. Thin, perky teenage girls wearing logo-emblazoned T-shirts and tight jeans grinned up from the screen. "How would you describe these models, Celeste?" I didn't know exactly what he was getting at, and so paused for a moment before muttering, "They're pretty." He said: "Pretty. Okay. How do you think the boys in your class would describe them?" I said: "The boys in my class would say those girls are hot." He smiled. "Right. And how would they describe you?" A little nervously, I replied: "Not . . . Not like that." "Correct," my would-be protector concluded triumphantly. "You're not hot, Celeste, you're *sexy*. That's more dangerous than being hot. And if you go to a secular college, you'll attract the wrong kind of attention. Not just from boys—from professors, from men."

I stopped eating just before graduating from high school in part because the many men who prophesied that trouble awaited me outside of our religious haven had inspired a foreboding, a mounting fear. Male lust was among the catalysts of this fear, but it was not exactly its object. I was not afraid of men, not yet. I was afraid of who I would become and what that development would cost me, how far it would force me from our haven and the ideal it preserved and protected. Leaving would mean admitting that I had no place inside the Jewish framework in which I had first encountered holiness. The term itself was bound up with that place, as were the concepts of goodness, beauty, and wisdom. My understanding of those ideals was entirely shaped by a world in which I did not belong. And so I could not conceive of those things existing in a world away from the one I knew, and I could not conceive of myself as consistent with any of them, since they were a part of a world the essence of which was inconsistent with mine. I could not have them—could not even imagine them—outside, but I corrupted them by staying.

What is to be done when one is fundamentally wicked? How can you honor the very values your nature violates?

The crime was not consciously conceived. I didn't decide that I was going to kill her. I merely stopped eating. I did that to purify myself of that physical, titillating fullness, to snuff out my own strength and all of its manifestations—intellectual, emotional, spiritual, and of course, sexual. Among the axioms that I absorbed from the normative profile of Jewish womanhood was that any sort of seriousness is fundamentally unfeminine, that a forceful woman is a guilty woman. When I finally left that little world, of course, I discovered that this understanding is fundamental also to the secular communities to which I fled. It turned out that *mechitzas* come in godless settings, too. The barriers abound, we just can't see them.

Starvation, as I say, was my form of absolution. Through the hunger I was absolved of responsibility for sex. I was doing nothing less than abdicating womanhood. Sexual power is a complex responsibility for anyone, but particularly for someone so young who wears it so openly. It was as if I was walking around naked no matter what I was wearing. Ever since I can remember, my presence made people feel in turns violated, excited, compromised, and defiled.

From ninth to twelfth grade the tension between the part of me that was forceful and provocative and the part of me that fetishized quiet cleanliness intensified. It manifested in odd ways—in explosions of energy that I at once feared and relished. I pity every teacher whose responsibility it was to look after me during that period. I was a liability, and a perplexing one, because I never did anything *technically* wrong. I didn't break the rules. Mine was a strange sort of subversion: I upset our wholesome ecosystem simply by staying inside it, putting on a pathetic performance of membership. Usually everyone pretended not to notice. Direct acknowledgment that I did not belong was rare. The memory of one such clash still resurfaces like a recurring nightmare: during my freshman year of high school, the head of secular studies called me into her office and told me that, though I hadn't broken the dress code, though my skirt covered my knees and my shirt covered my collarbone and elbows, still I "dressed promiscuously." I told her that, according to the handbook, dressing promiscuously was not a punishable offense and, proud and humiliated, I went back to class. That was the closest anyone ever got to telling me that I wasn't playing the part convincingly. No one else did me the cruel favor of saying it outright.

Most of the members of that world were wary of me. They weren't cruel, they were distant. If I sat with the other girls at lunchtime, they would not send me away, but they didn't naturally make space for me. Their eyes glimmered at jokes I did not understand, and their lips curled out of step with mine. In the social hall after services on Shabbat, if I were talking to a rabbi his wife would materialize like clockwork a minute or two into the conversation and tell him it was time to leave. There was no cataclysmic eviction, there were infinite tiny ones. Even in the mind of a teenage girl (especially in such a mind) one begins to detect a pattern and draw the proper conclusions. I was not despised, I was suspected.

Most were disturbed by me, but some of them were drawn to me against their better judgment. I coveted that magnetic pull, seduction's lifeblood. Even while I was disgusted by my energy, I indulged it. In casual conversations I would stare too long and too directly into the eyes of interlocutors who caught my interest, stripping them without loosening a button. Can I claim I was too young to be held accountable? That I could not adequately have understood this strange power? It must be partially true, because over the years I have learned to control it, to modulate or shut it off. I have, in other words, grown up. But even early on, I must admit the outrageous energy was fueled by a disquieting, precocious conviction, brazenly communicated, that I knew exactly what I was doing. They understood me: "All I want is privileged intimacy with the deepest parts of you. I don't need to touch you in order to have that. You can show it to me; your wife or your husband won't mind. They won't even notice." Can I claim that, *technically*, I hadn't done anything wrong? That even if I had, the power was out of my control—that I couldn't help it? I don't know. I didn't help it, I know that.

In my purer phases, I tried to channel the intensity into virtuous ends, telling myself that it was religious fervor. It was an elaborate, absurd game of imitation. In those periods I would wear long skirts and sleeves all the time, whereas when I first started high school I used to change into leggings and a T-shirt as soon as I got home. I began to pray three times a day, even though women are not obligated by Jewish law to pray with regular frequency, as the men are. There were many instances when I was the only person on the woman's side of the *mechitza*: a pious young girl. Once, at a service after an event at school, men had to build a makeshift *mechitza* for me because they hadn't expected any women to be there. Wasn't this the proper use of my maelstrom? Didn't this render it clean? Longing for union with God, longing for spiritual extremity—what was wrong with that? (How many others have disguised surfeits of libidinal energy as religious zeal?) But my religious solution failed. Piety ignited the powerful fullness that both thrilled and sickened me. There is a type of woman whose passion, no matter its catalyst, is always interpreted as a provocation. Whatever her intention, if she is forceful she is also seductive. Her excitation is illicit even when it is religious. The more intense her excitement, the more powerfully she provokes. I, a child inflamed by the possibility of touching the infinite, was like this. Fervor fed fervor. When I pushed myself to develop a religious passion, my sex got stronger too. I encouraged it by accident.

I did not mean to do this, and I was ashamed of it. I longed to be small and sweet, I longed to blunt myself. My shame was what perversely bound me to my community—not Judaism itself, which is a vast civilization that provides for all the varieties of souls, but Modern Orthodox Jews. Since I had come from a Conservative Jewish world in which members were, by orders of magnitude, less Jewishly educated than their Modern Orthodox counterparts, it was impossible for me not to associate Judaism itself with this particular community's construction of it. They certainly did know more, but the price of their knowledge was intolerance—they had riches to protect. As long as I lived inside their fold, the shame secured my space there. It was a pact: I wasn't like them, I possessed a disgusting vitality that compromised their purity, but so long as I was ashamed of it, I could still operate within their framework. I wanted to belong with them even while my membership in their ranks sapped me of the parts of myself that gave me strength.

I worried, though, that after I graduated and entered the world about which they warned us, the shame would dissipate, and I would be free but cast out. My nature would cost me my membership. What sins would I commit? What would I become? Who could forgive such a woman? Who could love her? She could be no one's wife, and certainly no one's mother. I knew that *out there* there would be nothing left to suppress my strange power. It would expand and mature in my new circumstances, and my connection to my community and all the uncomplicated goodness that it safeguarded would be destroyed.

IV

Starvation is another kind of extremity, so I was very good at it. Counting calories was my primary activity. I did everything else around that. I was stuck inside the calculations, the material metrics of self-worth, and I couldn't go anywhere else inside my own head. It felt like swinging in tiny, swift circles over and over and over again, and while trapped in those circuits the distant worry that my entire life was going to be swallowed up by numbers and hunger beat itself against the back of my brain.

After only a few months my spine would scrape against the backs of chairs. Bent forward, I could reach my hand around and run my fingers over the vertebrae, which I did often, ritualistically, to calm myself, to assure myself of my straitening progress. My hip bones jutted up above my legs, my hair began to fall out, my period stopped. I was cold all the time, dizzy, irritable. It was hard to concentrate, it was impossible to read. This was all a relief. This was very good.

I remember an afternoon lying face up on a couch in our living room staring at the ceiling, which appeared to be fading from bright white to baby blue and back again. (Colors and lights fluctuated mysteriously during those months, as if rebuking me for waging a war against my own nature.) The hunger was so fierce that the room was spinning. I knew that I was too dizzy to do any of the individual actions required to get food, and I also knew that even if I could manage to get to food I wouldn't permit myself to eat it. I was proud of all this.

The teachers in my small school had noticed that suddenly I was skinny. One woman, a very sweet and small woman, pulled me aside after class one day to express concern and support. Even in that deepening pit, I didn't respect other women just for being thin. On the contrary, I was contemptuous of skinny girls. Skinny girls, if they were not sweet, waif-life, and cherubic, if they were merely bony, were then, like me, afraid to be full. While I wanted a tiny waist and a jutting collarbone, I didn't admire those things. They were my punishment. If I were bony I would not be worthy of respect, and that was why I was doing all this.

Contempt colored my response to the concerned, tiny teacher. It didn't flatter or scare me that she was worried about my problem. I nodded and smiled back at her, simultaneously calculating the number of calories that I had permitted myself so far that day. (Between 340 and 350—there was a dispute among the nutrition websites pulled up on my phone and laptop regarding the caloric value of medium-sized navel oranges.)

Somebody convinced a rabbi, a man infamous for his acidic intellectual pride and snobbery, whom I revered for precisely those qualities, to intervene before I did serious damage to myself. After school one day he asked if we could talk. We sat in an empty room for a long while in silence, and then he said in an almost bored tone of voice: "Everyone knows that something is wrong with you. I'm not going to make you explain it to me. If you want to tell me, I'll listen, and if not you're free to leave." For years afterward I could not understand why his intervention worked. Now I suspect that it was his derisive tone, the disgust he exuded, which inspired my trust. The tiny woman had been loving, she had behaved as if the central problem was starvation—as if she didn't know that being skinny kept me from being something worse. What use was that to me? But this man with his detachment and his smirk radiated the same contempt for me that I had. It did the trick. A doctor's appointment was scheduled.

Naked beneath a thin paper smock, a nurse checked my vitals while I glared at the rolls of skin at the base of my belly. She shook her head and muttered, "Maybe the machine is broken. Sweetie, hold out your hand. I'm going to check your heart rate the old-fashioned way." The woman pressed her fingers hard against my wrist and stared at her watch for sixty seconds. "Is something wrong?" I asked, still focused on my stomach. "Just wait a second, honey," she anxiously said. "I'll get the doctor." The doctor explained that my heart rate was dangerously low, because "your body is not getting enough energy, so it's begun to suck the fat out of your heart and your brain. As your heart gets weaker it will lose the strength it needs to regulate blood flow. It will destabilize and you will be at risk for a heart attack."

I was taken to the Children's Hospital of Philadelphia. In the waiting room I wondered whether I would be back in time for poetry slam practice that evening. I was sure I would be home within a few hours, the next day at the latest. The dizzy seventeen-year-old in the waiting room had no idea what she had brought on herself. The next two weeks would be a boot camp in the rhythms of life as an invalid, a patient without the trust or freedom of a functional human being.

What a hell it was. The overwhelming associated sensation was of being filthy in a sterile place, which was exactly what my adolescence had been. I was filthy because for the first week I wasn't allowed to shower. I wasn't allowed to do anything that required excessive movement. There were strict rules to keep patients from burning calories. Those first days I was made to lie flat on my back in bed all the time. If I had to go to the bathroom I would be wheeled in a wheelchair and the door would be left ajar to keep me from forcing my fingers down my throat. When they finally allowed me to shower (praise God) I had to sit down on a plastic chair beneath the faucet so that I wouldn't burn calories standing. Predictably, meals and consumption were highly regulated: breakfast at 8:15, snack at 11:00, lunch at 12:15, snack at 3:00, dinner at 5:30, snack at 8:30. They warned that we were required to clear the plate entirely within thirty minutes and if the patient resisted, she would be force-fed high calorie protein shakes.

So, in a perverse sense, I had ended up exactly where I had hoped I would—in a hospital bed, hooked up to an EKG, unable to sit up or even read a book. ("The brain is a muscle, and you aren't allowed to exercise those.") That bed was a blunting booth, it was sanding down everything sharp in me, transforming my body and my brain into vats of jelly. I took orders, put my arm out when they wanted to draw blood, chewed and swallowed as directed. The hours stretched, and crawled forward on their bellies into one another. All along I had intended to reduce myself, but I have never again known such misery.

Nights were the most dangerous time, because one's heart rate slows while one is sleeping. If the numbers slipped below thirty, an alarm would sound to wake me up in order to prevent a heart attack. During my entire stay in the hospital, my mother kept vigil while I slept. From the moment I fell asleep until five thirty the next morning, when the nurse would awaken me to draw blood, my mother would stare at the EKG, silently ordering the numbers to rise. Toward the end of those two weeks, semi-deranged, incapable of gratitude or graciousness, I would sob and beat the floor, begging her to take me out of the damned cell.

V

I did recover. That particular battle ended, the hair and the weight came back, I got my period again (for which I was grateful exactly once). But the demons do not disappear, they merely regroup. This war is lifelong. My demons, like all people's demons, cannot be disentangled from who I am. No precise surgical removal, leaving only the strengths, is possible. A part of my mind, a sphere within it, is governed by a bottomless compulsion to self-sabotage. That injurious dimension of me is fully the match of my better elements in strength and in cleverness, and is nourished by the same wealth of human experience, which means it can never be defeated or satisfied. It can only evolve as I do, and be described correctly, and be managed by means of both reason and feeling. My objective is not to defeat my demons, but to study and to understand them. In high school, the sheer power of these two forces, my demons and their enemies (my angels?), both of which had only just become aware of themselves and each other, vastly surpassed their maturity, or rather my maturity, which is why the battle that I have just described was so crude, explosive, frightening, and perhaps ridiculous.

Whatever else it was, it was certainly a feverish response to coming of age in a system which regards women primarily as dangerous temptations. Even years after I left the world in which that conception had been imbibed, I conceived of myself and my womanhood first and foremost as a stumbling block for innocent but susceptible men. The men must be protected, the women must be blunted. And who must the men be protected from? From the women, of course—but not exactly. The truth is that the men had to be protected from the women because the men had to be protected from themselves—from their strength of desire and their weakness of will. And since they were incapable or unwilling to protect themselves, since the reality of their lust was regarded as an unalterable fact, a system was devised in which the women had to protect the men. They accomplished this by changing the way they looked and acted—the way they moved through the world as women. We lacerated ourselves and each other so as to leave men unblemished, and unencumbered by decency and restraint. We hurt ourselves and left them intact.

There was never an occasion to unlearn this system. I never discovered how to reconfigure my mental architecture. Moreover, the dangers of which the rabbis had prophetically warned me did find me: I have experienced awful violations. And it was the old system of womanly impurity, the old myth of female responsibility for male behavior, that dictated how I interpreted those violations. Inside my own mind I was already guilty—guilty before the skirt was lifted, guilty before the zipper was pulled down. Curled in a ball after the violence was over, it was myself whom I accused. I had not fallen victim to my assailant's entitlements and cruelties, he had fallen victim to my provocations.

Countless times alone in my room I howled, "Why am I like this? What is it about me that makes them do this?" Is it not obvious that guilt is an insane response to having been assaulted? But reason yields in this realm of raw pain, especially when one has been trained to doubt and even despise oneself. Empirically speaking, the self-torment of the victim is certainly not unusual. I need two hands to count the variations on the following conversation I had with friends after whispering the details of my unwilling role in the latest enactment of the old story. They would say, "Did you report it?" I would shake my head and then fall silent, wrestling with the barbed knot of reasons why I hadn't sought justice. And in that bewildered silence I would hear my friend say, "I didn't report it when it happened to me either."

There are still voices in my head which hector that if I had only stayed in that sacred haven, my origin bubble, these crimes would never have been committed—that they were the wages of my tastes for autonomy and curiosity, of my thirst for full strength and a larger horizon. But I cannot believe in such a merciless binary. Women must not be forced to choose between suppression and predation, between the blunting booth and an assailant's open mouth. Even now, after centuries of sweat and fury, we remain prisoners of our own misconceptions. Men, and bless the exceptions to this brutish rule, will always demand what is not theirs to claim—either unqualified access to and ownership of our powers, or their asphyxiation. But punishment for our strengths requires our own complicity. We are lost so long as we believe that a powerful woman is a guilty woman. It is not true, my friends, it is not true.

A Fist of Muscle

FROM *Chicago Quarterly Review*

TODAY, WANDERING THROUGH the local supermarket, I see my brother. Again. He is leaving one aisle just as I enter it from the opposite end. Though I only catch sight of the back of his head as he turns the corner, I have no doubt it is him. He has the same red-flecked hair, the same languid and unhurried walk, and, as always, the collar of his polo shirt is turned up to cover the nape of his neck. Without a second thought, I hurry to try and catch up with him. A pair of doddering trolleys blocks my path at the corner, however, and, by the time I have forced my way between them, my brother is nowhere to be seen.

I consider calling out to him, but I worry that any loud noise might break the spell and so make it impossible for me to find him among the high-stacked shelves. I may have set reason aside for a minute, but embarrassment isn't quite so easy to part with. I put down my basket and begin to push past the slower shoppers, desperately searching each lane before rushing on to the next. I am moving so fast that I almost stumble and fall into a tall stack of buy-one-get-one-free cola bottles on display at the head of one of the aisles. Several times I duck back upon myself, and more than once I return to the dairy aisle for a second look between the stacks of milk and yogurt. Not for a moment do I even entertain the idea that the man I am chasing might be a figment of my imagination. In fact, I am convinced of quite the opposite—that the past few weeks have been unreal and illusory, and that there is a perfectly logical explanation (as yet unknown) as to why we have all fallen prey to the ridiculous idea that my brother has died.

Soon I'm confused about which of the lanes I have already been down and which I have yet to search. I am walking through some elaborate labyrinth and might remain lost within it forever. After completing my third or fourth circuit of the main aisles, I decide that my brother has to be in the pasta section, since for the last few years of his life he not only ate pasta with almost every one of his meals but, in order to aid his obsessive desire to bulk up, he also regularly ate a large bowl of it as a snack after returning home from work or the gym. When I find my way to the pasta aisle, I discover that it is completely deserted. I hover there for a couple of minutes, waiting beside the packets of butterflies, spirals, cork-screws, and ribbons.

After a while I start searching again. I can no longer hear the heavy rain that was beating down on my way in. The stark glare of the supermarket lights seems designed to misinform the senses. Here it is impossible to tell whether it is the middle of the day or the darkest hour of night. It soon occurs to me that, without either phone or watch, there is no way of knowing how long I have spent in pursuit of my brother. Soon the supermarket light gives rise to the impression that the end of time has come and then passed and that this sterile place is all that remains of a forgotten civilization. Rows upon rows of tins and cans do nothing to alleviate the sense that something terrible has befallen the world outside and that the only people left on earth are a few anonymous survivors quarantined within. Even the hesitant and distorted voice crackling over the Tannoy sounds as though it is, like the first phonograph recordings, the last relic of a distant and unreachable past. I start moving with increased urgency and, more than once, I pick up a packet or bottle to scrutinize its expiry date.

Ten years ago, this supermarket caught fire. The blaze, which started in the adjoining petrol station, was not extraordinary in itself, but what was amazing was that when the supermarket re-opened some weeks later, it was impossible to tell which parts had been rebuilt and which belonged to the original structure. The reconstruction was, therefore, judged to be a great success, especially since it made it seem as if the events of the recent past had never happened. Supermarkets are designed to be uncannily similar to one another, and each time I enter one I take it for granted that I am setting foot within yet another copy and that the original was long ago lost among its countless simulacra. It is little wonder that so many people throughout the ages have posited that every life has been lived before and every conceivable action has already been carried out many times. Perhaps the world itself is a copy and there are an inconceivable number of other copy worlds. Perhaps there are more than a million copies, over a billion acts of creation abandoned by dissatisfied gods, a pluriverse of countless universes outside the limits of our vision, and no way to tell which was the first or whether all are duplicates.

I press on down the wine and spirits aisle, yet by the time I get to the fizzy drinks, I am convinced that the supermarket has been designed solely to unravel the loose tangles of my memory. Every shelf taunts me. First there are the fat loaves of bread that, as a child, my brother could not touch without falling sick, thus forcing our mum to spend hours every day making cornbread and gluten-free spaghetti. Next there are the protein shakes he drank each morning as though he was partaking in sacred communion with the savage and exacting god of bodybuilding. Finally, there are the fresh bouquets of flowers identical to those that have littered our house and garden ever since the funeral. I am dizzy and out of breath. I grab a bottle of water straight from a shelf. I gulp it down. The supermarket is a desert. This is my first drink in days.

Off I go again, off round the next corner, but my heart is no longer in the search. I am simply retracing my steps while my brother remains always a few aisles ahead of me, and it does not help that as I peer down each lane I encounter the same few faces staring back. But I must not give up. I begin to head back toward the dairy aisle and it is then, just as I am passing the pharmacy counter—where an old woman in an oversized raincoat is picking through a pile of crumpled prescriptions while the shop assistant toys with her nails—that I spot him. He is queuing up at one of the tills, his half-empty basket set down at his feet. I have to force myself not to run, as most of the shoppers around probably think I am sick or lunatic, though I cannot stop from increasing my pace.

He turns his head. I begin to raise my arm to wave to him. I have to catch his attention. I need to make him see. But then my rising arm falters. Stops mid-wave. It is not him. The man waiting at the checkout has a boxer's knuckle for a nose and bug-like eyes the color of wet seaweed. He is nothing like my brother. My arm slumps at my side. Only now does it occur to me that this man's hair is red, while my brother's hair had lost its fiery color and changed to a light brown. The person before me is tall and solid, as my brother had been in his adolescence and early twenties. He is not the bulky colossus my brother turned himself into during the last eighteen months. It is not him. I have been searching for my brother not as he was the last time I saw him but as he had been much earlier in life. It is not him.

I leave the supermarket in a hurry and dash through the rain to the car, without bothering to look for my abandoned basket nor the quickly scribbled shopping list it contains. After fumbling for a few moments unlocking the door, I climb inside and settle in the driver's seat without daring to turn the key in the ignition. How have I managed to become so confused? The ghost in the queue doesn't look like my brother at all, yet I have wasted close to half an hour attempting to track him down.

A world populated by doubles, I find myself thinking, would not be such a bad thing. In fact, the idea that every person might be a double of someone else is strangely comforting. Even though I know it will not change my own situation, I still hope there is a doppelgänger of my brother somewhere in the world who has managed somehow to circumvent his fate. This twin of my brother would not have grown so obsessed by bodybuilding, would not have sought to become a titan, a demigod. And in the process, he would not have pushed his heart to the breaking point.

More has been written about the heart than any other part of our anatomy. It has long been thought to be reckless and mercurial, the source of love, locked in battle with the more sober and restrained head. While the brain formulates careful plans, the heart gives sway to whims and passions. It is the enemy of restraint and rationalism, the furnace in which our desires are fired. The Romans even went so far as to formulate the idea that the heart is the place in which our best memories and ideas are stored. As for my brother's heart, I know it was saved, though not returned to us. In fact, I have no idea what happened to it after the autopsy. I know only that when his heart was removed, it was found to be close to three times the normal size.

The postmortem records that the walls and ventricles of the organ were so swollen that it was only with the most arduous labor that blood could be pumped through. His heart struggled, every day, until it could not go on. It was too big. So says the report. I read the same sentence again and again: *Histological examination of*

the left ventricular myocardium revealed widespread myocyte hypertrophy
with replacement fibrosis as well as an element of myocyte disarray. The
words mean little to me, even after a day and a night with a dictio-
nary stolen from a hospital. What, I wonder, do such words have to
do with the active and inexhaustible person that was my brother?
They are words that refuse to make sense. I simply cannot bring
myself to believe that the statement is about my brother—it might
as well be describing the orbit of a planet I have never seen, in a
universe far beyond my own.

Is this all the heart is? A collection of ventricles, veins, valves,
arteries, vessels, muscles, nodes, and tendons? What about the
rest? Everything else hidden within—his dreams and passions, his
quirks and idiosyncrasies? The report tells me nothing of why the
illness settled on him and not another—for example, myself. It
will not tell me why he in particular was chosen. It does not hint
at where the condition appeared from, or how long he might have
borne within him such a fatal secret. It does not say how he might
have felt, or how the disease changed him as time went on. The
only fact that makes sense to me from the autopsy notes is that his
heart weighed 886 grams. The same weight as a bag of rice. Or a
small watermelon. The weight is important, you see. The weight of
his lumbering heart. It is important not only because it must have
weighed heavy inside him for many months until the day that it
finally gave in, but also because it is by such criteria that lives were
once measured.

The ancient Egyptians, preparing the body for mummification,
would lay out the corpse and, after making an incision across the
abdomen and cleansing it with wine both within and without, would
remove lungs, liver, intestines, and stomach. Even the brain would
be removed, after which time the body could be coated with resin
and bound tightly in strips of linen. The only organ left in place
was the heart. This was for good reason: The soul could not travel
on into the next world without it. At the very beginning of the journey into the underworld, this most vital organ would be weighed, it
being well-known that all a person's sins and mistakes were written
within the heart. Greed, malice, hatred, envy; all these were thought
to make it grow fat and swollen. And on a great pair of scales the
heart was to be weighed against a feather that stood for truth and
fairness. If the scales did not balance perfectly, the heart was cast
aside to be devoured by a terrifying creature with the body of a lion

and the head of a crocodile. When this happened, the soul of the deceased would be trapped forever somewhere between death and life. Only those with the lightest of hearts were allowed to continue their passage on toward the next world.

My brother has travelled on without his heart. I suspect that he is better off without it. It only weighed him down, slowed his steps, until finally stopping him altogether. He had, as I say, a literally heavy heart, and it is tempting to think that his death was some-how connected to this. Did he sense what he was lugging around with him in those last months? Surely he must have felt it, the immense weight inside him like a stone, a cast-iron padlock, a fist of engorged muscle. Did he try his best to ignore it? Since his death, every time I wake in the night with my heart racing, I think instantly of him and wonder whether his heart's inevitable thump-ing ever scared him, or whether by the time he realized what was happening inside him it was already too late.

The word *record*, to note something down and store it for the future, is derived from the Latin *cor*, meaning heart. When we com-mit something to memory, we say we learn it by heart, and it was once believed that our heart recorded our longings, our ambitions, our regrets. It is not difficult, then, to see how a heart can grow heavy. And if his was weighed down, then now so is mine. I wonder whether my brother carried with him the weight of any regrets, or doubts, or mistakes. But what did he regret? I cannot say. My few guesses are feeble at best. Did he regret doing so badly at school? I am not sure. He had certainly been glad to see the back of the place, though in the last few years he worked hard at college courses to gain several advanced construction and design qualifications, of which he was certainly proud. Perhaps, though, he regretted his in-ability to control his temper. I think of the fights he and I often had in our teenage years, and of his legendary fits and rages that would cause us all to scatter and flee. Yet those were long in the past. In his final months he did not war with anyone. Not even me.

The more I think about the things that might have weighed heavy on his heart, the more I begin to think about how little I know of the person my brother had become at the time of his death. I cannot shake off the thought that I had lost or, if you will, mislaid my brother some years before he died. You will remember that the double in the supermarket looked not like my brother had in his last couple of years, but as he had been close to four years before. This makes me feel even worse. His heart was too big; mine, it seems, too small.

Not only have I now lost that future, but I also begin to worry that over time my memories of our shared past will grow increasingly hazy and that each day I will lose a little more of him. Yet at the same time I feel as though I cannot break away from him, and for many nights after the funeral, as soon as I close my eyes I am overcome with the sensation that he is still there, lying as ever in the bunk bed above me. If I listen closely, I can sometimes hear him muttering in his sleep. Occasionally I am even able to suspend disbelief enough to believe that at any moment he might swing his head down and suggest a midnight picnic, or ask me to tell him a story about the land of monsters we might find if we venture through the secret tunnel found at the back of the cupboard. Sometimes I even open my mouth to reply.

He can only have been three or four when we shared a bunk bed. We were living in a cramped terrace then, a house where the pipes gurgled and babbled all night. My brother and I had a raggedy stuffed toy that served as a doorstop so that our room would not be completely given over to darkness. We also had a cassette player, which told us fairy tales as we drifted toward sleep, and I can still remember the first time that I managed to force myself to stay awake (by repeatedly pinching my arm) until the story came to an end and the tape clicked off. A horrible silence settled over the room, as if a great bell jar had been lowered over us. I could hear my heart beating louder and louder in my chest. If I listened carefully, I could hear the sound of a door being opened somewhere on the other side of the house, and even though I knew that this was probably nothing more than my parents coming up to brush their teeth before bed, I could not stop my mind from running wild. I had soon convinced myself that there were burglars creeping through the house and that they were heading for our room—hence the dull snuffle of feet on the stair, the sigh of floorboards, and the hundred other odd noises that old houses possess in their armory. Each one my imagination seized upon as a sign of some approaching terror until, in desperate self-defense, I leapt out of bed, turned the cassette over, and pressed Play.

It is not, of course, so easy to calm an adult mind. My mum feels the same. Like the rest of us, she finds staying too long in the

wreath-filled house oppressive and overbearing, and so this afternoon she decides to head to the beach. She spends a long time at
the harbor, close to where the River Arun meets the sea, keeping
the dog on the lead while she stands looking down at the bevies
of swans and cygnets huddling in the crooks of shingle that rise
up where the river swerves at sudden angles. When the restless
dog finally succeeds at interrupting her thoughts, she turns and
follows the river down to its mouth before walking east along the
beach. The tide is slowly drawing in and the unleashed dog makes
a frantic dash across the sand, darting close to the edge of the
lapping waves and then sprinting back again, as though daring
himself ever closer to the water.

It is the dog that draws the young child away from his own family.
The little boy begins to follow our dog across the beach, zigzagging
as the dog does and calling out to it in delight. Meanwhile, my mum
is walking down the stony bank, looking out to sea and listening to
the sound of each wave following on upon the last. Her eyes are
trained on the distant point where the ashen clouds touch down
on the dark-green sea, and so it is only once the little boy is close
enough to snatch at the dog's tail that my mum notices him. He
is perhaps four or five, though it is difficult to be sure, since he is
dressed from head to toe in a Spider-Man costume.

It is almost identical to the costume my brother wore at the same
age. There were many days, in fact, when he would refuse to take it
off, even to go to bed, his one concession being to remove the red-
and-black mask and set it down beside him on the pillow. The only
visible parts of the child on the beach are two blue eyes staring out
from the holes in the mask. My mum freezes to the spot. When she
finally starts moving once more, she finds that the boy is moving
with her. For a few minutes he runs along beside the dog, and she
starts to worry that the boy might attempt to follow them all the way
home. It is only when his family starts calling out to him across the
beach that he leaves the dog alone and wanders away. Once he is
out of sight, my mum cuts short her walk and strides straight back
across the sand. Toward the car.

She tells us that it is not the thought that it might have been my
brother beneath the costume that has upset her but the knowledge
that it was not. It is as though her heart is being tested. Wherever
any of us goes, it is as though my brother is following. Time and
again something moves in the corner of our vision, a flicker of color,

a change in the light. Some days, in fact, it is almost impossible to leave the house without meeting someone who reminds us of him. The smallest thing is enough: a shock of red hair, a few freckles playing upon the nose and cheeks, or a laugh, or a boast. The rest of the day is then lost.

But at the same time nothing is lost. Because the certainty remains that the world is littered with the past, and so we will come across him—at the beach, in a queue for the cinema, in some cramped bar, at the supermarket—again, again, again.

SIGRID NUNEZ

Life and Story

FROM *The Sewanee Review*

LET ME BEGIN with an excerpt from a letter I once received from a former student:

> When people have interviewed you, have you ever been asked, why do you write? Another teacher asked us that and it really made me nervous. So I said that the question really made me nervous and then answered in a kind of inarticulate way—I think I said something about feeling present. I'm not trying to covertly ask you that question but was just wondering if you are comfortable with it. If the answer is yes that would be cool because then I can feel like I might evolve in that vein. And if it is no that would also be good because I would feel like I was not alone in my feelings.

Immediately I thought of Flannery O'Connor's response to a student who attended one of her lectures and who asked her this very question: "Miss O'Connor, why do you write?"

"Because I am good at it."

"At once," O'Connor said later, "I felt a considerable disapproval in the atmosphere. . . . But it was the only answer I could give. I had not been asked why I write the way I do, but why I write at all; and to that question there is only one legitimate answer."

I'm not sure why writers are so often asked to give their reasons for doing what they do. I don't believe the same question is asked with anything like the same frequency of, say, visual artists or composers or performers. I have at times said that I write because it is what I know how to do, or because it is who I am, or because it has fulfilled this or that desire or need, and I have always been painfully conscious of how unsatisfactory these answers are.

You can read between the lines of the letter from my student, who was still in her teens, and who has clearly been led to believe that if she wants to write she should be able to state her motives. I want her to know that, first of all, she is not alone, that the question makes a lot of writers nervous or uncomfortable, that the same writer may have many different motives for writing, that a writer's motives may change over time, and, above all, that the fact that she has no ready answer to the question is no reason for anxiety. I want her to know what George Orwell said, that "at the very bottom of [all writers'] motives there lies a mystery . . . some demon whom one can neither resist nor understand," perhaps "the same instinct that makes a baby squall for attention."

I *can* say that I don't remember a time when I did not want to write, and that it all began with being read to as a small child. Fairy tales, folktales, classical mythology, children's books—the ones about animals most of all. The wonderful Dr. Seuss. He was the first writer I ever tried to imitate, and I can remember saying exactly these words as a child: "When I grow up, I want to be Dr. Seuss." Indeed, for years after this declaration, I thought children's books were what I would write.

So, very early then, I equated reading with making people happy. And once I had learned to read, I discovered what a glorious thing it was to escape through a good book into some other world, at least for a time. It was a kind of double blessing: reading was a private, solitary experience, something you could withdraw into; and yet, when you were reading, you were never really alone. There was always the storyteller. There were always the characters. They were there when you needed them. They were your friends. And this corresponds to what I would one day learn about writing itself. The writing life appealed to me first of all because I saw it as something I could do alone, hidden, in the privacy of my room. But soon I discovered, as all writers do, that writing was an ideal way to escape the world and to be a part of the world at the same time.

Given what a rewarding childhood experience reading was for me, it was only natural that I'd want to create poems and stories myself. And, in the New York City public schools I attended, there was always some creative writing class or extracurricular literary activity in which I could participate and where my writing was encouraged, strengthening my desire to pursue a literary life. And, of course, there was no end of good books to read.

When I was old enough to read adult books, I fell in love with nineteenth-century so-called realist novels, those grand Victorian tomes, and among my literary heroes the most beloved was probably Charles Dickens. Here was proof that the possibilities for literature and the power of storytelling were boundless. He had all the gifts, and, losing myself in one of his capacious novels for long periods of time, I had no doubt: this was genius I held in my hands. No matter how exaggerated, his characters were utterly real to me, and Virginia Woolf was surely right when she attributed Dickens's astonishing power to make his characters so alive to the fact that he saw them as a child sees them. As for his elaborate plots, no matter how high the incidence of improbable coincidence on which they relied, I believed every word. Equally impressive were the beauty and precision of his prose, his concern for social justice, and the compassion with which he wrote about human suffering.

Among other things that literature could do, then, was this: show the reality of other people, and what those people might be going through—people who were completely different from oneself. As the Nobel laureate Orhan Pamuk has put it,

> Novels are political not because writers carry party cards—some do, I do not—but because good fiction is about identifying with and understanding people who are not necessarily like us. By nature all good novels are political because identifying with the other is political. At the heart of the "art of the novel" lies the human capacity to see the world through others' eyes. Compassion is the greatest strength of the novelist.

For a time when I was very young, I ended every story I wrote with the words *And then I woke up!* I remember distinctly the day a teacher told me I must stop doing that. You see, she explained, it's perfectly okay to write a story in which wild, impossible things happen without having it all turn out to have been just a dream. "And then I woke up" was not only unnecessary but in fact a disappointing way to end a story, didn't I see? It was one of those childish things that I must put behind me.

Now I think that I developed this bad habit at least partly because I was afraid that I might be seen as trying to pass off as reality something I had made up (and back then every story I wrote was completely made up; you won't find many little kids indulging in autofiction). As children we are taught that lying is wrong; a moral person always tells the truth. And I have always been curious: How and when does a child come to understand that it is not only permissible but a very good thing to make things up, to pretend that what never happened, happened? How and when does a person come to understand that fiction can be a way, perhaps one of the most important ways we have—perhaps even, in some cases, a better way—of getting at the truth, at the reality of human experience, than fact? After all, the main purpose of storytelling is to make us more aware of ourselves and of the world around us. To do this most effectively, you don't just tell what happened. You tell what might have happened, what should or should not have happened. What could happen. You write fiction to answer the question: *What if . . . ?*

When I got to college, though the practice of writing remained a passion, my feelings about becoming a writer changed. It was then that I learned what Thomas Mann meant when he said that a writer is someone for whom writing is harder than it is for other people; what Roland Barthes meant when he called a creative writer a person for whom language is a problem. I began to understand that, no matter what the rewards might be, from now on writing would always be a struggle. It wasn't all fun, as it had been in childhood. It wasn't play, it was work—it was very hard work. It wasn't an effort that was always going to be encouraged, let alone applauded, by my teachers—or by anyone else, for that matter. I was learning that frustration, failure, and rejection were a large and inescapable part of any writer's life.

People ask, Is it really that hard to be a writer, as we so often hear? Writers themselves, ever prone to exaggeration, have found vivid and dramatic ways of expressing it. Sportswriter Red Smith, for example: "There's nothing to writing. All you do is sit down at the typewriter and open a vein." David Rakoff once said that writing was like having his teeth pulled out—through his penis. "Writing is not a profession, but a vocation of unhappiness," declared Georges Simenon, at the time the best-selling author in the world. According to Joan Didion, "the peculiarity of being a writer is that the entire enterprise involves the mortal humiliation of seeing one's own words in print."

"Writing means always being wrong," said Philip Roth:

> All your drafts tell the story of your failures . . . To write is to be frustrated. You spend your time writing the wrong word, the wrong sentence, the wrong story. You continually fool yourself, you continually fail, and so you have to live in a state of perpetual frustration. You spend your time telling yourself, That doesn't work, I have to start again. Oh, that doesn't work either—and you start again.

Six years before his death, Roth told an interviewer that he was tired of it all and that he had given up. He'd stuck a Post-it on his computer: *The struggle with writing is over.* "I look at that note every morning," he said, "and it gives me such strength."

My own college writing teacher, Elizabeth Hardwick, used to tell her students that if there was anything else they could do with their lives instead of becoming writers—any other profession—they should do it. For her, though, the frustration of writing was as nothing compared with the frustration of teaching writing. "I tried to read your story," she once said to me. "I really did, but I just couldn't do it, it was just . . . too . . . *boring.*" And, to another student, about his story: "I'd rather shoot myself than read that again."

Here is another question writers are often asked: Where do you get your ideas? And here I like to quote Flannery O'Connor again: "You don't write a story because you have an *idea* but because you have a believable character or just simply because you have a story."

Like many of her students, I revered Elizabeth Hardwick—the first professional writer I ever met—and hung on her every word. I remember how enthusiastic she was about the work of a great number of writers. But now and then a name would come up, often a well-known name, and she would shake her head and say, "Well, he [or "she"] doesn't have any real ideas." And for these writers who had no real ideas Professor Hardwick clearly had much disdain. Whatever literary gifts they might have, however well they might be doing in the marketplace, these idea-less writers could not be taken seriously.

I remember that this caused me much anxiety. I wanted to be a writer. And I put the question to myself: Did I have any ideas? And if I did, were they the kinds of ideas Professor Hardwick was talking about—"real" ones, which of course I took to mean serious and important ones? Were my ideas serious and important enough to justify my desire to write? For I had reached a stage where I felt that I needed permission to write.

And how was this supposed to work, anyway? Did you come up with the ideas first, satisfy yourself that they were real, then find a story that would do justice to them? How daunting such a process seemed to me. How difficult. How strange. I knew this couldn't be right. But if you started a story without any real ideas in mind, how could you be sure they would come to you in the course of writing?

And so, when I first learned what the master storyteller Flannery O'Connor had said—you don't write a story because you have an idea but because you have a story—I felt considerable relief. For what she said made perfect sense to me, and I thought for sure she must be right.

Well then. Stories I had. And when I learned that O'Connor also said that anyone who has survived childhood has enough material to write for the rest of their life, I thought this, too, must be right. So: I had stories. And, like everyone else, I had a childhood, one that, as it happened, I wanted very much to write about (and that indeed one day I would write about). I had a childhood, and I had stories from childhood. Memories. Observations, reflections, opinions. I had a way—my own way—of remembering and of seeing. I had things I wanted to say about the world and about my experiences, and I wanted both to remember and to imagine all this into life on the page.

But were these memories and reflections of mine, were my way of seeing and remembering and so on, what Professor Hardwick would have called real ideas? I didn't think so. I only knew that, out of my own being in the world and, increasingly, out of the many great books I was reading, I wanted to be writing. And I now knew one other very important thing as well. I knew that if I spent every moment of the rest of my life trying, I would never come up with a Great Idea, and that if I thought too much about whether my ideas were real, whether they were deep or original or serious enough, I would never be able to write at all.

Of course, the more we read, the more we understand how much of literature deals with many of the same big questions as does philosophy: What is the role of human beings in the universe? What is the relationship between the individual and society? What is reality? Why are things as they are? What is the nature of good and evil? How should a human being live? What is death? If everyone must die, what is the meaning of life?

Much harder to say, though, is how much the worth of a literary work depends—or should depend—on the significance of its ideas and how successfully the author deals with them.

In the nineteenth century, the period widely regarded as the Western novel's golden age, the notion of the novel as a genre ruled by ideas was taken for granted, and among writers and readers alike there would have been general agreement with Victor Hugo's definition of a novelist as a historian of morals and ideas. But as we well know, it was one of Western Modernism's Big Ideas that ideas themselves must go. For an ardent Modernist like Virginia Woolf, the novelist should reject the mantle of intellectual authority and seek to write novels that were more like poems. And, once it had arrived, this new kind of novel, considered by most writers and readers to be more artful, not to mention hipper—or, as we might say now, sexier—than the old, was here to stay.

To the question, Where do you get your ideas? Vladimir Nabokov's response was to roll his eyes. "I've no general ideas to exploit," he insisted. "I just like composing riddles with elegant solutions." He did not think in ideas, he said, he thought in images. What mattered in a work of literature was strictly structure and style, according to Nabokov, who famously taught his college students that the notion of great ideas in a book was "hogwash."

For another writer, Milan Kundera, it is not Big Ideas that count in a novel but rather wisdom, and "the novel's wisdom is different from that of philosophy." The theoretical spirit is different from the spirit that gives rise to fiction, which Kundera sees as lightness, playfulness, and humor. Not ideas, but rather themes of existence, the enigma of existence, are the novelist's major concern, according to Kundera. And besides, a novelist can't be depended on to be the spokesperson of his or her own ideas, he argues, citing for example how, without changing his moral principles at all, in the course of writing *Anna Karenina* Tolstoy came to a very different understanding of his heroine, a deeper, wiser truth about her, than the one he had started out with.

In the end, it would be not so much through Hardwick's teaching as through her own writing—her exceptionally brilliant and beautiful writing, above all her autofictional novel *Sleepless Nights*—that she would remain an enduring influence on my work. As I never stop telling my own students, you will learn more from reading other writers than you'll ever learn from any craft lecture or writing workshop. Hardwick herself, who doubted that writing could be taught, insisted that reading was the *only* way to learn how to write.

It was after I had finished with school altogether that another very important mentor came into my life, someone equally formidable but very different from Professor Hardwick. This was the writer and cultural critic Susan Sontag, whom I met while I was working as an editorial assistant at the *New York Review of Books*, to which she was a frequent contributor. It was from Sontag that I felt that I received the permission I spoke of earlier: permission to take myself and my work seriously, long before I had published a word.

While it seemed everyone else wanted to know how I intended to earn a living, or when I was going to get married and settle down, Sontag was talking about something else. Put the writing first, she said. Teach if you must, but don't feel that you have to become affiliated with an institution. Don't give up your independence. Forget the safety of tenure. Forget safety, period. Forget everything but the work.

Let me return for a moment to Elizabeth Hardwick. I remember going to see her for the first time after I graduated from college. "Don't tell me you went and moved in with that boy," she said. "You girls today, you want to set up your domestic lives before you start your careers, but I'm telling you, it's a mistake." But as the years passed, I noticed that, whenever we spoke, her first question was no longer "How's the writing going?" but "Do you still have that nice young man?" I confess that long after it was untrue, I kept answering yes, just to avoid hearing her groan, "Don't tell me you've lost another one." Once, after not seeing her for several years, I told her that I was thinking of having a child, and I was moved by her response: "Now, that's *one* decision you'll *never* regret." Moved, but also anxious, because of what seemed to lie beneath that remark.

Several years ago, that boy Hardwick was referring to wrote to congratulate me on a new book. "I remember times," he said, "when you would struggle over five- or six-word sentences for hours on end." He does not say how that struggle used to annoy him, and what I remember is that it was when I was with this man that I got my first hint of what conflicts might arise from living with someone, as in a marriage, and working all those hours on sentences.

From Sontag I took the idea that to be devoted to the point of obsession to one's work was precisely how things should be, that one must think of writing not as a career but as a vocation—not unlike a religious vocation. To her, writing was a noble and even heroic activity; only those who understood this would ever come to know what Natalia Ginzburg meant when she called it the finest vocation in the world. And I was to pay no attention to those (and they were many) who said that one couldn't write and also be a voracious reader. On the contrary, she said: you must read everything.

Readers of fiction very often want to know whether a work is autobiographical, and if so, how closely it hews to the author's own experience. One of my favorite courses to teach is called "Life and Story," with an ever-changing reading list of writers who have, to one extent or another, included elements from real life in their fiction—writers as different from one another as Primo Levi, Jamaica Kincaid, Teju Cole, Garth Greenwell, Akhil Sharma, Tobias Wolff, Eileen Myles, Kathleen Collins, Renata Adler, Colson Whitehead, Weike Wang, and Alexander Chee.

What's the big difference between life and story? I like what the Israeli novelist Aharon Appelfeld has said in this regard: "In life you can say it happened, but in literature you have to give good reasons: Why did it happen?"

Once, after the first class of a graduate fiction workshop I was teaching, one of my new students came up to me and said, "I've read all your novels, and I have to ask you something." I thought for sure he was going to say something like, Is your writing autobiographical? Did any of what you wrote actually happen? Instead, he shocked me by saying, "Do you make some of that stuff up?"

Do I ever. I make a lot of that stuff up. In fact, I make up most of it. But in each novel I've written so far, like the writers I assign for "Life and Story," I also used at least some material from my own life. And I believe Edna O'Brien got it right when she said that "any book that is any good must be, to some extent, autobiographical, because one cannot and should not fabricate emotions; and although style and narrative are crucial, the bulwark, emotion, is what finally matters."

But no matter how autobiographical some of my writing has been, I didn't become a writer because I wanted to tell what happened. I became a writer precisely because I wanted to make things up. To spin yarns. To lie my head off. And it isn't memory that interests me most as a writer but rather invention. I became a writer so that I could use my imagination. Remember, I wanted to be Dr. Seuss.

Let me give you two instances of what I'm talking about.

As it happens, in the summer of 1969, I attended the Woodstock music festival in upstate New York. Thirty years later, however, when I was writing my novel *The Last of Her Kind*, part of which is set during the sixties, I had my characters head for Woodstock and then—as happened to so many people in real life—fail to get there. They end up missing the concert—just as I missed the Altamont Free Concert that took place in northern California later that same year. But that's where I sent my characters.

Now, given my own detailed and vivid memories, it would have been much easier for me to have my characters experience Woodstock. And in fact I have written nonfiction about Woodstock: an essay for an anthology called *The Show I'll Never Forget*. But instead I chose Altamont, about which I knew almost nothing, meaning, of course, that I would have to do research—as well as a whole lot of imagining about what the experience must have been like.

Another, earlier example: In my novel *Naked Sleeper*, I wrote about a couple who go through a crisis in their marriage and whom I wanted to send on a second honeymoon to Europe. At the time of writing I had been to Rome, I had been to Paris, I had been to London and to several other places that would have been perfectly suitable for a setting. But I had never been to Venice. That's where I sent my characters.

In each of these cases, I could have saved myself considerable effort by writing about what I knew. And of course, writing out of so much ignorance as I was, I could easily have gotten things wrong. I might even have made a fool of myself. But, as I say, I *wanted* the experience of imagining it all. And, in general, writing about what I don't know has had far more appeal for me than writing about what I do know.

In fact, I often work backward, as it were. Instead of beginning by researching something that I want to write about—what it's like to be an Army nurse, for example, what it was like to serve in Vietnam (the subject of my novel *For Rouenna*)—I try first to imagine it all. Using whatever knowledge I may already happen to have, I write the story, and only after I've got a draft down do I begin the research. I've tried doing the research first, telling myself that I'll thus be spared many hours of labor, but I've always found this very hard—so hard that I usually give up and go back to inventing. Later, I fix the errors to make the material accurate and more convincing. But though those errors might be numerous, I am no longer surprised at how much sheer imagination manages to achieve.

I suppose this is what makes me a fiction writer. And working like this, over so many years, has built up my confidence. Yes, getting the facts right is of utmost importance. (As the novelist Ron Rash puts it, in writing fiction, "if you don't get the small things right the reader won't believe the big lie.") But for me, at least, there appears to be nothing like ignorance to spur creativity. Soon after I had finished *Naked Sleeper* I did go to Venice, and as it turned out, about that part of the novel I didn't have to change a thing.

A related story: My first novel, *A Feather on the Breath of God*, is largely autobiographical. For public readings from the book I sometimes chose sections that were taken from real life, but other times I'd read one particular passage that was pure fiction. And I discovered that, whenever I read the purely fictional part, I'd worry that my voice might break or I might even start to cry. Yet there was never this danger while reading the parts that were taken from real life. I mentioned this, which seemed to me so strange, to another fiction writer, who did not find it strange at all. It's because our imagination is more powerful than our memory, he said. And to me this sounded right. And this may be why so many writers discover that when they are trying to re-create an experience exactly as it happened in real life, they find themselves flailing and needing to fix the problem by changing and elaborating upon the truth. It may also be why some writers find that they cannot write about an actual experience until they've reached a point in life when they've forgotten most of it.

And now a few questions writers often ask themselves: Why am I doing this? What makes writing necessary, when I could be doing something else with my time? How do I justify spending all these hours inventing stories about people who never existed, when I might be doing something not only more remunerative but more useful to the world, perhaps something of benefit to people who do exist, perhaps something to alleviate some of the suffering that so endlessly troubles humanity? It's not as if I didn't know that, were I not to produce a novel, it would not be missed. With tens of thousands of novels being published each year in the United States alone, who will say that what the world needs now is another novel?

Also impossible to ignore, what Calvin Trillin said: most books have "a shelf life somewhere between butter and yogurt."

Why write, then? Why *keep* writing? Flannery O'Connor's "because I am good at it" aside, the answer seems always to have been fraught with doubts. And in these times of extraordinary stress, as the world lurches from crisis to crisis, such doubts seem to me stronger than they have ever been.

In a recent interview, the novelist Sally Rooney said, "When you inhabit a time of enormous historic crises, and you're concerned about it, how do you justify to yourself that the thing to which you've chosen to dedicate your life is making up fake people who have fake love affairs with each other?" Like most answers to the question I have heard, hers isn't very satisfying: "I want to live in a culture where people are making art, even as everything else falls apart. It gives my life meaning." (Yes, but *how* does it give it meaning? And *what* meaning?)

If every poet sat down to write a poem about climate change tomorrow, I once heard someone say, it would not save one tree. No wonder every writer I know is experiencing high anxiety.

But as a friend of mine who is a poet rightly says, it is not the poet's job to save trees. It doesn't matter what's happening in the world, she says. We writers have our work, just as others have their work, and we must do it. And let us not forget: people write because they *need* to write, because there is something that obsesses them that will not go away until they write about it. To ignore that need is to court who knows what psychological danger.

All that said, I think anyone who is writing would do well to take to heart what another poet, Czeslaw Milosz, has said: "Before you print a poem, you should reflect on whether this verse could be of use to at least one person in the struggle with himself and the world."

I agree also with these words of the late Oliver Sacks, from one of the last pieces that he wrote: "I revere good writing and art and music, but it seems to me that only science, aided by human decency, common sense, farsightedness, and concern for the unfortunate and the poor, offers the world any hope in its present morass." In the same piece, Sacks offers his expert neurologist's view that what we are seeing in our age of digital addiction "resembles a neurological catastrophe on a gigantic scale."

I am reminded of something Philip Roth said in an interview many years ago. "The literary era has come to an end. The evidence is the culture, the evidence is the society, the evidence is the screen, the progression from the movie screen to the television screen to the computer." (To which of course we can now add other, increasingly smaller and more mobile screens.) "Literature," he said, "takes a habit of mind that has disappeared. It requires silence, some form of isolation, and sustained concentration in the presence of an enigmatic thing."

This, in turn, brings to mind another interview, one with the novelist Richard Powers. He cites how Terry Waite, who as an envoy for the Church of England went, in 1987, to Lebanon to negotiate the release of four hostages; he was then himself taken hostage and held for five years. When asked what was the main thing he had learned during his captivity, Waite, in an answer which shocked Powers, said, "Contemporary humanity has lost the ability to engage in productive solitude." Powers says,

> To me, his comment legitimized the process of reading and writing. The thing that makes reading and writing suspect in the eyes of the market economy is that it's not corrupted. It's a threat to the GNP, to the gene engineer. It's an invisible, sedate, almost inert process. Reading is the last act of secular prayer. Even if you're reading in an airport, you're making a womb unto yourself—you're blocking the end results of

information and communication long enough to be in a kind of stationary, meditative aspect . . . The destiny of a written narrative is outside the realm of the time. For so long as you are reading, you are also outside the realm of the time. What Waite said seemed like a justification for this unjustifiable process that I've given my life to.

The struggle with writing is over. The first time I heard Roth's story about the Post-it happened to coincide with what was probably the lowest point I'd ever reached in my own writing life. Like him, I had come to feel that I could no longer live in a state of perpetual frustration and failure. I remembered him saying that every morning he'd look at the Post-it and how it gave him such strength. I confess I could not resist. Hoping for at least a little much-needed strength, I stuck a Post-it on my own computer. *The struggle with writing is* almost *over.*

Many a morning I looked at it.

And then I woke up.

Eat Prey Love

FROM *The New Yorker*

IT IS ONE of the most famous murders in the history of cinema. A mother and her child are out for a walk, on the first warm day after a bitter winter. Beguiled by the changing weather, we do not see the danger coming. In fact, we never see it at all, because the man with the gun remains offscreen. We see only the mother's sudden alarm; her panicked attempt to get her child to safety; their separation in the chaos of the moment; and then the child, outside in the cold as snow once again begins to fall, alone and crying for his mother.

The film in question is, of course, the 1942 Walt Disney classic *Bambi*. Perhaps more than any other movie made for children, it is remembered chiefly for its moments of terror: not only the killing of the hero's mother but the forest fire that threatens all the main characters with annihilation. Stephen King called *Bambi* the first horror movie he ever saw, and Pauline Kael, the longtime film critic for this magazine, claimed that she had never known children to be as frightened by supposedly scary grownup movies as they were by *Bambi*.

Unlike many other Disney classics, from *Cinderella* to *Frozen*, this fright fest is not based on a fairy tale. It was adapted from *Bambi: A Life in the Woods*, a 1922 novel by the Austro-Hungarian writer and critic Felix Salten. The book rendered Salten famous; the movie, which altered and overshadowed its source material, rendered him virtually unknown. And it rendered the original *Bambi* obscure, too, even though it had previously been both widely acclaimed and passionately reviled. The English-language version, as translated in

1928 by the soon to be Soviet spy Whittaker Chambers, was enormously popular, earning rave reviews and selling 650,000 copies in the dozen-plus years before the film came out. The original version, meanwhile, was banned and burned in Nazi Germany, where it was regarded as a parable about the treatment of Jews in Europe.

As that suggests, *Bambi* the book is even darker than *Bambi* the movie. Until now, English-language readers had to rely on the Chambers translation—which, thanks to a controversial copyright ruling, has been the only one available for almost a century. This year, however, *Bambi: A Life in the Woods* has entered the public domain, and the Chambers version has been joined by a new one: *The Original Bambi: The Story of a Life in the Forest* (Princeton), translated by Jack Zipes, with wonderful black-and-white illustrations by Alenka Sottler. Zipes, a professor emeritus of German and comparative literature at the University of Minnesota, who has also translated the fairy tales of the Brothers Grimm, maintains in his introduction that Chambers got *Bambi* almost as wrong as Disney did. Which raises two questions: How exactly did a tale about the life of a fawn become so contentious, and what is it really about?

Felix Salten was an unlikely figure to write *Bambi*, since he was an ardent hunter who, by his own estimate, shot and killed more than two hundred deer. He was also an unlikely figure to write a parable about Jewish persecution, since, even after the book burnings, he promoted a policy of appeasement toward Nazi Germany. And he was an unlikely figure to write one of the most famous children's stories of the twentieth century, since he wrote one of its most infamous works of child pornography.

These contradictions are nicely encapsulated by Beverley Driver Eddy in her biography *Felix Salten: Man of Many Faces*. Born Siegmund Salzmann in Hungary in 1869, Salten was just three weeks old when his family moved to Vienna—a newly desirable destination for Jews because Austria had lately granted them full citizenship. His father was a descendant of generations of rabbis who shook off his religious roots in favor of a broad-minded humanism; he was also a hopelessly inept businessman who soon plunged the family into poverty. To help pay the bills, Salten started working for an insurance company in his teens, around the same time that he began submitting poetry and literary criticism to local newspapers and journals. Eventually, he began meeting other writers and creative types at a café called the Griensteidl, across the street from the national theater. These were the fin-de-siècle artists collectively known as Young Vienna, whose members included Arthur Schnitzler, Arnold Schoenberg, Stefan Zweig, and a writer who later repudiated the group, Karl Kraus.

Salten was, in his youth, both literally and literarily promiscuous. He openly conducted many affairs—with chambermaids, operetta singers, actresses, a prominent socialist activist, and, serially or simultaneously, several women with whom other members of Young Vienna were having dalliances as well. In time, he married and settled down, but all his life he wrote anything he could get paid to write: book reviews, theater reviews, art criticism, essays, plays, poems, novels, a book-length advertisement for a carpet company disguised as reportage, travel guides, librettos, forewords, afterwords, film scripts. His detractors regarded this torrent as evidence of hackery, but it was more straightforwardly evidence of necessity; almost alone among the members of Young Vienna, he was driven by the need to make a living.

Yet, like his father, Salten could be reckless with money. Anxious to seem like an insider, he insisted on eating, drinking, dressing, and travelling in the manner of his wealthier peers, with the result that he was constantly accruing debts, some of which he dispatched in dodgy ways—for instance, by "borrowing" and then selling a friend's expensive books. And he could be reckless in other respects, too. Inclined to be touchy, either by temperament or because he felt the need to prove himself, he spent much of his young life fomenting disputes (he once walked into the Griensteidl and slapped Kraus in the face after the latter criticized him in print), then resolving them via lawsuits or duels. Both his personal judgment and his critical judgment could be impulsive and errant; in his thirties, he borrowed prodigiously to produce a modernist cabaret, of the kind that was all the rage in Berlin, only to see it become a critical and financial catastrophe.

The production that brought Salten the most infamy, however, did not bear his name: *Josefine Mutzenbacher; or, The Story of a Viennese Whore, as Told by Herself.* Published anonymously in Vienna in 1906, it has been continuously in print since then, in both German and English, and has sold some three million copies. Despite the subtitle, no one ever seems to have entertained the possibility that it was written by a prostitute, or even by a woman. In Salten's life-time, nearly everyone thought he wrote it, except for those who liked him too much to believe he could produce something so filthy and those who hated him too much to believe he could produce something so well written. Salten himself twice claimed not to have been responsible for it but otherwise was silent or coy on the subject. These days, everyone from academics to the Austrian government regards him as the undisputed author of the book.

Written in the tradition of the ribald female memoir, à la *Fanny Hill*, *Josefine Mutzenbacher* recounts the sexual adventures of the title character beginning when she is five years old, and continuing after her turn to prostitution in her early teens, following the death of her mother. Today, what is most shocking about the book is Josefine's youth. At the time, however, most of the scandal concerned her unapologetic embrace of her career, which she both enjoyed and credited with lifting her out of poverty, educating her, and introducing her to a world far wider than the impoverished Vienna suburbs where she (like Salten) grew up.

Perhaps inevitably, scholars have tried to draw parallels between *Josefine Mutzenbacher* and *Bambi*. Both title characters lose their mothers while still in their youth; both books introduce readers in detail to urban borderlands—the poor suburbs, the flophouses, the forests—about which most proper Viennese were largely ignorant. Still, for the most part, such comparisons seem strained. *Josefine Mutzenbacher* occupies much the same place in the Salten oeuvre as his homage to carpets: the one that lies at the intersection of ambition, graphomania, and penury.

But the place of *Bambi* is different. If there is a through line to Salten's scattershot career, it is his interest in writing about animals, which was evident from his first published work of fiction: "The Vagabond," a short story about the adventures of a dachshund, written when he was twenty-one. Many other nonhuman protagonists followed, most of them ill-fated: a sparrow that dies in battle, a fly that hurls itself to death against a windowpane. Salten's novel *The Hound of Florence* concerns a young Austrian man destined to spend every other day of his life as the archduke's dog; in the end, he is stabbed to death, in his dog form, while trying to protect a courtesan he loves from assault. (In an even more drastic transformation than the one *Bambi* underwent, this story became, in Disney's hands, *The Shaggy Dog*.) *Fifteen Rabbits* features, at first, fifteen rabbits, who debate the nature of God and the reason for their own persecution while their numbers gradually dwindle. *Renni the Rescuer*, about a German shepherd trained as a combat animal, features a carrier pigeon traumatized by its wartime service. And then, of course, there is *Bambi*—which, like these other stories, was not particularly suitable for children, until Disney bowdlerized it to fit the bill.

If you haven't seen the Disney version of *Bambi* since you were eight, here is a quick refresher: The title character is born one spring to an unnamed mother and a distant but magnificently antlered father. He befriends an enthusiastic young rabbit, Thumper; a sweet-tempered skunk, Flower; and a female fawn named Faline. After the death of his mother the following spring, he and Faline fall in love, but their relationship is tested by a rival deer, by a pack of hunting dogs, and, finally, by the forest fire. Having triumphed over all three, Bambi sires a pair of fawns; as the film concludes, the hero, like his father before him, is watching over his family from a faraway crag.

Bambi was not particularly successful when it was first released. It was hampered partly by audience turnout, which was down because of the Second World War, and partly by audience expectations, since, unlike earlier Disney productions, it featured no magic and no Mickey. In time, though, *Bambi*, which was Walt's favorite among his films, became one of the most popular movies in the history of the industry. In the four decades following its release, it earned forty-seven million dollars—more than ten times the haul of *Casablanca*, which came out the same year. Perhaps more notably, it also earned a dominant position in the canon of American nature tales. In the words of the environmental historian Ralph Lutts, "It is difficult to identify a film, story, or animal character that has had a greater influence on our vision of wildlife."

That vision is of an Eden marred only by the incursion of humankind. There is no native danger in Bambi's forest; with the exception of his brief clash with another male deer in mating season, and maybe that hardscrabble winter, the wilderness he inhabits is all natural beauty and interspecies amity. The truly grave threats he faces are always from hunters, who cause both the forest fire and the death of his mother, yet the movie seems less anti-hunting than simply anti-human. The implicit moral is not so much that killing animals is wicked as that people are wicked and wild animals are innocent. Some years ago, when the American Film Institute compiled a list of the fifty greatest movie villains of all time, it chose for slot No. 20—between Captain Bligh, of *Mutiny on the Bounty*, and Mrs. John Iselin, of *The Manchurian Candidate*—the antagonist of *Bambi*: "Man."

Unsurprisingly, *Bambi* has long been unpopular among hunters, one of whom sent a telegram to Walt Disney on the eve of the film's release to inform him that it is illegal to shoot deer in the spring. Nor is the film a favorite among professional wilderness managers, who now routinely contend with what they call "the Bambi complex": a dangerous desire to regard nature as benign and wild animals as adorable and tame, coupled with a corresponding resistance to crucial forest-management tools such as culling and controlled burns. Even some environmentalists object to its narrowness of vision—its failure to offer audiences a model of a healthy relationship between people and the rest of the natural world.

But perhaps the most vociferous if also the smallest group of critics consists of devotees of Salten, who recognize how drastically Disney distorted his source material. Although the animals in the novel do converse and in some cases befriend one another across species, their overall relations are far from benign. In the course of just two pages, a fox tears apart a widely beloved pheasant, a ferret fatally wounds a squirrel, and a flock of crows attacks the young son of Friend Hare—the gentle, anxious figure who becomes Thumper in the movie—leaving him to die in excruciating pain. Later, Bambi himself nearly batters to death a rival who is begging for mercy, while Faline looks on, laughing. Far from being gratuitous, such scenes are, in the author's telling, the whole point of the novel. Salten insisted that he wrote *Bambi* to educate naïve readers about nature as it really is: a place where life is always contingent on death, where starvation, competition, and predation are the norm.

That motive did not make Salten go easy on human beings. On the contrary: his depiction of our impact on nature is considerably more specific and violent than the one in the film, not to mention sadder. Consider the moment when Bambi, fleeing the hunting party that kills his mother and countless other creatures, comes across the wife of Friend Hare, in a scene that reads like something out of *Regeneration*, Pat Barker's novel about the First World War:

"Can you help me a little?" she said. Bambi looked at her and shuddered. Her hind leg dangled lifelessly in the snow, dyeing it red and melting it with warm, oozing blood. "Can you help me a little?" she repeated. She spoke as if she were well and whole, almost as if she were happy. "I don't know what can have happened to me," she went on. "There's really no sense to it, but I just can't seem to walk . . ."

In the middle of her words she rolled over on her side and died.

What purpose are scenes like that one serving in this book? Salten maintained that, despite his own affinity for hunting, he was trying to dissuade others from killing animals except when it was necessary for the health of a species or an ecosystem. (That was less hypocritical than it seems; Salten despised poachers and was horrified by the likes of Archduke Franz Ferdinand, who boasted of killing five thousand deer and was known to shoot them by the score as underlings drove them into his path.) But authors do not necessarily get the last word on the meaning of their work, and plenty of other people believe that *Bambi* is no more about animals than *Animal Farm* is. Instead, they see in it what the Nazis did: a reflection of the anti-Semitism that was on the rise all across Europe when Salten wrote it.

As a textual matter, the best evidence for this proposition comes from two parts of *Bambi* that never made it onto the screen. The first concerns Faline's twin brother, Gobo, who was written out of the movie. A fragile and sickly fawn, Gobo cannot flee during the hunting rampage that kills Bambi's mother and Friend Hare's wife. For several months, he is presumed dead. Then one day Bambi and Faline spot a deer making its way across an open meadow with reckless nonchalance, as if oblivious to any possible peril.

This newcomer turns out to be the grown-up Gobo, who, we learn, was rescued by a member of the hunting party, taken into his home, and nursed back to health. When Gobo returns, the other forest animals gather to hear him describe the kindness of the hunter and his family, the warmth of the dwelling, and the meals that were brought to him every day. Most of them think that Gobo's time among humans has made him dangerously naïve, but he is convinced that it has made him wiser and more worldly. "You all think He's wicked," he tells them. (In Salten's books, humans are typographically styled the way God is: singular and capitalized.) "But He isn't wicked. If He loves anybody, or if anybody serves Him, He's good to him. Wonderfully good!"

Every subjugated minority is familiar with figures like Gobo—individuals who have assimilated into and become defenders of the culture of their subjugators, whether out of craven self-interest or because, like Gobo, they are sincerely enamored of it and convinced that their affection is reciprocated. Such figures often elicit the disdain or the wrath of their peers, and Salten leaves little doubt about how he feels: Bambi "was ashamed of Gobo without knowing why," and the half-tame deer soon pays the price for his beliefs. One day, ignoring the advice of other animals, Gobo strolls into the meadow even though the scent of humans fills the air. He is confident that they won't harm him, but he is shot in the flank while his love interest looks on. As she turns to flee, she sees the hunter bent over Gobo and hears his "wailing death shriek."

One understands why Disney left that part out. So, too, a scene in Salten's book where a dog kills a fox, which unfolds at a horrifyingly leisurely pace. The fox's paw is shattered and bleeding, and he knows he will die soon, but he pleads with the dog: "Let me die with my family at least. We're brothers almost, you and I." When that fails, he accuses the dog of being a turncoat and a spy. The dog works himself into a frenzy defending the virtue and the power of his master, then itemizes all the other animals who serve humankind:

> "The horse, the cow, the sheep, the chickens, many, many of you and your kind are on His side and worship Him and serve Him."
> "They're rabble!" snarled the fox, full of a boundless contempt.

It is easy, in light of these scenes, to see why some people interpret *Bambi* as a covert account of the crisis facing European Jews in the 1920s—a story about innocent creatures forced to remain constantly vigilant against danger, from would-be betrayers within and proto–Brown Shirts without. Some of Salten's biography supports that reading, starting with the fact that he knew a thing or two about assimilation. "I was not a Jew when I was a boy," he once wrote; raised in a household that prized European liberalism, and educated in part by pious Catholic teachers who praised him for his knowledge of the catechism, Salten only really began to identify as Jewish in his late twenties, when he grew close to Theodor Herzl, a fellow Austro-Hungarian writer and the father of the Zionist movement. He claimed that it was Herzl's pamphlet "The Jewish State" that made Salten, as he wrote, "willing to love my Jewishness."

If so, that love was, to say the least, complicated. On the one hand, Salten began writing a weekly column for Herzl's Jewish newspaper, in which he grew more and more critical of the assimilationist impulse that had shaped his childhood; on the other hand, he wrote it anonymously and refused to set foot in the newspaper's offices. In later years, his increasing willingness to embrace his Judaism corresponded, not coincidentally, with the increasing anti-Semitism in Vienna, which made it impossible for Jews to forget or deny their religious background.

In 1925, three years after *Bambi*, Salten published *New People on Ancient Soil*, the product of a visit to Palestine and a book-length tribute to his friend's dream of a Jewish state. A decade later, his books, together with countless others by Jewish authors, were burned by the Nazis, and two years after that, following Germany's annexation of Austria, he moved to Switzerland. Salten died in Zurich, at the age of seventy-six, four months after Hitler killed himself.

Does all this make *Bambi* a parable about Jewish persecution? The fact that the Nazis thought so is hardly dispositive—fascist regimes are not known for their sophisticated literary criticism— and, for every passage that supports such a reading, numerous others complicate or contradict it. Many critics see in *Bambi* different or more diffuse political sentiments, from a generalized opposition to totalitarianism to a post–First World War commentary on the brutality of modern combat. All these readings are plausible, including the specifically Jewish one and Salten's own interpretation of his work as a plea for greater understanding of and greater care for the natural world. Yet the most striking and consistent message of the book is neither obliquely political nor urgently ecological; it is simply, grimly existential.

Whatever else *Bambi* may be, it is, at heart, a coming-of-age story, cervine kin to *Oliver Twist, Little Women,* and *Giovanni's Room.* In the language in which it was written, however, it is often described not as a bildungsroman—a general novel of maturation—but more specifically as an *Erziehungsroman*: a novel of education and training.

The agent of that education is a character known as the old Prince, the oldest surviving stag in the forest, and the lessons he imparts are not subtle. When he first encounters Bambi, the latter is still a fawn, dismayed because his mother has lately grown distant—pushing him away when he tries to nurse, and walking off without caring whether he is following. Thus rebuffed, he is by himself in the middle of the forest bleating for her when the old Prince appears and scolds him. "Your mother has no time for you now," the old Prince says. "Can't you stay by yourself? Shame on you!"

That, in two sentences, is the ultimate message of *Bambi*: anything short of extreme self-reliance is shameful; interdependence is unseemly, restrictive, and dangerous. "Of all his teachings," Salten writes, "this had been the most important: you must live alone. If you wanted to preserve yourself, if you understood existence, if you wanted to attain wisdom, you had to live alone." This is not *The Lorax* or *Maus*. This is *The Fountainhead*, with fawns.

Most panegyrics to the solitary life written by men have an element of misogyny in them, and *Bambi* is no exception. Seemingly brave and vivacious in her youth, Faline grows up to be timid and lachrymose; she "shrieked and shrieked," she "bleated," she is "the hysterical Faline." When she and Bambi are (for lack of a better word) dating, the old Prince teaches Bambi to ignore her calls, lest they come from a hunter imitating the sound. Like Gobo, the romance between the childhood friends is doomed by the logic of the book. "Do you love me still?" Faline asks one day, to which Bambi replies, "I don't know." She walks away, and "all at once, his spirit felt freer than for a long time." All other relationships with the female of the species have a similarly short life span; fatherly love is enduring and ennobling, motherly love juvenile and embarrassing. *Bambi* ends with its hero importuning two fawns, just as the old Prince had importuned him, to learn to live alone.

The curious thing about this insistence on solitude is that nothing in the book makes it seem appealing. The chief trajectory of Bambi's life is not from innocence to wisdom; it is from contentment and companionship—in his youth, he cavorts with Gobo and Faline, with magpies and Friend Hare, with screech owls and squirrels—to isolation and bare-bones survival. Stranger still, this valorization of loneliness seems unrelated to the book's second explicit moral, which concerns the relationship between human beings and other animals. In the final pages, the old Prince takes Bambi, himself now old and beginning to gray, to see something in the woods: a dead man, shot and killed by another hunter. (Amazingly, Walt Disney planned to include this scene in his film, excising it only after the sight of the corpse made an entire test audience leap out of their seats.) With the old Prince's prompting, Bambi concludes from this experience not that we humans are a danger even unto one another but, rather, that other animals are foolish for imagining that we are gods merely because we are powerful. "There is Another who is over us all," he realizes while contemplating the dead man, "over us and over Him." The old Prince, satisfied that his work is done, goes off to die.

This vague gesture in the direction of deism has no antecedent in the book, no moral or theological trajectory to make Bambi's insight meaningful or satisfying. On the contrary, the book is at its best when it revels in rather than pretends to resolve the mystery of existence. At one point, Bambi passes by some midges who are discussing a June bug. "How long will he live?" the young ones ask. "Forever, almost," their elders answer. "They see the sun thirty or forty times." Elsewhere, a brief chapter records the final conversation of a pair of oak leaves clinging to a branch at the end of autumn. They gripe about the wind and the cold, mourn their fallen peers, and try to understand what is about to happen to them. "Why must we fall?" one asks. The other doesn't know, but has questions of its own: "Do we feel anything, do we know anything about ourselves when we're down there?" The conversation tacks back and forth from the intimate to the existential. The two leaves worry about which of them will fall first; one of them, gone "yellow and ugly," reassures the other that it has barely changed at all. The response, just before the inevitable end, is startlingly moving: "You've always been so kind to me. I'm just beginning to understand how kind you are." That is the opposite of a paean to individualism: a belated but tender recognition of how much we mean to one another.

What are we to make of this muddy, many-minded story? Zipes, in his introduction, blames some of the confusion on Chambers, contending that he mistranslated Salten, flattening both the political and the metaphysical dimensions of the work and paving the

way for Disney to turn it into a children's story. But that claim is
borne out neither by examples in the introduction nor by a compar-
ison of the two English versions, which differ mainly on aesthetic
grounds. Zipes is knowledgeable about his subject matter, but he
is not a lucid thinker or a gifted writer (a representative sentence
from the introduction: "Salten was able to capture this existential
quandary through a compassionate yet objective lens, using an in-
novative writing technique that few writers have ever been able
to achieve"), and the Chambers translation, from which I have
quoted here, is much the better one.

In both versions, the *Bambi* that emerges is a complex work, part
nature writing, part allegory, part autobiography. What makes it
such a startling source for a beloved children's classic is ultimately
not its violence or its sadness but its bleakness. Perhaps the most
telling exchange in the book occurs, during that difficult winter,
between Bambi's mother and his aunt. "It's hard to believe that it
will ever be better," his mother says. His aunt responds, "It's hard
to believe that it was ever any better."

It's tempting to read those lines, too, as a commentary on the
Jewish condition, if only because—to this Jew's ears, at least—they
have the feel of classic Jewish dark humor: realistic, linguistically
dexterous, and grim. Yet no one alive today can regard such a sen-
timent as exclusive to any subgroup. It is simply a way of seeing the
world, one that can be produced by circumstance, temperament, or,
as in Salten's case, both. Reading him, one suspects that the conventional interpretation of his most famous work is backward. *Bambi* is
not a parable about the plight of the Jews, but Salten sometimes regards the plight of the Jews as a parable about the human condition.
The omnipresence and inevitability of danger, the need to act for
oneself and seize control of one's fate, the threat posed by intimates
and strangers alike: this is Salten's assessment of our existence.

One of the forgotten novelist's most forgotten novels, *Friends
from All Over the World*, is set in a zoo that is maintained by an
enlightened and humane zookeeper yet remains, intrinsically, a
place of suffering and cruelty. The animals within it, Salten writes,
"are all sentenced to life imprisonment and are all innocent." That
is a lovely line, and one that seems to apply, in his moral universe,
to all of us. In the forest—that is, in a state of nature—we are in
constant danger; in society, tended and cared for but fundamentally compromised, we are still not out of the woods.

Thirteen Ways of Listening to the Rain

FROM *New England Review*

"I do not know which to prefer,
The beauty of inflections
Or the beauty of innuendoes,
The blackbird whistling
Or just after."
　　　　—Wallace Stevens

1.

MY MOTHER AND I sat listening to our breathing over the phone. If I asked a question, she gave the shortest answer possible, placing the words down with slow exactitude, like a row of coins scrounged from the bottom of her purse. "Did you get out for a walk today?" I asked.

"To the fruit stand." The stand on the corner was the limit of her territory now, the border of her remembered world. Beyond that corner, she couldn't find her way back.

"What did you get?"

"Bananas."

She had been an overwhelming talker in the old days, hyperfluent, hungry for attention, unfiltered, exhausting. It was awful, but better than this. "You used to talk more than anyone on the planet," I said now, trying to sound amused—playacting for myself, not for her. "It was a veritable tsunami of words. You could drown people. You *did* drown people."

"Now I like to be quiet."

I shifted in my seat, unsure what to do. Silence had always meant anger in our family, but now it just meant silence. For a thing to be so exactly what it was—nothing less and nothing more—it was as if she had somehow stepped outside the cage of language and was standing beside it, peering in.

2.

At the time, I was living in a small city in Virginia, in an apartment building by the railroad tracks. After one of our calls, I would go downstairs and walk beside the freight cars as they dreamed past, like children's blocks the size of houses, an unthinkable, dark weight sleeping inside them. *Here, here, here,* they sang, and then *gone, gone, gone,* and then there was nothing but the sound of my breathing filling the cold street.

3.

A part of me recognized that I could give in and let the phone line stand empty between us for a few minutes, that it would hurt no one, that it would be like moonlight in a darkened room. But another part of me became electric with fear and began to talk about anything, everything, trying to fill us up with words.

4.

I told my mother about the hike my wife Karen and I took outside of town: the long gravel road, then the path that wound steeply upward through the trees, a sort of green tunnel, and the deer down by the stream at the bottom of the ridge. And when I couldn't come up with anything more, I finally asked, "And what have you been doing?"

"Me? I went hiking on the mountain."

"Mom, you're in the middle of Manhattan. There is no mountain."

"But I do have a mountain, and I hike there."

For a second, I thought she was making fun of me, and then I wasn't sure what to think. "There is no mountain on Twenty-third Street," I said, trying to keep my voice even.

"If there is no mountain, how do I hike on it?"

It was dark and starting to rain, long heavy drops that glowed in the light of the streetlamp below my window. She was filling in the gaps with whatever bits of language she could scavenge from our conversation, trying to cobble together a bridge that could take us from here to there without falling. "Well, I see your point," I said.

"It was a very nice hike," she replied.

5.

Karen and I had walked in silence, breathing hard because the trail was steep. The trees met at their tops to form a sort of lattice-work roof, and the light filtered down, bluish-green, the color of silence. No sound from the outside; our own footsteps inaudible. The feeling was of enclosure: a winter garden filled with a forest, or maybe a memory box by Joseph Cornell the size of the world. It contained a creek and a little wooden bridge at the bottom of the ravine and then a tree the size of an ancient Roman pillar that had fallen over the path, hanging over our heads as we passed underneath. We are here, I thought, one part of the composition, but we can't read its meaning. We'll never know whose dream we describe.

6.

After the conversation with my mother, I sat at the window, thinking. Wasn't there something a little odd about the way I kept forcing her to talk when she didn't want to, as if I weren't merely checking on her, as if there were something specific I wanted her to say? And then I noticed a long chain of flatbeds coming down the tracks at the end of the street, carrying strange metal armatures two stories high. One was just a curved steel wall like a Richard Serra sculpture, floating with great ceremony into the darkness.

7.

That night I dreamed that somebody gave me a big scary dog to take care of, a Rottweiler like the one my brother used to keep— all teeth and muscle, but strangely vulnerable, too, pathetically eager to be loved. Not sure what to do with him, I put him in an empty apartment I happened to own and then promptly forgot him, and I didn't remember him again till many days had gone by. I was in a guilty panic, afraid the dog had starved to death, so I sent a woman I knew to check on him. She came back and reported that the dog was fine, healthy and well fed, but it soon became apparent that she had made a mistake, gone to the wrong apartment and seen the wrong dog: this dog was not *my* dog. Now I would have to go to the apartment myself, alone, would have to find the body stretched on the floor, the ribs showing through the skin, the scratches on the door from when he tried to claw his way out. The dream was so intensely real that I woke up gasping for air. I actually said aloud to myself, "It isn't real, it's a dream, just a dream," and felt gratitude fill my chest like sunlight in an empty glass.

8.

There were times when my mother seemed momentarily restored to language, if only long enough to say something unbearable before retreating back into silence. Once when we were on the phone, neither of us speaking, out of nowhere she said, "It's like I'm becoming a blank."

"You're not a blank," I replied.

"Even if I can't remember who I am?"

My mind started to move very fast, trying to find a way to make the question into something else, something that wouldn't hurt us. "Stop and think about this logically," I said. "If you don't remember what you ate for dinner, does that mean you didn't eat?"

"I'm not sure."

"If you don't remember your birthday, does that mean you weren't born?"

"Maybe. I don't know."

"Does a rose even *know* it's a rose?"

"But I'm not a rose."

9.

That night, I was woken by a human voice: high-pitched, wordless, keening, mournful, terrified. Karen's eyes were still closed, but her mouth was wide open and she was sobbing in her sleep. I shook her very gently, then a little harder, and then I tried to wrap her in my arms; she shrugged me off, and by the end I was reduced to whispering, "It's a dream, it's a dream," as if she might hear me and understand. By that point, I was shivering with fear, unable to stop; my heart was beating like a boot kicking at the door. I lay back, completely still until light came through the window.

10.

I told her about it in the morning and she said she didn't remember the dream, didn't remember being frightened, had had a deep dreamless sleep and felt fine now, great, in fact, without a hint of fear or sadness.

11.

The next night, the same thing happened: I was pulled from sleep by a sound that was uncanny in its sheer nakedness, its lack of civilized veneer. It was the sound you make when somebody has a grip on you, when you are struggling. Her eyes were closed but her face was anguished. I tried to hug her, but she shook me off, and I lay back in bed, waiting for dawn. Eventually I realized it was raining, the rain lashing the window.

12.

The night after that, my eyes opened spontaneously, as if on a timer. "When will she begin?" I thought, listening for that distinctive sound, ready for it, my chest tight, my heart like the drip of a sink. But her face remained placid, the room silent, and I hung there in confusion. It felt like her scream had been erased from my own throat.

13.

The detail too confusing to mention to my mother: Karen and I had been up to the top and were almost back at the bottom. It was dusk and the fungi attached to the trees seemed to be lit from within, orange and yellow. I could hear the rush of water, almost like a waterfall, though I couldn't see a source, and then I realized that it was raining, that I was hearing the sound of rain slapping the uppermost branches above our heads. Nothing reached us down below, and we remained completely dry the whole way, walking through a kind of hazy green light, until we came to the trailhead and stepped out onto the gravel road. There, the rain was coming straight down, a silvery curtain with its fingers deep into the gravel, and we were instantly soaked cold.

SCOTT SPENCER

Dreamers Awaken

FROM *Chicago Quarterly Review*

ON THE SOUTH Side of Chicago, the students attending my public school were predominately second-generation Americans, many with family roots in Eastern Europe—Poland, Yugoslavia—though no one waxed nostalgic about the Old Country. It was the mid-1950s and still close to the time when Europe was basically a hellhole, and that door to the past was closed. We were all dug in and secure in our unhyphenated identity as Americans. No one who wasn't white stepped foot in our school without a broom and a dustpan, and on the block where I lived, my guess is that no one except my parents even knew anyone who was Black. The crazy, angry dream of an All-White World was alive in the carpenters, bricklayers, roofers, plumbers, and electricians who had built the neighborhood, the people who worked the shops we frequented, and every father, mother, and child who lived and played there. Every once in a while, a Black housekeeper could be seen getting off the bus with a paper sack holding her lunch, and there she would be again at the end of the day, waiting for the bus to take her back to her home, with the paper sack, empty now, carefully folded so it could be used again.

We began the school day pledging our allegiance to the American flag. It was around this time that, in a burst of anti-Communist virtue, the words "under God" were inserted into the pledge by congressional decree. I wasn't aware of anyone else in the school having a quarrel with this addition to the morning ritual, but I silently mouthed those two words; I was being raised to disbelieve in God, and I was also being taught to keep that unbelief a secret.

Our teachers were the usual mix of dedicated educators, public-sector lifers, and cheerful younger teachers doing their best to teach us to add and subtract, write legibly, and learn the names of the presidents and the state capitals.

The students were of varying abilities, but nearly all of us were obedient and relatively easy to teach. We completed our homework assignments, and no one made remarks without first raising their hand, except, occasionally, me. I was the designated pain in the neck of the fourth grade—a distinction that would follow me through elementary and high school. I wanted to be a blend of Marlon Brando and Jerry Lewis, and my bad reputation puzzled me. I had never been tardy, or fought in the playground, or cheated on a test, yet it was clear to me that most of the teachers actively disliked me, a disdain that caught on with many of the other students, resulting in my feeling underliked.

In the spring of that year, plans were being made for a schoolwide assembly organized around the theme of American folktales. The teachers had already chosen a freckled girl to be Johnny Appleseed, another girl with straw-colored hair for Casey Jones, a tall boy for Paul Bunyan, but the role of John Henry, the Black steel-driving man who worked himself to death in his attempt to outwork a steam drill, was still up for grabs. I told the music teacher I wanted to try out for the part. It was my chance to be seen as I wanted to be seen—not as a discipline problem but as someone creative, talented, and interesting.

I had a leg up because my parents owned a recording of the guitar-playing Josh White singing the folk song about John Henry—"he could whistle, he could sing, / he woke up every morning just to hear his hammer ring." Josh White was not particularly militant and outspoken—he was no Paul Robeson—but he was a Black man who was hounded by the very red-baiters who repelled and frightened my parents, giving him a kind of favored-nation status in our household.

I was glad my parents liked someone singing and playing a guitar, but, really, anyone who could entertain had favored-nation status with me. I was an only child, with a passion for any and all forms of show business, but I'd learned to be careful when I watched the TV. We had a snug little house—four rooms and a kitchen—and my parents heard everything that was happening on the set: the laughter, the applause, and the dialogue, too. There were things I didn't dare watch if they were home, such as *Davy Crockett*, a show every kid in my school loved but which my parents (accurately, depressingly) said was a bunch of lies about a guy who was nothing but a vicious, coldhearted Indian killer. As much as I enjoyed Jack Benny, I would have been mortified to be caught watching his program because Rochester, his house servant, who spoke in a screeching, funny voice, would have offended my parents. *Amos 'n' Andy* was out of the question. And blackface? Blackface was an abomination. When they came upon Al Jolson singing and dancing in one of the old movies I used to watch on TV, or Eddie Cantor doing a similar act on one of the new variety shows, my father would say, "That's disgraceful," and my mother would add, "He's making fun of Negroes. Do you think that's the right thing to do?" And in their presence it became what it actually was—the inky, shining black face, the insane, goofy eyes, the wildly exaggerated lips, the hopping, the jumping, the childish patty-pat-pat of hands in bright-white gloves. It became grotesque.

I told my parents I had a featured role in the upcoming school assembly, and I was going to portray John Henry, singing the song they had taught me to love. They seemed quite pleased. They might not have been pleased had I told them I was going to be made up so my skin would be black. In fact, they might have forbidden it, and probably that's why I kept that detail to myself. I didn't want them to yank me the hell out of that pageant, which I continued to dream about as if it were going to be a tremendous turning point in my life.

The afternoon of the performance, it was time to blacken my face. The art teacher supplied the charcoal, and she and two other teachers circled around me, clearly enjoying themselves, giving me the tingling sensation of positive attention for once.

The art teacher was a soft, well-powdered woman in her forties, with a wide face, light-brown eyes, and bangs that had grown out too long, forcing her to continually toss her head like a horse. She was a kindly soul who disliked me noticeably less than most of the other teachers. She used Kleenex to protect her fingers while she gently went over my face with a charcoal stick. I stood at attention, dressed in the torn shirt and patched trousers that made up my costume, and held in one hand a broom handle upon which a hammerhead had been fashioned out of aluminum foil.

I was a bit nervous, but I knew the song "John Henry" about as well as I knew "The Star-Spangled Banner." I had sung it fifty times at least, in the shower and for my parents, and, over the past week, I'd rehearsed it with the music teacher, who was going to accompany me on the piano. She had promised prompting whispers to anyone who might forget a word or a line, but I doubted I would need her prompts. I knew that song cold.

The whole school would be there to see the show, and some of the parents would be there, though not mine. My parents kept a low profile. I don't think the phrase "flying under the radar" was widely used at the time, but there certainly was radar looking for enemy planes in the sky, and a more insidious kind of radar searching for what J. Edgar Hoover called the enemies within, and my parents were doing what they could to fly beneath it.

And in the meanwhile, two women, both appointed members of the board of education, and both Black, were driving toward our school in a two-door Plymouth. Richard Daley, who'd been elected mayor a couple of years before, and would remain mayor of Chicago for another two decades, was consolidating his power and making savvy moves. Daley needed to pull in votes from people in the Black community, so he put a few Blacks on the board of education, in a small gesture that would not likely offend the sensibilities of the white ethnic voters who were his base.

And as two of those appointees were closing in on my school, three teachers and the librarian hovered around me, and the gentle art teacher put the finishing touches on my face. I silently ran through the song while Mrs. Adams (circumstances prohibit me from using her real name here) moved the charcoal stick over the wings of my nose. She was really getting into it, taking little voilà swipes at me and then lifting the charcoal and stepping back a foot or two, like someone in a movie about a great artist.

Louise Gluck has written that the best occupation for a child is to observe and listen. I did a bit of that, but mainly my energies went into seeking approval. That a teacher had a home life would have made sense to me if someone had mentioned it, but on my own it never crossed my mind. In my narrowly self-centered imagination, the teachers were basically a twenty-headed gorgon, a scolding authority whose affection I had no chance of earning and whose ire I was continually hoping to evade.

Yet here in this makeshift green room, getting ready for my star turn, I was aware of the interplay between the teachers. I noticed that even though Mrs. Adams was solely responsible for blackening my face, Miss Michaels and Miss Benson (also not their real names) diligently monitored. Miss Benson, whom I liked because she was pretty—slender, young—smiled at me, and when she brushed back her hair, her left ear emerged. I listened to the friendly hum of their conversation. You missed a spot. We have five more minutes. I'm hurrying. Oh, wait, you missed another spot.

At that moment, Miss Fitzgerald, the third-grade teacher, burst into the library, urgency radiating off of her. She was so upset, and the situation was so urgent that she didn't want to waste a moment by taking Mrs. Adams aside, or speaking sotto voce. "Clean him up," she said, in a tone better suited for *Man overboard!* or *The British are coming!* The other teachers looked at her blankly. "Two women from the board of education just arrived," she said. She waited for a moment and then said the rest. "Colored."

It took only a moment for them all to realize the gravity of the situation. No one said, "That's great," and no one said, "So what?" Instead, they seemed to know what to do if a Black person appeared, just as we'd practiced what to do if the Russians dropped the bomb on Chicago.

Mrs. Adams raced to the teachers' lounge across the hall. The rest of us waited in silence. We were like bank robbers who hear the Doppler whoop of approaching sirens. We had only a minute or two to save ourselves. Mrs. Adams returned, her eyes wide with purpose, holding a cloth towel thoroughly wetted down with water. The teachers worked in concert. Miss Fitzgerald said she would get another towel, Miss Michaels spoke to Mrs. Adams in a calming murmur, and Miss Benson—this was the moment's saving grace— held my shoulders steady to keep me from falling over while Mrs. Adams scrubbed at my face.

Some of the charcoal came off, much of it remained, though lightened and smeared. As they worked, the teachers debated among themselves whether to cancel my part of the show or send me out as-is. I was slow to realize that no matter what happened, my dream of impressing the school was not going to come true.

"Why did they have to come here on this of all days?" wondered Mrs. Adams as she scrubbed me.

"To ruin everything," opined Miss Fitzgerald.

"We're saying John Henry was a good man," said Mrs. Adams. "That's the whole point of the song." She fell silent for a moment and then added, barely audibly, "It's for Mr. Henry. Not against."

I marched into the assembly, a filthy, frightened boy shielded inside a moving box of teachers. I looked up at their necklaces, their chins, their freeze-dried smiles. My teachers had lost their privacy from the non-white citizens of our city, and now they were like people in a dream who had come to school naked.

"How were we supposed to know?" Mrs. Fitzgerald asked.

"We didn't do anything wrong," said Miss Benson, glancing down at me, smiling.

We made it to the front, and I slowly walked up the four steps that led to the side of the stage, joining the other American folk heroes waiting to go on. Everyone could feel that some sort of trouble had come to us, and there they were: invaders in heavy blue dresses, accusers in hats with the veils pinned up, spies with black patent leather handbags large as reel-to-reel tape recorders resting on their laps.

At first, they had seemed indistinguishable, twins. But now I saw that one was older and larger than the other. The older one had broad shoulders and a wide face and wore a necklace made of large colored stones. Her hair was smooth and shiny and went back in three waves. She wore large dangling earrings that matched her necklace, heavy ovals that pulled down on her lobes. The younger board rep rubbed her hands together as if to warm them. She wore pink lipstick and blue eye shadow. Her hair was a blackish gray, pulled tight and gathered in a bun.

I got through the first verse of "John Henry" without flubbing so much as a syllable. My dream of school-wide stardom was over. The only real goal was to get through to the end. It's not a short song. Ten days before, the music teacher had found a version of "John Henry" that was even longer than the version I had memorized. The song as I had known it ended with John Henry's death, but now there were three more verses about his wife, his son, and his immortality.

When I'd first been presented with the new verses, I'd been happy that my time onstage would be extended. Now, however, the extra verses loomed ahead of me like a rock face I was meant to climb. I didn't know them nearly so well as I knew the earlier verses, and I was suddenly sure I would flub them. When I lost heart and my voice got smaller, the visitors from the board leaned forward, smiling and nodding encouragingly.

Every once in a while, I looked away from the two Black faces, just to make certain that my parents hadn't surprised me and slipped into the auditorium. I scanned the rows. There were plenty of parents in attendance, mostly mothers. Ponytails, babushkas, harlequin glasses, sitting with whatever class their child was in, towering over the children like cypress trees.

Finally—it felt as if an hour had passed—I got to "He died with a hammer in his hand, Lawd, Lawd." I was careful to translate the "Lawd" into "Lord," lingering over the *r*, as if to light it with neon, lest there be any mistaking my intentions. And that was as far as I could go. The music teacher was already playing the first chords of the next verse, but I put down my broomstick with its tinfoil hammerhead, and, with one hand on my belly and the other on the small of my back, I made the low bow.

Our principal, Miss Taylor, a strict, deeply traditional product of Chicago public schools, came quickly onto the stage and announced her enthusiastic appreciation of all of the students and teachers who had made today's assembly possible. Stately, impenetrable Principal Taylor stood near me as she brought the assembly to a close and then did something I found extraordinary. She picked up my pathetically unconvincing steel-driving hammer and handed it back to me. "If you will, please," she said, smiling at me warmly, with a sympathy I had never seen in her before—we had gone through something together and as far as she was concerned, we had all survived it.

As we had practiced, John Henry, Casey Jones, and the others joined hands and bowed our heads for a final thank-you to the audience, and then the cast, except for me, jumped off the stage and ran to their mother, their mother, their mother and father, and their mother. I stood alone for a few moments, relieved that my parents were not here and experiencing the familiar shame of being different, then hopping off the stage and placing myself in front of the two visitors from the board of education.

"I'm sorry," I said.

The auditorium seemed to twitch for a moment; one of the fathers had taken a souvenir picture and lit it with a flashbulb.

"You made a wonderful John Henry," the smaller of the two women said. Her hands were still cold, and she continued to rub them together.

"I never knew that song had so many verses," the larger woman said. Her voice was deep, and after she spoke she raised her eyebrows.

"There's even more," I said.

"Oh," said the larger woman, stretching the word out.

"Well, you were very good," her friend said.

I touched my face.

"You sang it well and very clearly," the larger woman said. "We could hear every word."

We stood in the awkward silence that followed their two-star review of my performance. I'm sure they wanted to get out of there and go home, but it was clear to them that there was something I wanted to say, and they were kind, very kind. As for me, I was waiting for something, some recognition that did not and could not come. I had wanted to be seen as someone worthy of applause, and now what I needed was to be seen as someone worthy of forgiveness. I wanted them to tousle my hair, give my arm a little friendly squeeze. I could hear the shuffle of feet and the teachers reminding everyone to stay with their class as the auditorium emptied. Normally, I would have been sharply reminded to march out with the rest of my class, but for now I was ignored. In a few moments the auditorium was empty except for the three of us.

We stood to one side, halfway between the stage and the exit doors, smiling uncertainly. We were in our own little impromptu pageant, folktales from the future, and we were waiting for the invisible proctor to tell us in a whisper, or perhaps with some urgency, what to say next.

Care Credit

FROM *New England Review*

I WAS STILL lying on my back, the white nylon bib around my neck, the sour taste lingering in my mouth, when the hygienist said, "Oh honey, you're beautiful. You should take care of your smile." The dentist had just given me a twenty-five-thousand-dollar estimate to get all of the problems with my teeth fixed. "It's like buying a car," he said. And I wondered what kind of car he thought I owned. The most expensive vehicle I had ever bought was the nine-year-old Toyota Corolla that I scored for five thousand dollars. I was proud of myself, too, for finding that bargain with three months of saved up overtime cash and weeks of ad-scouring for a low-mileage number with front-wheel drive and working air-conditioning. But teeth are not like cars. There are no bargains to be found if you want a pretty smile.

The dentist told me about CareCredit—a card specifically made for dental- and health-related needs. Conveniently, I could apply right there in the office. "Okay," I said, knowing that even at forty years old my credit had never scored above six hundred. But I complied and filled out the paperwork anyway. What did it matter? I had already been humiliated walking into that office with a mouth full of cavities and missing teeth. It surprised me when the dentist came back and told me I was approved for four thousand dollars. Working full-time as a community college professor for six years had made a difference, I guessed. That, combined with the full allowable withdrawal of three thousand in flex spending, he told me, would get me one implant for one tooth. And then we could move on from there. At that rate, it would take me years to fix all the damage.

I tried not to think about how long it would take. I tried to shut out the condemnation that echoed in my head. The dentist put a temporary fix on my molar, then we made a plan for the implant over the next six months and also to get my teeth whitened. I think he added the whitening as a bonus to keep me coming back. He had already pegged me as a flight risk. I drove home that day a sobbing mess—the Novocain's punch still swollen on my face, the gauzy white pad reddening my uncontrollable spit, and a deep shame I couldn't explain.

Our teeth tell stories about us, about the way that we have lived, about where we come from, about our habits, our health, and status. Teeth are stronger than bones. Even thousands of years after the body is gone, the narrative cemented into the layers of enamel can chronicle a life, like the rings inside trees. Cavities catalog a long history of carbohydrates and sugar consumption; the wearing of enamel reveals poor diet and nutrition; micro-wear on teeth shows the way a person chews. Archaeologists can tell, for example, that Neanderthals lived through high-stress events that disrupted the enamel formation during childhood. Events like illness or malnutrition that have lasted up to three months can appear on teeth.

When I was in my twenties and had my first tooth pulled, the dentist, upon looking inside my mouth, said I must have had a high fever when I was in grade school. I was surprised at how he knew this, at how accurately my enamel told the tale. But what it didn't tell him was that my mom had left my dad again. Their relationship had blossomed at AA meetings, and after they got married it was marked by days-long fights and periodic trips to rehab and the psych ward. But even though they split up often, they always ended up back together. Mom couldn't make enough money by herself to take care of both my sister and me. This time, Mom had taken us to a shelter where there were dozens of other mothers and their children sharing rooms and common areas. Gina and I were maybe six and seven. My first permanent molars might have been just erupting at that point. I had been sick for over a week, and when my fever rose to 105 and I was shaking in my bed, delirious, the women pooled their money so that Mom could taxi us to Emergency. The doctor diagnosed me with strep throat, said it was good we caught it in time; otherwise, I was at risk of getting rheumatic fever. I spent most of that night lying behind a curtain on a gurney in Emergency, Mom and Gina by my side. Together we waited until the antibiotics and Tylenol brought my fever down.

When I was ready to be discharged late into the morning, it was Dad who picked us up. Mom had called him from the hospital. We had been gone for only a few weeks that time, but it felt like no time had passed, because everything seemed right again when we got into the house and there was ice cream waiting for us.

Like millions of Americans in poverty, my parents never had dental insurance. Even when both of them were working, they had jobs that did not offer that kind of remuneration. Dental care and prevention were always lowest on the list of our problems. I was in sixth grade when my family moved to Berlin Street. It was a roach-infested upper level of a duplex on Rochester's northeast side. Mom had just gotten back from another sixty days in the psych ward and Dad had lost his job again.

Those eight hundred square feet were the cheapest Dad could find on our welfare allotment. Once a month, the landlord, who thankfully lived below us, scheduled the exterminator, which always turned into two days of hell for me and Gina. Our little family of four spent the evenings prior removing all of our dishes, silverware, and food from the cupboards to place into boxes on the table. We pulled the furniture away from the walls so the spray could get into every crevice. The fumigation was usually scheduled for a weekday to be sure everyone would be out of the house for six or seven hours. When we got home, we'd have to deal with the death—thousands of roach carcasses on their backs, some still squirming, unable to turn over. Armed with brooms, dustpans, and large garbage bags, we moved from room to room opening the windows to dissipate the chemicals and sweep those hard-shelled, six-legged monsters that multiplied by the thousands.

Roaches weren't the only pests our family lived with. In our many apartments, we often had mice and rats. We learned to keep our cereal, pasta, and cookies in recycled plastic and glass containers so that the little chewers wouldn't munch through the bottom corners and force us to waste precious food. There were always ants, spiders, and flies too. Back in the seventies, Dad bought those dangling fly-traps. In the mornings, we'd help him open the little cardboard cylinders and pull out the twirling sticky flypaper so he could hang them in the kitchen like decorations. By the evening, they'd be packed full of buzzing and wiggling flies trying to break free of the molasses-like attractant. None of those things bothered me, though, not even the flypaper dangling from our kitchen ceilings or the mice that Dad found each day stuck headfirst in snap traps. It was the cockroaches that haunted me.

You always knew that even if you didn't see them, the roaches were there, hidden within the walls, skittering in the darkness waiting for the light to go down, feeding on the scraps, reminding you of where you came from. They weren't seasonal like flies, and they did not live in corners, like spiders, making beautiful webs. They could never be the heroine in a favorite children's book. They weren't like the Southern roaches either, those slower, bigger, heat-loving cousins called palmettos. No, the German cockroach in New York had a narrative unlike any other. That little six-legged insect that shuns the light with its two threadlike antennae and those hairy legs told a story of filth, of disgust, of poverty and shame. Unlike the Southern roaches, they only lived in certain households and, in my child's mind, they brought with them a label that stitched itself onto every fiber of my being.

After I pulled out of the dentist's parking lot, the blue folder of shame detailing my work plan and pricing scheme on the passenger seat next to me, I drove first to the liquor store then the grocery store. I had called in sick that day. When the Novocain wore off, I was going to drown my sorrows in comfort food and whiskey. Before my appointment I told a friend about my cavities. She said, "I get mine cleaned every six months, and I've never had a cavity." In the car, I wanted to punch her too. I wanted to punch anyone who had ever believed that cavities were a sign of dirtiness, of choice rather than of inequities within our healthcare system. Nobody chooses to have cavities.

As I walked into the store with my swollen face, I was reminded of another cavity I had suffered just before I turned thirty. That cavity took up space on my right incisor very close to the gum. Though it was small enough that I could show some teeth when I smiled, it was still big enough to tear away at my self-confidence. I had been living in a roach-infested two-room studio, working two to three part-time jobs, and paying for community college. In my first few semesters, I couldn't afford to buy my books, so I stood in the bookstore aisles at night to read my homework. Other times when I couldn't get the readings online, I borrowed other students' books and made copies on the faculty copier. When the manager in my low-rent apartment building moved out, I offered to oversee the building temporarily if the owner would let me live there rent-free. Even with the other part-time jobs and the extra money and free rent, I still had no health or dental insurance.

In my last semester at the community college, I was awarded a full scholarship from the Gates Foundation to transfer to any school of my choice. I picked a program in Costa Rica that was embedded in ideals of experiential learning and human rights. But like many universities, this one didn't disperse scholarship money until six weeks into the semester, after the school's census data proved that students had indeed attended. This meant I had to pay out of pocket for upfront costs like travel, books, a laptop, and the first two months of meals. I could barely afford to eat back then. What was the use in getting a full scholarship to college, when the money wouldn't even become available until two months into the first semester? I wrote frustrated letter after letter, trying to explain to officials in financial aid that their system was flawed, but there was no give. (Years later I learned that the school fixed this inequity in their financial aid process.)

But while I was still a student at that college, there was no way I could even consider getting my cavity fixed, forget about buying a laptop. It was all I could do to earn and save up the cash for the flight, all the shots and meds needed for international travel, the books and supplies, and then the first two months of lunches and dinners. All of that added up. But I was so desperate to get out, to experience something new, that when renters in my building moved out, I painted, cleaned, and fumigated the roaches on my own for extra money under the table. I offered to clean houses for my friends and professors. By the time August rolled around, I had no choice but to board the plane, broke, with that ever-growing cavity.

I hoped that I could hide that blackening incisor until the next year when I could use the leftover scholarship money to fix it. But

I stood out in too many other ways for people not to notice. Most of the students were white and rich and very young. I was a brown woman, and by the time my plane touched ground in Costa Rica, I was thirty years old. Other students had brought spending money with them to take salsa lessons or photography courses or to taxi to San José for nice dinners. They all had their own laptops and cameras and hiking gear. They went away to the coast on weekends and they had parents who sent them money when they ran out. I had less than a hundred dollars to last me the next two months. I ate the breakfast and dinner allowed by my homestay, and a few days a week I bought a bottle of Cherry Coke and thirty-cent tacos from the taqueria near the school. Every time someone pulled out a camera there was another person asking me to smile, someone else saying you're so beautiful. Someone else watching from the side, waiting to get a glimpse of my rotten tooth. I knew they saw it—that growing black hole defining the essence of my humanity.

Humans have four kinds of teeth: incisors, canines, premolars, molars. Each tooth has a specific job to do and each one can tell a different part of the story about the way a person has lived. While most of our molars are formed when we are babies, the third molars—otherwise known as wisdom teeth—are the last ones to appear and don't often erupt until our late teens to early twenties. Consequently, researchers can tell where a human was during each of these formations and eruptions. The minerals from the geographic area are literally cemented into the layers of the burgeoning enamel. Based on how long it takes for all of our permanent teeth to erupt, researchers have also learned that humans take longer to grow up than any other primates.

So much of our evolutionary history was spent eating hard foods harvested by hunting and gathering. Our teeth weren't adapted to a soft and sugary diet. It wasn't until the Industrial Revolution that molar impaction and tooth misalignment became ten times more common than it ever was before. Plaque buildup and cavities are a product of a more contemporary diet crammed with refined carbs and an overabundance of sugar. Food habits mark our smiles in such deep and enduring ways that anthropologists have begun to see our teeth as landscapes of histories.

I wonder what my record would say a thousand years from now, after that blue folder disintegrates, after the skin and hair goes back to earth. Would it reveal that I never had roots in any one place, that I left my foster home before I graduated high school, moved in with my boyfriend at seventeen, that I got up every morning of my life and drank coffee with powdered cream and extra sugar before work, that I got by on freezer food and pasta? Where in the layers of my enamel is the evidence that I lived in Costa Rica and traveled throughout Central American countries for over a year? I wonder how that evidence would conflict with the evidence of poverty plaguing my mouth in the form of missing teeth and cavities.

After a few months on Berlin Street, Gina and I began scheming ways to stay out later on extermination days. Before we left for school, we'd steal all the change on Mom and Dad's dresser, tell them we were going to a friend's house after school. When the bell rang at the end of the day, Gina and I met at the front door and walked through the neighborhood to the bodega on the corner. We'd spend every cent on penny candy. Each of us selecting FireBalls, Gobstoppers, Dubble Bubble, banana Laffy Taffy, Smarties lollipops. Sometimes we splurged on red Wax Lips, Now and Laters, Pixy Stix, Ring Pops, and Pop Rocks. When we had extra money, we'd each buy a pack of the bubblegum cigarettes—smack them upside down on our palms like Dad did. My favorite was Astro Pops, those cylindrical-shaped syrupy suckers in three flavors. Nothing made me feel more like an adult than walking into that bodega, choosing my candy, paying for it, and waltzing out with that little paper bag in my hands. Sometimes we'd walk the streets with candy cigarettes between our fingers, blowing out the powdered sugar and pretending we were smoking.

One day, Gina came home with her friend Latisha. The three of us hung out in our bedroom—candy wrappers everywhere, the Go-Go's on LP—smoking our pretend cigarettes and sucking on our Ring Pops when a string of roaches skittered across the back wall behind our bunkbeds. Latisha didn't see them, but Gina and I were mortified. Gina immediately moved so that Latisha's back was against the wall. In school, nobody ever talked about their own infestations; instead, the existence of cockroaches in our classrooms were used as bully's tools. Whenever one of us spied a roach, some bully would find an especially vulnerable kid to blame it on. Though so many of us lived on welfare in the same kind of detestable conditions, no one was willing to admit it.

*

In the grocery store, I picked up some pasta, sauce, garlic bread, and a Sara Lee Cake. Then in the soda aisle, I grabbed a two-liter of Cherry Coke to mix with my whiskey. I didn't know if I was going to be able to eat dinner that night, but I was sure going to try. And if I couldn't chew, then I was going to drink my sorrows away.

Mom had taught us how to make her coffee; "scalding hot with powdered cream and three tablespoons of sugar," she'd say, "and don't spill it." She'd be on the couch, legs up, watching the morning news. We were nine years old when she finally let us pour our own cups. We'd sit on the cushions and curl our legs just like her, blow the heat from the mug, and dip our buttered toast into the sweet creamy mixture. On Fridays, when there was money, Mom and Dad went shopping. They replenished our pantries with Dino Pebbles and Cocoa Puffs, our refrigerator with two liters of generic cola, black cherry for me, root beer for Gina. When there was no money for soda, we bought eight packets of Kool-Aid for a dollar. Lime was my favorite. Once Dad came home with two cases of Ragu sauce. One of his friends at AA came upon a whole truckload of the stuff. When Gina and I arrived home from school, we'd put the sauce on Ritz crackers, slice some government cheese over it, and bake it in the oven like mini pizzas. When there was money, Dad picked up a dozen doughnuts with the Sunday paper. The four of us would each pick three and take a newspaper section, the comics for me and Gina, the news for Mom and Dad. Junk food was our life, the remnants of which spilled over into my twenties and thirties when I still chose soda over water and doughnuts over salad.

Like so many children in the United States, Gina and I were practically weaned on sugar. But what put us into a different category is that we never went to the dentist, not for regular cleanings, not for X-rays, not for any reason. The cost was too much. And to make matters worse, our parents rarely enforced teeth brushing and flossing. Mom was diagnosed with paranoid schizophrenia in eighth grade and spent the next twelve years in the psych ward. She had lost so many teeth that it was hard for her to chew her food without moving it awkwardly around in her mouth. Gina had chipped a tooth at eleven, falling face-first roller-skating down a hill. She never got that chip fixed and the tooth next to it had a brown cavity for years.

Dad had already lost all of his teeth. When I was very young, he wore dentures. He'd take them out and put them on his bed stand at night. But he lost those too in one of our many moves. I don't remember Dad with teeth. I mean, I don't remember what his face looked like with a pearly smile. I only remember those dentures outside of his mouth—sitting on the table or the bathroom sink. I remember the way he gummed his food, the way his lips were sunk in, the way he turned down the nuts because he couldn't chew them. He never got another set. Maybe he couldn't afford it, or maybe he just grew comfortable gumming his food. That's the thing about humans, we can get used to almost anything, even a cavity eating away at a tooth until severe pain forces a trip to Emergency.

When I finally got back to the States from Costa Rica to fix my incisor, the dentist told me that both my front teeth needed crowns and that the bill would be well over a thousand dollars. Because I had prepaid for so many of my college costs, I had enough leftover scholarship money to pay for it. By then I had already lost two other teeth: my second premolar on the upper right and the third premolar on the bottom right. Neither hurt my smile, neither made it hard for me to chew. I could go through life without those two molars and no one would ever know. It was the front teeth that bothered me. It was those front teeth that would form every perception of me in the future.

After the drilling, when the dentist got up to leave the room and I'd rinsed the blood and ground bone from my mouth, I tongued the empty space around my incisors. Two points poked out of my gums like fangs. I wondered what would happen if he never came back, if some disaster forced us to stop right then. What would the students back in Costa Rica say if they saw me and those two nubbins hanging down from my gums? What would my face look like without those two front teeth? Would my mouth sink in like Dad's? Would I start chewing like Mom? I was thirty years old and still had three more semesters of college. Could I even get a job looking like that? I told myself that if I were to walk out of the dentist office with those half teeth, then it would be my punishment for all the years of neglect.

On Berlin Street, we had so many cockroaches, they came out during the day, especially after Mom cooked a greasy meal. By the dozens they would blacken the sides of the stove and kitchen floor where hamburger or bacon grease spattered. The sight of them moving unnaturally tortoise-like and feeding horrified me. I'd scream for my dad to pick me up and carry me out of the kitchen, make him kill every one of the roaches before I'd walk back in there. At night, if I had to go to the bathroom, I'd scream for Mom to turn all the lights on between my room and the toilet so I wouldn't accidentally step on any.

When we finally moved out of that place, Mom and Dad had both been working long enough to save up for a security deposit and first month's rent for a place just outside of the city in Gates. Dad had a knack for finding nice apartments in our budget range. This was a full house in a commercial section on the corner of a busy road. We didn't care, we were just glad to be out of Berlin Street. Our new house was the last residence in a row of three directly across from the highway's exit ramp. In fact, all the houses were so perfectly aligned with the ramp that our neighbors' front door had been smashed in by a car going too fast off the highway. To the right of our rental was a bakery and large parking lot. Gina and I each had our own rooms and there was even a little yard. And, because we were outside the city boundary, we could go to the suburban school.

By then we had already moved so often that we had rarely spent a full year in the same district. It didn't change the way we felt about our new home. Every time we progressed to a nicer apartment, it felt like a fresh start. This kitchen had two ovens right on top of each other and an island countertop. The seventies architecture reminded me of the Brady Bunch house, which made it seem even more dreamlike. The living room, with a fireplace at one end, was so big that our little furniture suite from Berlin Street seemed to be swallowed up by the room. The most important thing about this house was that it had no roaches.

The bakery next to us made doughnuts in the mornings and stromboli in the afternoons. I had never had a stromboli, but after that first bite, it became a weekly event. We'd sit around our little kitchen table like a normal family and eat those freshly baked ricotta pepperoni pizza pockets, which were worlds above our slapped-together Ragu-slathered Ritz and lime Kool-Aid.

It wasn't long, however, until the first roach appeared in our kitchen. It was just after dinner. Mom was cleaning when she yelled at the "little motherfucker" on the counter. "Goddamned roaches followed us here," she said, as she slammed her fist down on its hard shell. I was disgusted. How could we have gone so far and still have them? Dad said we probably brought them in our furniture and belongings. I begged them to bomb the house immediately. I never wanted to see another roach again. We were going to a different school with new kids from normal families. Now we couldn't invite any of them over. If they knew we had roaches, they would know what kind of people we were.

Cockroaches have been around for over three hundred million years. They are a vector of human disease because they feed on waste. They can track bacteria all over a house and multiply at dizzying rates. The German cockroaches, the ones most prevalent in homes all over the world, are most often equated with low-income urban housing; they have also been blamed for allergies and asthma in urban children. In the 1970s and '80s, before Combat came along, it was almost impossible to get rid of a cockroach infestation, even with regular fumigation.

I don't know what made me think that just moving from one place to the next would alter our situation, but that was my first lesson on the nature of change. In my child's way, I learned that evolution is layered and multifaceted and takes years to actualize. Life doesn't just flip like a quarter when the situation improves. It's more like a process of reconstruction, in which only after decades of layering one small change over the last does a new veneer emerge.

By the time we moved out of Gates, I had learned to look for signs of cockroaches in every new apartment we moved into. Even when I moved out on my own years later, in every new apartment I'd pull out the refrigerator and stove to search for forgotten carcasses, scour the cupboards beneath the sinks for the little pepper-sized droppings, comb through the bathroom for the babies with their spotted shells and oblong bodies. I learned how to shake out my clothes before packing in boxes, to inspect the furniture before putting it into the truck.

Years later, when I moved out of my two-room studio to go to Costa Rica, I put everything I owned on the curb, except for some boxes of mementos that I painstakingly took outside one by one to seal into plastic containers. I shook every notebook, every letter, every page of every novel before placing it neatly into a plastic bin.

Then I let them sit outside for a few weeks before packing them away in a friend's attic. I wanted desperately to leave the roaches behind, the last vestiges of my old identity.

I was forty years old when I walked down the aisles of that grocery store with a Sara Lee cake in my basket, the blue folder on my front seat—exactly ten years after moving to Costa Rica with a rotten incisor. In the past decade I had gotten a master's degree, landed an adjunct teaching gig, then a full-time tenure-track position at the same community college I attended. I had become a career woman with healthcare and a retirement plan, but even at forty it wasn't enough. Our dental plan, like so many others, barely covers serious periodontal issues. Contrary to popular belief, being a professor, especially at the lower levels and especially at a community college, isn't a high-paying job. I made less money than most of my friends who didn't work in academia.

It's no surprise that Black and brown children and those who grew up poor feel the inequities of healthcare in deeper ways than children from higher-income families; but what's not so obvious is what happens to those children when they grow up. They often repeat the patterns again and again. Though I had shed one of the markers of poverty in my life, I had amassed debt from graduate school, from all those years in my twenties and thirties when I had to pay for dental bills out of pocket, or when I had to pay cash for bad brakes on my twelve-year-old car, or when I accumulated dozens of parking tickets for alternate-side parking—sometimes by only eight minutes. Every time one of those extraneous bills popped up, something else had to give: a late payment on the gas and electric, a missed grace period on the rent, a bounced check to the phone company, a year of smiling for photographs with a blackened tooth. And each one of those tiny acts affected another and another until all of the pins of economy, of status, of credit and career fell into a vicious cycle of struggle. I didn't even get my first credit card until I walked into that dentist office at forty years old.

That twenty-five-thousand-dollar dental bill was devastating, not just because it was a lot of money, but because I had falsely believed my past was behind me. It was the kind of news I'd learned to fold up again and again, to make so tiny that I'd forget it ever existed. But bad teeth aren't the kind of thing one can leave behind.

*

I bought my first house a few years ago. But before I put my offer in, I inspected the cupboard beneath the sink, searched the floor behind the refrigerator and stove. Flashlight in hand, got on my hands and knees and inspected every baseboard in the kitchen and bathroom, all despite the fact that I hadn't seen a roach in over fifteen years. After I moved into this house, with its little backyard, I dug a five by seven plot, which grows a little bigger each year. Last fall I harvested enough tomatoes to make eight quarts of sauce; and between the pepper, eggplant, zucchini, cucumbers, and herbs, I have enough vegetables to eat whole, organic, and healthy for most of the summer. I still have missing teeth and can only chew hard foods on the left side. But those last two empty spaces on the right are currently fitted with metal posts, one purple and one blue, drilled earlier in the year. The dentist says that I have to wait some months for them to heal before permanent crowns can be formed over them.

The Americas They Left Me

FROM *The New York Times Magazine*

IN 2015, I moved into a small back house in California, a necessary step in a divorce that was ugly and would remain so for nearly a year. At first I traded spaces with my soon-to-be ex. Then, for a year, I lived above a garage in Pomona on a pullout couch. These were awful times. One night, all three of my children were asleep, nested, innocent, seemingly safe, but I couldn't sleep. Earlier that day fourteen people were murdered and more than twenty wounded nearby in San Bernardino, and I was suddenly afraid: for my kids, for myself (as the person, impossibly, who was supposed to protect them), and for the country.

And I wondered, in that moment, what my parents would do if my life were theirs. It was hard to imagine them together, though they had been together for twenty-four years of my life. Even so, in my mind I couldn't put them in the same room or the same attitude, about anything. When they were divorcing, I went for a walk and stumbled on them sitting in lawn chairs near the family's sweat lodge. They were there, literally, to pull the lodge apart. I was shocked, because it was the first time I could remember them being in something close to agreement. They were both sad, both contemplative, both staring at the frame of sticks that had once been theirs and was symbolically a representation of their union.

My life felt as if it was being pulled apart, too: between the one I had been living (with my children and my soon-to-be ex) and the one—unknown and unknowable—to which I was headed. It was as if some dispassionate tinkerer had made a series of small cuts and extracted the spine, the plot and structure of my life as if to say, "Let's see what happens *now*." In a strong bid for mimesis, the same cuts seemed to be happening to America, the country that, like my parents, both birthed and plagued me: the same unknowing, the same uncertainty, the same darkness descending on the horizon and creeping ever closer.

I didn't know how to deal with any of this, and I'm not sure I even knew how to *be*. But I did know this: I was the sum of my parents' faults and ambitions. My father was nothing if not intense—a deep feeler whose emotions often ran a little too close to the surface. Despite his emotional architecture or perhaps because of it, he approached his jobs and his life as an opportunity to make the world better. Much of that drive had to do with the fact that America had, undeniably, saved his life. Austria, the country of his birth, tried to kill him during the Holocaust. It had turned against him.

But then there was my mother, a Native woman who grew up as an outsider in her country and for whom America was a constant threat—a country seemingly determined to grind her down and against which all of her skeptical ferocity was aimed. And so I grew up—the recipient of both my parents' attitudes about the republic—perplexed, confused, almost paralyzed.

My mother would be dead in five years; my father, in the final throes of Alzheimer's, in mere months. There I was, with my kids asleep in the next room, sitting in that outer dark, blinking confusedly in the light of my personal and patriotic wars. What to do about this country that saved my father's life and tried to destroy my mother's? What to do about myself? These questions plagued me, defined me, and redefined my relationship to my parents. I never would figure out how to answer them until they both were gone.

My father, Robert Treuer, was born in Vienna in 1926. His earliest memory was of crouching, terrified, in his seat at the Wiener Staatsoper during a production of *Don Giovanni*. He recalled (vividly and often) how scared he was when the winged demon dragged Don Giovanni (unrepentant) to hell; how my father grabbed his mother's hand; how she laughed at him. It was only a few years later, in 1934, that Fascists would come into power (also remembered vividly and often).

My grandfather dipped into the family's meager savings to pay for English lessons for my father, delivered in the back of the stationery store he managed in their working-class neighborhood. My father was taught how to cook, how to mend his socks and sew on buttons, how to navigate public transportation. "We won't be able to stay here for long," my grandfather told him. "And the future lies in the West, and the future is spoken in English." He wasn't wrong.

After the Anschluss in March 1938, things got worse. Just before the Nazis smashed the windows on Kristallnacht, the family itself broke apart. My grandmother and father fled, sometimes together, sometimes separately, through Germany, Belgium, England, and Ireland, where my father found refuge at a Quaker boarding school in Waterford. My grandfather went into hiding in the Austrian countryside posing as a farm laborer. And, with the exception of two cousins and an aunt and uncle, the winged demons came for the rest of the family. They were, eventually, turned to ash.

Against all odds, my grandparents and father were reunited in Southampton, and in 1939, they sailed on the S.S. *Westernland* under a Nazi flag, docking in New York Harbor in February of that year. By 1940, the family settled in Yellow Springs, Ohio. In those early days, they bought the only house they could afford, in the Black part of Yellow Springs, across from an AME church. My father's closest friends were his neighbors and the other outsiders in their integrated high school. He hadn't been in the country more than a few years before he joined sit-ins at lunch counters around Yellow Springs and Dayton. He had been a second-class citizen in Austria, and so he made common cause with the second-class citizens in Yellow Springs.

When he turned eighteen in 1944, a lot changed: My father became a father, a soldier, and an American citizen. The Army, in its infinite wisdom, pulled this fluent German-and-English speaker from his unit en route to Belgium, taught him Japanese, and sent him to the Pacific, where he served in the Philippines and, later, in Okinawa. Even there he managed to find common cause. He made friends with a few Japanese POWs and, in Japanese, asked them to install a hidden kill switch on his jeep, a vehicle that was easy to steal at the time.

My father was a small, compact, powerful man. And he possessed a kind of intense charm. There was a great power in his legs and arms; it wasn't until he was seventy and I was twenty-six that I could honestly say I could outwork him. His power, I think, was a result of his energy. The man never seemed to stop moving. After the war, he returned to Ohio—suddenly home and just as suddenly the father of three young boys with his first wife, Nancy—and entered a new chapter of life as the Zelig of civic engagement. He found work in a steel mill outside Chicago, as a shop steward and as an organizer for the AFL-CIO.

He and Nancy and their three sons eventually moved to northern Minnesota, where my father got his teaching degree and took a job as an English teacher at Cass Lake Senior High School on the Leech Lake Reservation. It was the only school that would hire this German-and-English-speaking Austrian immigrant. He taught Shakespeare to Native American children. I'm unclear why his job as a teacher came to an end after a few years. He says it was because he decided to teach *The Communist Manifesto*. ("If these kids are going to hate Communism, they should know something about Communism!" he told me.)

After his job at the high school, he worked for the Bureau of Indian Affairs and the Community Action Program, which was a part of President Lyndon Johnson's War on Poverty. As a soldier in that war, ferociously committed to helping people, he traveled to reservations all over the state—White Earth, Leech Lake, Red Lake, Bois Forte, Fond du Lac. He once delivered roses to an elder at Nett Lake in January by keeping them on his lap for the entire two-hundred-mile icy drive. She had never received roses or flowers of any kind.

Eventually, my father and Nancy divorced. I still don't know why. And he and my mother began dating. My mother suspected there was overlap between the end of his first marriage and the start of the second, beginning a theme that would define their relationship and their divorce. My mother shared, with great bitterness, how during their first "date," he told her that he and Nancy were through, and yet my mother came downstairs in the morning and noticed Nancy's bathrobe, slippers, and things all over the house. After a few years—having run out of jobs in Minnesota—he and my mother moved to Washington, DC, in 1967.

Of all the things a person could do during America's postwar boom, my dad cleaved to public service: labor unions, teaching, social-service administration, community building. But by 1978, after they'd been living in Washington for ten years and my three siblings and I had been born (my older half-siblings were grown long before we arrived), my mom wanted to move back to our reservation, Leech Lake, in northern Minnesota. So we moved. My father loved Native people in a curiously modern way—unpaternalistically. I once asked him how it felt to be on the reservation, to be among us. He spread his hands wide. "I had been kicked out of my country and persecuted," he said. "So had they. We understood one another."

Here was a man who, back when he lived in Washington, stood in line to have a flag he had purchased himself fly over the US Capitol for a day. Every Memorial Day thereafter, he flew that flag over our house on the reservation. He loved this country in spite of everything he knew about it. He loved it in a way I never felt I could. Because, however much I was my father's son, I was also my mother's.

My mother, Margaret Seelye, was born at the Cass Lake Indian Hospital in 1943. She grew up in a 12-by-14-foot cabin in our ancestral village of Bena. She and her four siblings were drastically poor. They had electricity but no plumbing or heat. They survived the way most of their neighbors survived: by harvesting and selling wild rice, snaring rabbits, and hunting partridge and deer. She often told me stories of how the Native kids at Cass Lake High School did not have to begin the school year until after the wild-rice harvest was over, usually in mid-to-late September. When she returned for her senior year, she was walking down the hallway to her first class and the principal passed her and asked her what she was doing. "Going to class," she said.

"Why?" he asked.

"Why what?"

"Why bother?"

She bothered anyway and graduated in 1961, attended St. Luke's nursing school in Duluth, and then returned to Leech Lake, where she founded our reservation's Community Health Program, established an ambulance service, and wrote the grants that funded Red Lake Reservation's nursing program.

After marrying my father, she moved to Washington with him, and after my brother and I were born, she enrolled in law school at Catholic University. She went on to become the first American Indian woman lawyer in Minnesota and the first American Indian woman judge in the country.

There is much I still don't understand about her. I don't understand how someone who had been told, in ways direct and indirect, that she wasn't supposed to achieve anything could end up driven by so much ambition. She was simply wired to want, despite the country's attempts to prevent it. My father seemed to labor under a vow of engagement with the country and its institutions, but my mother was moved by something else.

For her the answer was not engagement but armor, and the best armor wasn't what money could buy; it was money itself. She was obsessed with it. Having it. Having more of it. Making sure more was coming in than was going out. Accumulation, for her, was key. Money—and nothing else—was going to keep her safe. In 2002, Walmart came, at long last, to Bemidji, Minnesota. She was pretty excited about it. I chided her by asking if she wouldn't rather support local businesses. "Local businesses?" she sneered. "You mean the ones owned by the people who used to follow me around to make sure I wasn't stealing when I was kid? No thanks."

One story she fixated on, the one that would come up regularly no matter what we were talking about, was how, when she was twelve, the sheriff stole her rice. Every fall the extended family went, en masse, to harvest rice in the old way: in boats that were pushed along the weedy margins of lakes and rivers by a long pole while another person used carved cedar knockers to beat the ripe rice into the bottom of the boat. It's arduous, even under the best circumstances. At the end of the season, the rice was sold by the pound, and that was pretty much the sole source of income with which to buy school clothes, kerosene, lard, and flour to get them through the winter.

One fall, they spent a few days camping and ricing at Raven's Point on Lake Winnibigoshish near the village. The weather was terrible: stormy and windy and cold. My mother and her ricing partner had been given a flat-bottomed plywood duck boat to use. It was awkward, and the wind caught it and blew them sideways. My mother, who weighed less than one hundred pounds, leaned on the pole and tried to keep them on course. By the time they got back to the landing, everyone was exhausted, hands numb and tingly from gripping the pole and the knockers, covered in rice beards and rice worms, but content: they had managed to collect hundreds of pounds.

Waiting for them at the landing was the sheriff. He told them they had been ricing illegally, and he confiscated the harvest. Everyone knew, because everyone knew him, that he was going to take the rice and sell it himself and keep the money. But there was nothing she or anyone else could do. I think this small episode stood in for what the country was "up to." It was, to my mother and to my community more generally, never up to any good. As for the "community" itself, it was made up of our relatives and neighbors and the village of Bena as well as the other smaller villages at Leech Lake and White Earth in a loose constellation of relatedness. But it was principally among the family where my mother was comfortable. She would be tight, rigid with distrust the farther away from Bena she traveled. Back among her uncles and aunts and cousins, she would really laugh.

And so I inherited from her the same distrust, the same belief that it was a matter of time before the country came for me. I did all the "right" things: I achieved, I barely misbehaved, I earned and I kept my hands, metaphorically and literally, where they could be seen. I inherited, too, for better or worse, that desperate wanting. Ambition and greed, for her and for me, were the armor that protected us from the spears that would pin us to the ground if they could.

I came of age in the 1990s with the different and warring natures of my parents' attitudes fighting for room in my head. While I was in college, the multicultural wave crested, and I couldn't help angrily noting the superficiality of it. It seemed that all anyone wanted from Native culture was the "three F's": food, folklore, and fashion. As part of that multicultural process I, my mother's son, was skeptical of even the adoration that was beginning to creep into how people thought of me, my tribe, my reservation, and, by extension, Native Americans generally: exoticized others who were interesting in direct proportion to our suffering. So it became easy to align myself with my mother's response to America. She never wanted to run for tribal or governmental office, and unlike my father, who was an aggressive institution joiner and builder, she would never put herself in a position in which anyone had control over her.

Around this time, when I was home for the holidays in December 1990, there was a memorial walk and ride, culminating in a vigil at the Bemidji waterfront commemorating the hundred-year anniversary of the murder of more than three hundred men, women, and children at Wounded Knee, South Dakota. My father was one of the organizers, and he roped me and a college friend into tending "the sacred fire," which had been built on the ice near the statues of Paul Bunyan and Babe. It was bitterly cold, as it was at Wounded Knee a century earlier. I was just as bitter at having to stand out there and tend those flames, and it occurred to me then that if there was ever a better metaphor for the country, I had yet to see it: a fire built on top of lake ice, the flames purely decorative and not powerful enough to warm us or melt the ice underneath.

My father gave a speech to the few people around the fire. He was a man who savored words, and he was in no hurry. I don't remember the substance of his speech. I don't remember any of his speech, actually, except his repeated use of the word "justice," which he gave an extra spin by landing on the "-ice" for a few beats too long. Justissss. My friend and I laughed through the frost of our breath, and it became something we repeated to each other over the years as an inside joke. My father's earnestness, his complete lack of irony, his belief in the rightness of things and the improvability of both our nature and our republic—it all embarrassed me.

My mother was not at the memorial. She did not stand by the fire. She was, I imagine, at home smoking the cigarettes that would help kill her a few decades later. Even my parents' choice in cigarettes betrayed them. My father smoked Winners. My mother favored Merits.

But though my father believed this country was ultimately a just place, he never avoided its history, either. He wasn't naïve. As we drove into Bemidji, following the lake past the waterfront, my father would remind me regularly of burial mounds in the area that had been destroyed to make room for the city. When a nearby road was being widened, he heard, a number of graves were found, and the construction workers had wired skulls to the radiators of their bulldozers. When driving to Minneapolis, he rarely failed to mention how in 1850, the government forced nearly three thousand Ojibwe to travel 150 miles from Wisconsin to Sandy Lake, Minnesota, to receive the annuities they depended on. They arrived in October and had to wait until December. Overcrowded, underfed, and exposed to the weather, more than a hundred died waiting, and 250 more died on their long walk home.

Not that I really needed him to tell me that Indians were expected to suffer. I felt it in the very low expectations my teachers had of me. I heard it in my band teacher's voice when he told my class that all "Indians were lazy and on welfare and should return to Canada where they're from." I saw it in the bruises on my uncle's arms, neck, and ribs after he was "detained" by Bemidji police. I was immersed in it when I went to reservations like White Earth, where many of our people were relocated in an effort to terminate and dismantle other reservations.

I felt it, too, on my way to and from college in the smug towns all across Wisconsin, Illinois, Indiana, Pennsylvania, and New Jersey—towns with Indian names but no Native Americans at all: our lowness, our abjectness, and the social and governmental structures that tried to keep it that way. This great dreamy country squatted like a rock, like grief itself, on my chest and made it hard to breathe.

My parents divorced not long after the Wounded Knee memorial. They had been living separate lives inside the house for years before that; my mother went so far as to renovate the house so that she had her own room, ostensibly because my father snored. Really it was because they didn't like each other anymore. When they finally divorced, they both came to me with their disappointments. My mom felt betrayed by my father's adultery, and my father felt that my mother simply didn't love him anymore. Both of them were right.

After the divorce, they each—in their houses about a mile apart—began their respective declines. In 2001, my mother was diagnosed with lung cancer, which she managed to beat. People will always surprise you, but they will never break character. Instead of feeling as if she won the lottery, which was my reaction to her remission, what her cancer taught her was that death was indeed coming. She was overprescribed oxycodone, which dampened, shaped, and authored the end of her life in March 2020. It was the oxy—not her lung cancer, and not her subsequent bout with pancreatic cancer, which she also beat—that did her in.

My mom lost her life because she lost her body, but my father lost his because he lost his mind. One time, weeks before my father's final decline, he and I were having lunch. We were at the tail end of things, and I knew it. His Alzheimer's had taken most everything by then. The stories he told were getting fewer and fewer—the tapes he played, that we all play, as we narrate the meanings of our lives, had been degraded to the point that only a few remained.

Pausing between bites, I asked my father about the food in the Army. Was it as bad as everyone says? He shrugged. "I had no complaints," he said. This was not surprising: he was one of the least complaining people I had ever known. "For the first time in my life I got three meals a day, as much as I wanted to eat!" That was not surprising either: he had an indiscriminate palate.

Then, when I least expected it, he kept talking and told a new story, or at least one that was new to me. When he was at the base in Okinawa back in 1945, the kitchen staff would haul huge oil drums into the mess, and the soldiers, my father among them, dumped their scraps there. Off the base, meanwhile, the Japanese and Okinawans were starving. They would line up near the waste barrels outside and pick the trash clean. "They were so poor!" my father said, the tears starting to come. "They were so poor they didn't even have bowls. But they put the food in whatever they had: shell casings, bags, baskets, even their hats."

The base commander got wind of it and began ordering the cooks and orderlies to douse the leftover food with bleach. "They were so thin! They were starving to death, Dave!" He, unlike most of the other soldiers, had a good relationship with the Black cooks and dishwashers, so he asked them to disobey the order and set the food aside, and he would take care of it. Together they hauled the barrels outside the base and the Japanese lined up down the block. They bowed to the kitchen workers and they bowed to my father.

His tears were flowing freely now. I asked him if it was, I don't know, *weird*, or if he felt weird, considering what the Japanese Army had done in China in Nanking, and to American soldiers at Bataan and in the Philippines and Malaysia and Korea. He pounded the table. "These were people, David. Starving people! That was enough. That was all I needed to know."

I had been so ashamed of him for so long: ashamed of what I considered to be his weaknesses, ashamed of the surplus of feeling. And now, finally, I had managed to be ashamed of myself. "How can you stand the things this country does?" I asked. "How can you live with it?" I was thinking of the base commander who ordered the food doused in bleach. I was thinking, too, of myself. I hadn't chosen America any more than it had chosen me. To abandon it would be to abandon my tribe and tribal homelands. Something I couldn't possibly do.

"You chose this place," I said, gesturing to the house, the birds, the pine trees scratching the screens. "You chose this country. So how can you stand the things it does?"

He stopped eating and put down his silverware and spread those great gripping hands of his. "No one else wanted me," he said. "I was hunted down in Austria, barely tolerated in England and Ireland. But America saved my life. It saved my *life*. So it's my job to save it from itself. That's the deal. That's the bargain."

After that lunch, in January 2016, the same month he was to have turned ninety, my father died. I think he was ready to die. We knew it was coming, too. Because of his Alzheimer's, he had been dying by degrees. The blood vessels in his brain had become brittle. (For much of his life, he smoked two packs of cigarettes a day.) They'd been snapping like dried spaghetti. Snap. Snap. Snap. Even before the onset of his Alzheimer's, he was given to extravagant moans and exclamations.

I lived with him and helped take care of him for about five months. Every morning when I came down the stairs, he looked at me with surprise and wonder. "Dave!" he said. "What are you doing here?" I would tell him I was living there. Then his tears would come. "That's great news, Dave. Just great. But"—and then he sighed in that way of his, so familiar to me—"I've got bad news." Pause. "I have Alzheimer's."

"Ah, that's a tough break, Pops. But I'm here, and we'll be okay. You'll be okay."

But he wasn't. After I returned to California, the family hired help. A home-health aide cleaned him and bathed him. His driver sat with him as he noted and counted the birds at the feeder. He had two strokes and didn't talk much after the second one.

He was eventually moved into my brother Paul's house in Duluth, 140 miles from the home he built on the edge of the Leech Lake Reservation. Paul had done the lion's share of coordinating his care before the move and took care of him almost single-handedly after the move. It was there that things got worse. I wasn't around to see it, but according to Paul, our father sometimes woke at night, disori- ented, crying out and screaming. He began to wander, but not far. One place he was drawn to was the refrigerator. My brother would find him there, lit by its glow. He also found him on the back deck, staring at Lake Superior, moved to tears by the water.

My father ultimately died in bed. Slowly, suddenly, all at once: he was gone. Everyone, it seemed, came to Duluth to pay respects. My brother kept my father's body, unembalmed, in the downstairs bedroom until all of us had the chance to spend some time with him before he was cremated. It was winter, and cold, which was convenient. I visited with the family and—to show I was really okay—got as many people as I could involved in a game to see who could stand on one leg the longest. Finally, my brother An- ton looked at me and said, "Shouldn't you go back there and say goodbye?"

Some of the objects in his room were so familiar, had moved from place to place with him. The same painting that hung in his childhood room in Vienna graced the wall here. It had not only survived the war but survived the many separations the war entailed. There was also the walking stick with ribbons and eagle feathers that meant something to him for reasons I disparaged while he was alive. His slippers were there, too.

There was no avoiding it—there he was. His mouth was open. His eyes were closed. He was dead in the manner he had slept. My father's sleep had been something epic for him and for those of us condemned to need him *while* he was sleeping. As kids, when we woke him up, he did so with terrified energy. His hands shot out to the sides and his eyes bounced around the room wildly, and he asked, "What WHAT WHAT IS IT?" I always thought his frustra- tion had to do with me and what I wanted. I didn't understand his panic had more to do with him.

For someone who had escaped so much, for whom safety was not something given as much as it was something stolen; for some- one who endured so much loss and against whom such vast forces of the state had been mobilized; for whom death was assigned at such an early age, sleep must have been the great, unavoidable helplessness, a daily unbridling of consciousness in exchange for the possibility (but not the certainty) of waking up the next day to do it all over again.

Here was a boy who fled the Holocaust; someone who had started fresh over and over again; whose status as a survivor turned him into something of an idealist; someone who saw that this country had a lot to offer; someone who could be in this country in a way that I—a Native who grew up on a reservation and had my own relationship to the government that put me there—could not. I looked at my father's shrunken face, his jaw dropped down onto his throat, and missed his tears.

Then I left. Back to New Mexico where I was living temporarily. Back to my own divorce that was almost done. (Slowly, suddenly, all at once: it was gone.) Back to 2016 and a country that felt as if it were falling apart.

In the months after his death, I had a chance to visit my old writing mentor at her home. She asked about my father, of whom she was terribly fond. I said he'd passed away. "The living elude us," she told me, "and it's only possible to understand people after they're dead, because it's only then they sit still long enough for us to see them clearly." She, too, would be gone in a few years.

It was only after he "sat still" that I could see him clearly and could see, also, that I had begun to absorb some of his worldview. By degrees—not epiphanically, not pegged to any one thing—his belief in this country stopped seeming ridiculous to me. The polarities within me were in the process of being reversed. I could no longer write off this country as my mother had. I couldn't see it as a place that existed only to exercise its worst impulses. Hope, of all things—for my country and myself—began to filter in. It was, perhaps, the best and only way I could honor my father.

My ideals, and those of the country, weren't merely notional or aspirational. They had some kind of visible substance, and you could, sometimes, see them in practice. In order to survive, I needed to hold within me two opposing ideas: I needed to believe in my mother's version of things, that America will always try its best to break us down, and we must stand guard against it. I also needed to hold on to my father's vision that America can, and sometimes does, nurture and sustain us.

This country is a terrible country, and this country is not. This country has done its best to take and conquer and kill my Native life, and at the same time it has saved my father's life and created mine. There is a great ugliness on the land and also a great beauty.

This country would and will do its worst at the same time it embodies the most nurturing habits our civilization has to offer. There is no reconciling these contradictions; they cannot be reduced or done away with. I must, *we* must, find a way to contain both. And I had, as we all do, the dead to guide me—first in 2016 and again in 2020—when I left my parents' sides for the last time and traveled back home to my children.

Contributors' Notes

Notable Essays and Literary Nonfiction of 2022

Notable Special Issues of 2022

Contributors' Notes

CIARA ALFARO is a Chicanx writer, romantic, and descendant of magicians from Texas. Her work has appeared in *Cutthroat*'s *Puro Chicanx Writers of the 21st Century*, *Water~Stone Review*, *swamp pink*, and elsewhere. Most recently, she won *Iron Horse Literary Review*'s 2022 PhotoFinish Contest. Her work has been supported by awards and fellowships from Colgate University, the Anderson Center, Hedgebrook, and others. She holds an MFA in creative writing from the University of Minnesota. Currently, she is at work on a memoir about queer mestiza girlhood, monsterhood, and magic.

JILLIAN BARNET'S poems and essays have appeared in *North American Review*, *New Letters*, *Nimrod*, and *Image*, among others. She holds an MFA in poetry from Vermont College of Fine Arts, is a Pushcart Prize nominee, and the author of the poetry chapbook *Falling Bodies*. Links to some of her work can be found at jillianbarnetwrites.com. She taught writing and literature at Pennsylvania State University and Chatham University, and now lives on a tiny farm in the Finger Lakes where she is at work on a memoir.

SYLVIE BAUMGARTEL is the author of *Song of Songs* (FSG, 2019) and *Pink* (FSG, 2021). Her poems have appeared in *The New Yorker*, *Paris Review*, *Financial Times*, *The Nation*, *The New York Review of Books*, *Subtropics*, *Raritan*, *Harvard Review*, *Ploughshares*, *The Virginia Quarterly Review*, the PEN Poetry Series, *The Unprofessionals: New American Writing from the Paris Review*, and elsewhere. She lives in Santa Fe, New Mexico.

ERIC BORSUK is the author of *American Animals* (Turner, 2020), the memoir featured in the acclaimed motion picture of the same name. He has written for such award-winning publications as The Marshall Project, *Vice*, and *Virginia Quarterly Review*. Borsuk's essay, "Bidders of the Din," which chronicles his experiences in the US federal prison system, received the 2022 Sidney Award from David Brooks of *The New York Times* and was featured in *Longreads' Best of 2022*. He works with organizations around the US to spotlight stories of individuals impacted by the criminal justice system and incarceration. Borsuk lives in Brooklyn, where he serves on the board of directors of Die Jim Crow Records (DJC Records), the nation's first nonprofit record label for prison-impacted musicians.

CHRIS DENNIS is the author of the story collection *Here Is What You Do*. A regular contributor at *Granta*, his other stories and essays have appeared in *Paris Review*, *Playgirl*, *McSweeney's*, *Astra*, *Lit Hub*, *Bull*, and *Guernica*. He is the recipient of an NEA Fellowship and a *New York Times* Sidney Award for long-form journalism. He lives in southern Illinois and works in public health as a recovery and overdose prevention coordinator.

XUJUN EBERLEIN is an immigrant writer who has lived in two different worlds. Recipient of the artist fellowship in fiction/creative nonfiction from the Massachusetts Cultural Council, a fiction scholarship from the Bread Loaf Writers' Conference, and a Goldfarb Nonfiction Fellowship from VCCA, Xujun is the author of the story collection *Apologies Forthcoming*, and an essayist whose writing has been recognized with special mentions in the Pushcart Prize anthologies and as notable in *Best American Essays*. Her work can be found in *AGNI*, *American Literary Review*, *Brevity*, *The Iowa Review*, *LARB*, *New England Review*, and elsewhere. She holds a PhD in Transportation Science from MIT and an MFA in Creative Nonfiction from Emerson College. Currently, she is at work on a memoir and teaches creative writing at GrubStreet in Boston.

SANDRA HAGER ELIASON was raised on the Iron Range of northern Minnesota and graduated from Augsburg University in Minneapolis with a degree in English. She then took classes for her premed credits at North Dakota State University, and graduated with an MD from the University of North Dakota School of Medicine. She practiced as a family physician for more than thirty years before retiring in 2017. Since then, she has been writing full-time. In 2016, she won the Minnesota Medicine Magazine Arts Edition writing contest, and she has been published in *Bluestem*, *West Trade Review*, and *The Linden Review*. She has been anthologized in *Tales from Six Feet Apart*, *Pure Slush*, *vol. 23*, and *True Stories About Love*, *vol. 2* by Chicago Story Press, and had three articles in the *Brevity Blog*. Her book reviews have appeared in *Rain Taxi* and the *Brevity Blog*. She is also a book reviewer for *Hippocampus Magazine*. Dr. Eliason lives with her husband in Minneapolis, where she has a garden in the summer and a cat to warm her

lap in the winter. Look for her on Instagram @sheliasonmd, or dreliason
writer.com.

GEORGE ESTREICH's publications include a book of poems, *Textbook Illus-
trations of the Human Body*; the Oregon Book Award–winning memoir *The
Shape of the Eye* (2011); and *Fables and Futures: Biotechnology, Disability, and
the Stories We Tell Ourselves* (2019), which NPR's *Science Friday* named a Best
Science Book of 2019. He's also the coeditor, with Rachel Adams, of Alison
Piepmeier's posthumously published book, *Unexpected: Parenting, Prenatal
Testing, and Down Syndrome* (NYU, 2021). He lives in Corvallis, Oregon,
where he teaches in the MFA program at Oregon State University and
plays guitar in the band Mule on Fire.

MERRILL JOAN GERBER has written thirty books including *The Kingdom of
Brooklyn*, winner of the Ribalow Prize from *Hadassah Magazine*, and *King
of the World*, winner of the Pushcart Editors' Book Award. Her fiction has
been published in *The New Yorker*, *The Sewanee Review*, *The Atlantic*, *Made-
moiselle*, and *Redbook*, and her essays in *The American Scholar*, *Salmagundi*,
and *Commentary*. She has won an O. Henry Award and a Wallace Stegner
fiction fellowship to Stanford University. She retired in 2020 after teaching
writing at the California Institute of Technology for thirty-two years. Her
literary archive is now at the Beinecke Rare Book Library at Yale. A new
book of her essays, titled *Revelation at the Food Bank*, will be published in
December 2023.

DEBRA GWARTNEY is the author of two memoirs, *Live Through This*, finalist
for the National Book Critics Circle Award, and *I Am a Stranger Here Myself*,
winner of the Willa Award for nonfiction. She is the recipient of two Pushcart Prizes and her essay "Fire and Ice" was included in *Best American Essays
2022*. She lives in western Oregon.

EDWARD HOAGLAND, a contributing editor of the *American Scholar*, is the
author of many books of essays, travel, and fiction. His most recent novel
is *In the Country of the Blind*.

LAURA KIPNIS is a critic, essayist, and the author of eight books, most
recently *Love in the Time of Contagion: A Diagnosis* (2022). She lives in New
York.

PHILLIP LOPATE is the author of four essay collections (*Bachelorhood,
Against Joie de Vivre, Portrait of My Body*, and *Portrait Inside My Head*) and the
editor of *Art of the Personal Essay, The Glorious American Essay, The Golden Age
of the American Essay*, and *The Contemporary American Essay*. His other books
include *Being with Children, Waterfront*, and *Notes on Sontag*.

CELESTE MARCUS is the managing editor of *Liberties*.

SAM MEEKINGS is a British novelist and poet. He is the author of *Under Fishbone Clouds* (called "a poetic evocation of the country and its people" by the *New York Times*) and *The Book of Crows*. He has also been featured on the BBC website, in *The Independent*, on *Arena* on Radio 1, and in *National Geographic*. He recently received an award from the Society of Authors, and he has been published in a number of international magazines and academic journals. He has spent the last few years living and working in China and the Middle East. He balances his time between teaching, raising two kids as a single father, and drinking copious cups of tea.

SIGRID NUNEZ is the author of nine novels, including *The Friend*, a *New York Times* bestseller and winner of the 2018 National Book Award; *What Are You Going Through*, and *The Vulnerables*, which is scheduled for publication in November 2023. Nunez is also the author of *Sempre Susan: A Memoir of Susan Sontag*. She has been the recipient of a Whiting Award, a Berlin Prize Fellowship, the Rome Prize in Literature, and a Guggenheim. Her books have been translated into thirty languages.

KATHRYN SCHULZ is a staff writer at *The New Yorker* and the author of *Being Wrong: Adventures in the Margin of Error*. She won a National Magazine Award and a Pulitzer Prize in 2015 for "The Really Big One," an article about seismic risk in the Pacific Northwest. Her other essays and reporting have appeared in *The Best American Science and Nature Writing, The Best American Travel Writing*, and *The Best American Food Writing*. She served as the guest editor of *The Best American Essays 2021*. Her most recent book is *Lost & Found: Reflections on Grief, Gratitude, and Happiness*. A native of Ohio, she lives with her family on the Eastern Shore of Maryland.

ROBERT ANTHONY SIEGEL is the author of a memoir, *Criminals* (Counterpoint), and two novels, *All the Money in the World* (Random House) and *All Will Be Revealed* (MacAdam/Cage.) His work has appeared in the *New York Times, Smithsonian, Paris Review, The Drift*, and *Ploughshares*, among other magazines. He has been a Fulbright scholar in Taiwan, a Mombukagakusho fellow in Japan, a writing fellow at the Fine Arts Work Center in Provincetown, and a Paul Engle fellow at the Iowa Writers' Workshop. Other awards include O. Henry and Pushcart Prizes.

SCOTT SPENCER was raised in Chicago and now lives in New York State's Hudson Valley. He has taught at the Writers' Workshop at the University of Iowa, Columbia University, the University of Virginia, Williams College, and the Bard Prison Initiative. His journalism has appeared in *Rolling Stone*, the *New York Times, First of the Month, The New Yorker*, and many other periodicals. He is the author of fourteen novels, including *Preservation Hall, Endless Love, A Ship Made of Paper, Man in the Woods*, and, most recently, *An Ocean Without a Shore*. Currently, he is writing, and rewriting, and rewriting again a novel set in Chicago in the mid-1950s through the early 1960s.

ANGELIQUE STEVENS teaches creative writing, literature of genocide, and race literatures. Her nonfiction can be found in *The Best American Essays 2022, LitHub, New England Review*, and *Granta*, among others. She holds an MFA in Creative Nonfiction from Bennington College and an MA from SUNY Brockport in Literature. Her other honors include an alumni fellowship from Bennington College's MFA Program; fellowships from Bread Loaf, Tin House, Sewanee, and Kenyon Review Writers Workshops; a fellowship from the inaugural cohort of the Periplus Collective; and a fellowship from the Lighthouse Writers Book Project. She is a founding member of the Straw Mat Writers; and she is a member of the board of directors of Water for South Sudan. She finds inspiration in wandering—being in places that push the boundaries of comfort, experience, knowledge, and hunger.

Bestselling author DAVID TREUER is Ojibwe from Leech Lake Reservation in northern Minnesota. He graduated from Princeton University in 1992 (where he wrote senior theses in both anthropology and creative writing) and three years later published his first novel, *Little* (Graywolf). After receiving his PhD in anthropology, he published two more novels, *The Hiawatha* (Picador, 1999) and the award-winning *The Translation of Dr. Apelles* (Graywolf and Vintage, 2006). He is also the author of a book of criticism, *Native American Fiction: A User's Manual* (Graywolf, 2006), a work of nonfiction, *Rez Life: An Indian's Journey Through Reservation Life* (Grove, 2012), and a fourth novel, *Prudence* (Riverhead Books, 2015). His most recent book, *The Heartbeat of Wounded Knee: Native America from 1890 to the Present* was a *New York Times* bestseller, a National Book Award finalist, a Minnesota Book Prize winner, a California Book Prize winner, shortlisted for the Carnegie Medal, and a *Los Angeles Times* Book Prize finalist. His essays and stories have appeared in the *New York Times, Granta, Harper's, Esquire, the Washington Post, Lucky Peach,* the *Los Angeles Times,* among other outlets. He divides his time between his home on the Leech Lake Reservation and Los Angeles, where he is a professor of English at USC.

Notable Essays and Literary Nonfiction of 2022

SELECTED BY ROBERT ATWAN

Sandy Pool
   If Body/Dora, *Room*, #45/3
Dacia Price
   Mitosis, *Forge Literary Magazine*,
   November 21
Emily Raboteau
   Exodus, 2020, *Bomb*, #159
Hugh Raffles
   On Stones, Big and Small, *Orion*,
   Winter
David Raney
   Ink and Memory, *bioStories*,
   December
Kate Ravilious
   Priestess, Poet, Politician,
   Archaeology, November/December
Matthew Raymond
   The Father, *New Letters*, 88/3&4
Amy Reardon
   Stuck, *Believer Logger*, February 25
Jeremy Redmon
   Tell the Kids I Love Them, *Oxford
   American*, 117
Will Rees
   Waiting Room, *Granta*, #158
Robin Reif
   To the Woman Whose Body I
   Washed, *Off Assignment*, August 9
Alexis Richland
   My Body, My Theology, *The
   Gettysburg Review*, 33/4
Diane Roberts
   Miss Betty, *Oxford American*, #116
Sandy Roberston
   If You Weren't There, *Colorado
   Review*, 49/3
Elizabeth Lindsey Rogers
   Shame, *The Cincinnati
   Review*, #19/1
James Silas Rogers
   The Erratics of Early Reading, *Oh
   Reader*, Winter
Lee Ann Roripaugh
   Re-Membering: An Archaeological
   Catalogue, *South Dakota Review*,
   #56/3

Laurence Ross
   The Star Essay, *The Georgia Re-
   view*, 76/4
Becca Rothfeld
   For the Sake of Argument: Defend-
   ing Debate, *The Yale Review*, 110/2
Anuradha Roy
   About the Dogs, *Freeman's*, October
Nicole Rudick
   A Glamorous Patron Saint, *Oprah*,
   March 25
Brandon Rushton
   The Unincorporated Bridge,
   Terrain.org, June
Witold Rybczynski
   Portrait of a Marriage in Six Homes,
   The American Scholar, 91/1
Siavash Saadlou
   My Mom Told Me, *Southeast Review*,
   #40/1
Joe Sacksteder
   Against Quirky Writing, *Michigan
   Quarterly Review*, #61/1
Amory Rowe Salem
   Family Poker, *Solstice*, Summer
Annie Sand
   Of Metaphors and Snow Boots,
   Guernica, May 23
James Scales
   Cicadas, *The Hopkins
   Review*, 15/2
Adrienne Ross Scanlan
   Questions of Gratitude, *Pangyrus*,
   June 7
Suzanne Scanlon
   The Moving Target of Being,
   Granta, #160
Lindzi Scharf
   My Baby Girl Is Gone, *Los Angeles
   Times*, July 29
Mattathias Schwartz
   The Ayahuasca Diaries, *Insider*,
   June 26
Amy Lee Scott
   How Do You Name a Hurricane?
   New Ohio Review, #31

Notable Special Issues of 2022

Alta, The Joan Didion Issue, eds. William R. Hearst III & Blaise Zerega, #19

American Poetry Review, 50, ed. Elizabeth Scanlon, 51/6

The American Scholar, Ulysses at 100, ed. Sudip Bose, 91/3

Aster(ix), Mothers Unearthed, eds. Emily Raboteau & Tanya Shirazi, September

Astra, Ecstasy, eds. Nadja Spiegelman & Samuel Rutter, #1

The Baffler, Reality Minus, ed. Jonathon Sturgeon, #64

Belmont Story Review, Witness, ed. Sara Wigal, VII

Bennington Review, Return to a Meadow, ed. Michael Dumanis, #10

The Boston Review, The Politics of Pleasure, eds. Deborah Chasman & Joshua Cohen, 47/3

Capsule Stories, Swimming, ed. Carolina VonKampen, Summer

Creative Nonfiction, Experiments in Voice, ed. Lee Gutkind, #78

Denver Quarterly, Indigenous Voices, ed. W. Scott Howard, #56/4

Ecotone, The Ocean Issue, ed. David Gessner, #33

Epiphany, The Illusions Issue, guest ed. Jose Diego Medina, Summer

Exposition Review, Flux, eds. Anniee Ellingston & Mellinda Hensley, VII

The Fiddlehead, Creative Nonfiction Issue, ed. Rowan McCandless, #292

Freeman's, Animals, ed. John Freeman, October

The Georgia Review, Southern Post Colonial (SoPoCo), ed. Gerald Maa, #76/1

Granta, Sister, Brother, ed. Sigrid Rausing, #161

The Hedgehog Review, Hope Itself, ed. Jay Tolson, 24/3

Indiana Review, Folio: Borders Between Worlds, ed. Shreya Fadia, #44/1

Iron Horse Literary Review, Bliss Issue, ed. Leslie Jill Patterson, #24/2

Jelly Bucket, Indigenous Voices, guest ed. Annette Saunooke Clapsaddle, #12

Kenyon Review, Angry Mamas, guest editor Emily Raboteau, XLIV/4

The LARB Quarterly, What Is L.A.? ed. Boris Dralyuk, #33

Meat for Tea, Electric, ed. Elizabeth MacDuffie, 16/4

Michigan Quarterly Review, Fractured Union: American Democracy on the Brink, guest editor Davan Maharaj, #61/4

The Missouri Review, Rescue Me, ed. Speer Morgan, #452

The New Atlantis, Saving the Real, ed. Ari Schulman, #68

The New Republic, Democracy in Peril, ed. Win McCormack, May

The New York Times Magazine, The New York Issue, ed. Jake Silverstein, June 5

Notre Dame Magazine, Fifty Years, ed. Kerry Temple, 50/4

Orion, Microcosms, ed. Sumanth Prabhaker, Winter

Oxford American, Celebrating 30 Years, ed. Danielle A. Jackson, 118

Plough, Made Perfect: Ability and Disability, ed. Peter Mommen, #30

The Point, What Is the Military For? editorial staff, #27

Psychotherapy Networker, Listening to Women, ed. Livia Kent, November/ December

Room, Ancestors, ed. Serena Lukas Bhandar, #45/1

Root Quarterly, Lions & Lambs, ed. Heather Shayne Blakeslee, III/4

Salmagundi, On Adam Phillips, eds. Robert Boyers & Peg Boyers, #216–217

Stranger's Guide, New Orleans, ed. Kira Brunner Don, #15

The Summerset Review, 20th Anniversary, ed. Joseph Levens, Fall

The Threepenny Review, A Symposium on Invisibility, ed. Wendy Lesser, #171

Virginia Quarterly Review, Color & Shade, eds. Paul Reyes & Allison Wright, 98/4

Water~Stone Review, How Quiet Burns, ed. Meghan Maloney-Vinz, #25

The Yale Review, Folio: On Ownership, guest editor Eula Biss, 110/2

ABOUT
MARINER BOOKS

MARINER BOOKS traces its beginnings to 1832 when William Ticknor cofounded the Old Corner Bookstore in Boston, from which he would run the legendary firm Ticknor and Fields, publisher of Ralph Waldo Emerson, Harriet Beecher Stowe, Nathaniel Hawthorne, and Henry David Thoreau. Following Ticknor's death, Henry Oscar Houghton acquired Ticknor and Fields and, in 1880, formed Houghton Mifflin, which later merged with venerable Harcourt Publishing to form Houghton Mifflin Harcourt. HarperCollins purchased HMH's trade publishing business in 2021 and reestablished their storied lists and editorial team under the name Mariner Books.

Uniting the legacies of Houghton Mifflin, Harcourt Brace, and Ticknor and Fields, Mariner Books continues one of the great traditions in American bookselling. Our imprints have introduced an incomparable roster of enduring classics, including Hawthorne's *The Scarlet Letter*, Thoreau's *Walden*, Willa Cather's *O Pioneers!*, Virginia Woolf's *To the Lighthouse*, W.E.B. Du Bois's *Black Reconstruction*, J.R.R. Tolkien's *The Lord of the Rings*, Carson McCullers's *The Heart Is a Lonely Hunter*, Ann Petry's *The Narrows*, George Orwell's *Animal Farm* and *Nineteen Eighty-Four*, Rachel Carson's *Silent Spring*, Margaret Walker's *Jubilee*, Italo Calvino's *Invisible Cities*, Alice Walker's *The Color Purple*, Margaret Atwood's *The Handmaid's Tale*, Tim O'Brien's *The Things They Carried*, Philip Roth's *The Plot Against America*, Jhumpa Lahiri's *Interpreter of Maladies*, and many others. Today Mariner Books remains proudly committed to the craft of fine publishing established nearly two centuries ago at the Old Corner Bookstore.

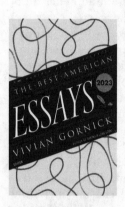

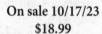
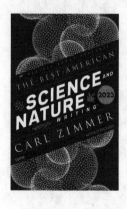